"This truly is an absolutely wonderful book. I know my daughters will thank you, the women and men who are supporters, sponsors, mentors – you are making a huge difference to the future of all."

Susan St. Amand, President & CEO,
The Sirius Group

"Post Lean-in, post #MeToo, COVID-19, the at-home economy... 'Dear Chairwoman' courageously calls on tribal elders with engaging folklore to guide leaders through a rite of passage, in a time like no other."

Lisa Hammitt, Executive Vice President, AI
Davidson Technologies

1

WITH IMMENSE GRATITUDE

---

*This amazing project would not have been possible
without the incredible support, bright insights, and
tremendous help from these extraordinary contributors:*

SYLVIANE GRANT
MONIK MIDDLETON
ARNA GUPTA
BARB MIKELS
JENN LEBLANC
and
ALL OF OUR SUPPORTERS OF
BOARDSEATMEET

Book Design
YUIKO SUGINO

Letters

ALEXIS HERMAN

Board of Directors: The Cola-Cola Company, MGM Mirage, Cummins Inc.

"When we bring women in, it's not just the right thing to do. It's the smart thing to do."

Dear Chairwoman:

When I was a little girl, my daddy used to say:

"No child ever becomes anything that he or she has never heard of."

I grew up in Mobile, Alabama, in a family of activists. My father was the first African American elected to any office in the Deep South in the 1940s. It influenced me to devote my whole life to taking risks to open doors for others.

My own activism started when I got expelled from high school at age fifteen. Catholic schools were segregated at that time. I disrupted the Archbishop and got expelled. After my reinstatement, I began protesting. My parents and many others

7

joined those protests, which led to the desegregation of the Mobile, AL, Catholic school system.

That moment was my first insight into the power of risk-taking. When you take a stand for something that is right and just, and people support you in the process, you can be a force for change and for good.

After college, I worked in the shipyards in Pascagoula, Mississippi. I cared about securing real jobs for young African American men and helped open up the first apprenticeship opportunities for African Americans in the Deep South. Ray Marshall, head of the School of Economics at the University of Texas at the time, contacted me after hearing about my experience. He became one of the top influencers in my life. His academic specialization was in the building trades apprenticeship, and he wanted to know how I had integrated the trades in Mississippi. He wrote the story of my experience. I was twenty-three years old.

Ray soon asked me to move to Atlanta, Georgia, to help open doors for women of color. In 1972, I researched all the major companies in the Deep South. Not one had a single woman of color in any managerial, professional, or technical job. We helped place the first women of color into managerial jobs across the Deep South at General Motors, Delta Airlines, Coca-Cola, and more.

At this time, I was running the Minority Women's Employment Program nonprofit. A few of my mentors told me I needed the help of a board. They were right because I certainly didn't know everything I needed to know. They introduced me to Dorothy Height, one of the Big Six of the Civil Rights Movement. She became the chairwoman of my first board.

I was twenty-five. She taught me the concepts of nonprofit work, boards, minutes, records, documentation, and advocacy. She introduced me to a network of women who became my support base. I was blessed to have such a mentor at an early age. Dorothy stayed in my life until her death at the age of ninety-nine.

Thanks to my work with her, I explored everything from women in apprenticeships to women in business to women on boards, focusing on non-traditional roles for women.

My work and connection with Ray Marshall led me to become Director of the Women's Bureau under President Carter's Department of Labor. Carter created the first Women Business Owners 'Initiative. I was tasked, along with the head of the Small Business Administration, to recommend a policy for this initiative.

We learned a lot about the status of women business owners at that time, and the results were shocking. Women couldn't even obtain a loan or credit from a bank unless their fathers or husbands co-signed. President Carter was willing to remove the enormous regulatory barriers facing women.

We talked to women about what it meant to own and operate their own businesses. We explained how to put a board together and led workshops to teach business skills. We'd ask:

What are you trying to sell?

What's your value proposition?

What type of influences do you need on a board to help grow your business?

What about finances?

The biggest difference between nonprofit and for-profit boards is the fiduciary responsibility to stakeholders on for-profit boards. A for-profit board member can be legally liable as can an owner of a for-profit business.

Running a nonprofit requires discipline and a focus on finances, because even a nonprofit can become a multi-million-dollar organization. You need to account for expenditures. You can't be frivolous. You must ensure your spending supports your cause. Your goal as a nonprofit board member is to support the nonprofit's cause and mission. It's a different mindset and a different lens.

When I think of the increased involvement of women on boards, I go back to my father's quote:

"No child ever becomes anything he or she has never heard of."

When you're no longer the only woman in the room, you're no longer the pioneer. Your mere presence helps lower barriers and opens the door for other women.

When we bring women in, it's not just the right thing to do. It's the smart thing to do. Businesses are increasingly aware of the purchasing power of women and especially that of the younger generations of consumers. If no one on the board understands these purchasers 'mindsets, habits, goals and passions, the business will not succeed.

In addition to gender and age inclusion, racial inclusion would be extremely beneficial to boards. We must fight for a fully inclusive roster. This is, without a doubt, a tough challenge.

Historically, African American women have not been included on boards. This makes it more difficult for them to gain the access needed to build relationships with board chairs. The African American history comes from the slave tradition. We were bought and sold. Our men were not allowed to fight for us, so we learned to fight to protect our bodies and our children. The tradition of slavery and abuse is very much still in the psyche and history of black women, which is why they often preach the need to fight for what they want, even today.

I will leave you with this: You have to work hard. You have to be intentional, conscious, and purposeful. You need to have a community of support around you and a plan. It doesn't automatically happen.

But I also know this is our moment. This is our day. We have to recognize our power. The more we raise our own thresholds of understanding about the power in our hands, the greater our success will be, not just in the boardroom but for women in every walk of life in general, today, tomorrow, as well as for the child looking forward to the great thing they want to become.

Yours truly,

Alexis

Alexis Herman has been a Director of The Coca-Cola Company since 2007. Alexis is the Chair and Chief Executive Officer of New

Ventures LLC, a corporate consulting company, and has held these positions since 2001. She served as Chair of the Business Advisory Board of Sodexo, Inc., an integrated food and facilities management services company, through 2013 and serves as a member of Toyota Motor Corporation's Diversity Advisory Board and Global Advisory Board. As Chair of the Company's Human Resources Task Force from 2001 to 2006, Alexis worked with the Company to identify ways to improve its human resources policies and practices following the November 2000 settlement of an employment lawsuit. From 1997 to 2001, she served as U.S. Secretary of Labor. She is also a Director of Cummins Inc., Entergy Corporation and MGM Resorts International.

KATHY WALLER

Board of Directors: Delta Airlines, Beyond Meat, CGI Inc.,
Cadence Bank

"Honestly, I don't understand why companies are challenged in identifying women for boards. I meet talented women all the time...Adding racial diversity initiatives in addition to gender diversity makes it even more difficult for them. Companies are going to have to address racial and gender diversity in their boardrooms and in their management ranks."

Dear Chairwomen of Tomorrow:

I am now retired, but in a former life, I was the Chief Financial Officer of the Coca-Cola Company. My life has been a series of directional changes that led to a great career and more.

As an Atlanta native, I attended all-black schools until I went to college in NY State at the University of Rochester. The school was a total culture shock for me, both in terms of its black population (which was approximately 5 percent) and its ice-cold, no-sunshine winters.

13

The weather, cultural and other challenges I encountered helped me learn to navigate various environments and prepared me to work in corporate America.

I had planned to become a lawyer from the time I was six years old having been inspired by Perry Mason, a role model I had seen on TV. When I was young, there were no black role models in business on television. Because I grew up in a relatively protected environment, I did not focus on race in my younger years. As a black person, I knew to be careful, but my exposure to other races was limited. I think people really learn about racial differences when they start interacting with other races. They learn because of the way they are treated and made to feel different. That treatment starts to work its harmful magic, which compounds year to year, experience to experience.

In college, I majored in history with the plan of going to law school. I took a year off after graduation to study for the LSAT and took a job at the City of Rochester in the Budget Bureau. I loved the work and changed direction, deciding to pursue an MBA instead of a law degree.

In graduate school, I enjoyed the accounting courses and decided to follow the public accounting route and get my CPA license. After obtaining my MBA, I joined Deloitte, Haskins, and Sells (now Deloitte) in Rochester, NY, where I then earned my CPA.

I worked for Deloitte in Rochester for three and half years before transferring to Deloitte in Atlanta. Within six months of my move home to Atlanta, a recruiter introduced me to Coca-Cola. At that time, I was enjoying public accounting and wasn't ready for a change in direction, but I interviewed for the job at Coca-Cola because I knew I would eventually leave public accounting. During the interview, I realized the job was not going to be as fulfilling as my job in public accounting, and I turned the job offer down. A week later, I received a call from a different manager at Coca-Cola. That manager offered me what I considered to be the perfect job for me. It was in the accounting research department of the Controller's Group, and it was like public accounting but working on internal SEC filings, acquisitions, and divestitures.

In October 1987, I happily started my job at Coca-Cola in the accounting research group, tasked with SEC filings and other financial matters. Shortly after I joined the company a new CFO started. He worked hard to be incredibly good at his job, especially in his quarterly presentations to the board of directors. He would rehearse his presentations in front of various audiences, often including associates from the Controller's Group.

One afternoon I was invited to a rehearsal. I have always believed that if someone is trying to improve themselves, you should help them. During this rehearsal, the CFO was asking for feedback, so I shared my careful but constructive observations with him, which he seemed to appreciate and took into consideration as he went through his presentation again. For the next three years, I worked with the CFO preparing his board presentations and helping him rehearse. The job gave me a lot of exposure to other senior leaders in the company and started the journey for me to come full circle and eventually become the CFO of The Coca-Cola Company.

So now, after thirty-two years at The Coca-Cola Company, I am retired. I get enthusiastic reactions from those who ask me how I am spending my retirement and hear that I serve on public and not-for-profit boards. I learned about public board service through my various roles at Coca-Cola that allowed me to interact with and work for the company's Board of Directors. Had I not had this exposure, I would likely have had no idea what it means to serve on a public board.

Over the years, I have encountered many people who potentially have an interest in board service. Those individuals who have had limited or no exposure to public boards don't fully understand the level of caution companies exercise when deciding to bring on new board members. Board members are engaged in the inner decisions of a company during good times and challenging times. However, that isn't the only reason for caution. Bringing in the wrong board member can be highly disruptive and can cause the board to focus on issues that have little to do with governing the company for which they serve. Boards do want candidates who will think differently and bring different perspectives, but they also want people who can bring those perspectives in a non-disruptive manner. Although I fully understand why boards are so cautious about how they choose board members, I do not accept the lack of diversity.

I currently serve on four public boards. All of them have some level of diversity and are actively seeking more diverse board members. Research shows diversity matters and the number of diverse board members matters. The research also shows that when there is more than one woman in the boardroom, the dynamics in the room change as the two women support each other. However, the magic number to experience the full advantages of having a diverse boardroom appears to be at least three. When there are three diverse board members, there is a greater level of overall acceptance and support. Although each board is different, being the only woman in a boardroom or on a management team is often challenging. If the only diverse person in the room has a dissenting opinion from the majority, that person must work hard not just to be heard but to be understood.

Over the years, the governing bodies of public companies have been changing as companies have been broadening their search criteria for board members. In the not-too-distant past, boards were primarily composed of CEOs of other public companies who were primarily white males. Given efforts to diversify boardrooms, boards have broadened their search criteria to include other "categories" such as C-suite executives, consultants, educators, and people from government service. When boards were comprised of CEOs who had boards of their own, there was no perceived need to have programs to train these CEOs how to be effective board members. Now that public companies are broadening their searches, there are many programs to train prospective board members.

As you pursue a role in corporate governance, know not all board training programs are equal. There is nothing wrong with participating in a training program. I have found some of the best programs offer some skills and governance training and also offer exposure to current board members. Most of the courses I have experience with are offered primarily, if not solely, to women, given we are having the most difficulty being recognized as a board candidate. In the current environment where the search criteria have opened to non-CEOs, non-diverse candidates also need training and exposure, although they may not experience the same difficulties obtaining a board role.

Fortunately, gender-diversity initiatives are having a positive impact as it relates to management roles. Honestly, I don't understand why companies are challenged in identifying women for boards. I meet talented women all the time. I have no idea why companies are finding it so challenging to locate them. Adding racial-diversity initiatives in addition to gender diversity makes it even more difficult for them. Companies are going to have to address racial and gender diversity in their boardrooms and management ranks. They have to do both. As with gender, addressing racial diversity within management will help solve the disparities inherent to the current boardrooms as more senior-level executives would be available for board roles. Until diversity is prevalent in all levels of organizations, the excuse that they can't find diverse individuals to fill board roles will continue to be used.

Recent legislation requiring companies to add gender-diverse board members is helping accelerate the gender initiative. It is unfortunate that for some it took legislation to enforce the issue. However, research bears out having more diversity is the right thing to do as it helps companies and boards get better answers and results. I can imagine there will be a day when companies with no female board representation will be outliers. At that point, I think those companies will adapt rather than remain outliers.

There are many organizations that support women's efforts to secure public board positions by helping women learn how to market their experience. Women who haven't had previous corporate board experience but who have served on not-for-profit boards often have transferrable skills. Knowing how to talk about those transferable skills is key.

I also think current board members would want to engage in an organization like BoardSeatMeet. I see men and women board members who can and want to be part of the solution of diversifying boards. This is especially true for retired board members like me, where we have more time. A great way to spend some of that time is to support others trying to achieve more during their careers.

One great way to get board experience is to join the board of a young public company or a start-up. The constant across all boards, regardless of size, is good governance. Lots of start-up companies achieve various levels of success. Not all of them fully appreciate the requirements of being a public company, but a public company's shareholders have given their money and want value back, including governance. Many talented women are available for board service who can and will make sure these companies are doing the right thing.

There seems to be lots of board opportunities. Some opportunities are the result of new public and private companies being formed, and some are the result of companies refreshing their boards as their current board members reach age limits. It seems many companies have age limits. Sometimes it is waived for a short period of time to enable the company to avoid losing needed skills or losing too many knowledgeable board members at one time. Regardless, an age limit does allow the company to refresh the board. Some boards have term limits, which also provide an opportunity for board refreshment. Regardless, there is no shortage of board opportunities available now or coming available soon.

Given the abundance of opportunity, choosing which boards to join isn't easy. There are many great companies to consider. When you are ready for board leadership, think about the criteria you will use and choose your boards thoughtfully. My current boards are in different industries and all have strong leadership. For me, the company's culture, people management philosophy, and company governance philosophy are important. You have to decide what your criteria will be.

While things have come a long way since the day I took the role at Coca-Cola that defined where I would be today, we have a lot more work to do on diversity in the boardroom. With support and commitment, companies can successfully address the racial and gender disparities in their boardrooms and in their management ranks fairly quickly, if they are so inclined.

I cannot wait to see how you and future leaders will embrace these challenges and make a better tomorrow for all of us.

Yours truly,

Kathy

Kathy Waller is a Chief Financial Officer and Board Member with over 35 years of broad financial and operational leadership experience within the consumer and retail sectors.

Kathy retired in March 2019 after 32 years with The Coca-Cola

Company where she was the Chief Financial Officer and President, Enabling Services. In these roles, she led the company's global finance, technical and shared services organizations, and represented the company to investors, lenders and rating agencies. Kathy also serves as a Board member for Delta Airlines, CGI Group, Cadence Bancorporation and Beyond Meat.

Kathy joined The Coca-Cola Company in 1987 as a Senior Accountant and assumed roles of increasing responsibility. She was named Executive Vice President and Chief Financial Officer in 2014 and added the role of President of Enabling Services in 2017. In addition to her c-suite role, Kathy was the founding chair of the Coca-Cola Company's Women's Leadership Council.

Kathy is also a member of the Board of Trustees of Spelman College, The University of Rochester, The Woodruff Arts Center, Achieve Atlanta, The Atlanta Symphony Orchestra and The Girl Scouts of Greater Atlanta.

She holds a Bachelor of Arts degree and a Master's degree in Business Administration from the University of Rochester and is a Certified Public Accountant.

PAM LENEHAN

Board of Directors: ATN International, New Residential Investment Corp

*"A CEO once said to me that, when a new fish is added to the fish tank,
everybody swims differently."*

Dear Future Chairwoman of Tomorrow:

Work for organizations with diverse pipelines of talent.
I am the product of equal opportunity. I was a highly educated white woman who had earned two degrees in four years from an Ivy League school. I had never faced any prejudice. During the spring of my senior year in college, I started interviewing. I thought everyone would be happy to hire me. Unfortunately, I was in for a surprise.

Unbeknown to me, I was being judged by the engagement ring on my left hand. While I was at one interview at an accounting firm, the HR person, a Black man, let me read my file. It read that I was highly qualified, but it would be a waste to hire me because I was getting married and would leave soon to have children. He said

22

they might offer me a job, but I had to think about whether I would want to take it. Instantly, I realized I was being prejudged based on what others thought I would do.

Thankfully, I got two job offers: one from a women-run consulting firm and the other from Chase Manhattan Bank. Chase was under a consent decree at the time from the U.S. government, which required them to increase the number of women and minorities. I joined a wonderful training program for bank officers with twenty-two people: two were white men, and twenty were women and people of color. I believe I would not have gotten that job had it not been for some form of equal opportunity.

Assume responsibility for your career path.

I entered the banking world from a non-business family. My father was a doctor, and my mother was an actress. I did not know an asset from a liability. After being hired, I was in a grueling training program for a year, which taught me everything I needed to be a good banker. Then I became a manager in the training program, and, after that, I had my pick of where I wanted to go. I picked technology because that team was different.

My boss had hair longer than mine. He was a guy with different perspectives than most and gave me lots of freedom. Within five years, I built a $2-billion loan portfolio for rising technology companies. I traveled all over the country. I'd go out to California for five days a month and see five companies a day. It was a fantastic experience.

I thought I would stay there forever until I got pregnant with my first child. I was given eight weeks of maternity leave. At the end of the seventh week, the head of the corporate bank called me and said that, if I was not back by Monday, I would be fired. Also, the promotion list came out and my name was on it. However, when they realized I was on maternity leave, the list was retracted and reissued without my name. I went back to work and started taking calls from recruiters. A year and a half later, I went to work for the firm now known as Credit Suisse.

Take risks in your career.
I was at Credit Suisse for fourteen years doing mergers, acquisitions, and financings for technology companies. One of the things I have always loved about technology, from a service provider point of view, is the technology companies did not care what gender or color you were. If you understood their business and their needs and could bring the resources of your organization to solve their problems, they gave you their business. I have always looked for places that respect you for your work and not for what you look like.

The first fifteen years of my career were in New York. Then I transferred to Boston and have been here ever since. After a while, the firm closed the Boston office. I thought I would go to another investment bank. However, I met an incredibly smart CEO who was running a $200 million New York Stock Exchange-listed manufacturing company. I decided I would never have the opportunity to work with someone that smart again, so I took a huge pay cut and went there. It was the best job I ever had.

We more than doubled the company's size and sold it to Corning for an impressive price. Then I went to a high-tech start-up and became CFO of a communications company. I was there before the first product shipped and left when it had about a $30 million run rate. We did a major financing, filed the IPO and, when the market crashed, pulled the IPO and downsized.

Bring all of your experience – personal and professional – to work.

I joined my first board while I was CFO of the start-up. It was a terrible time to join a board from a personal perspective. I had recently remarried and was trying to blend a family with four teenagers. I worked for a CEO who did not support the idea of my serving on a board, and he told me that if I wanted to be on a board, I could use my vacation days to do it. I joined the board anyway and, since then, I have been on six other boards. I have learned a lot along the way and realize you bring both your personal and professional experiences into the boardroom.

Question, analyze, decide – then proceed as a team.

The best board training I had was when I was in the C-suite of the public company and attended every board meeting. We had an impressive board where the directors were all former CEOs and former U.S. cabinet members. This incredibly smart, articulate board really focused on creating shareholder value.

The management team would throw ideas on the table and look at the issues from all different perspectives and bring our recommendations to the board, who would ask insightful questions. That's what happens in a good board. Each director brings different views on how to solve a problem. The board is not telling management what to do. The board is asking probing questions. The directors look at the issues from the different perspectives they bring into the boardroom, and then management and the board collectively converge on a solution or strategy.

Then everyone gets behind it, whether you agree or not. As a board member, you have two choices: support the strategy or leave the board. One key lesson is that being a director is like being a member of a sports team. You may not win every game, but you are all part of the same team. When you leave the boardroom, you need to be united. It is important to note that in the end, it is not about the board. It is about the company, the shareholders, the employees, and the customers.

Treat people well, especially during challenging times.
I have been the first woman on most of my boards. Fortunately, I have not been the last one. I think women inherently bring a different perspective to the table. Most of us are mothers, and I think we look at the world more "humanely." I grew up on Wall Street, and people will tell you I am pretty tough. However, I am not embarrassed to bring up the human side of the equation.

I have served on several compensation committees. When management says they cannot believe someone they considered a team player is leaving, I always tell them that team number one is that person's family, and they have to think of that first. You need to consider what is essential to that person before deciding if they can do a good job.

For example, in the COVID situation, we need to be sensitive to the fact there many working parents are at home right now. It is a lot harder to do your job if you are trying to homeschool children than if you are sitting by yourself at your computer all day. If you treat people well during the most challenging times, including when they are under stress, when they are having children or dealing with sick parents, they will remember those times and feel valued by the company. I ended up leaving a job I loved because of an issue related to my taking maternity leave. Let's just say these kinds of moments leave an indelible imprint on you and on your regard of the organization—as a leader or otherwise.

Reach out, listen to all the voices, and be willing to learn.
When we talk about diversity, people always think about gender and ethnicity, but there are other ways to slice "diversity." A critical one for board work is diversity of communication. The best article I read about the subject is the article "The Power of Talk: Who Gets Heard, and Why" by Debra Tannen. In the article, she talks about how communication styles are affected by more than gender and ethnicity. Factors such as where you grew up and how people there interact differently also play a part.

In her example, a woman from Texas was used to polite meetings. When she moved to the East Coast, where the style was more aggressive and people jumped into conversations, it was challenging for her, and she was viewed as unsuccessful. So there is the critical aspect of diversity in communication styles. In the boardroom, the chair needs to step forward because some directors may dominate the conversation due to their speaking styles. Those of us who grew up in New York will make sure our opinion is heard. However, we need to remember other people who communicate less aggressively may have some of the best ideas. Every voice in the boardroom should be heard.

My style is that at the end of every board meeting, we go around the table and ask each person about their opinion or unanswered questions so that when we walk out of the meeting, we have heard from everyone. When you walk into a boardroom as a new board member, you need to understand the board already has a way of communicating. A CEO used an analogy to explain to me the addition of a new director. He said it's like adding a new fish to the fish tank. Everybody swims differently. You all will adjust to each other. However, you cannot change the culture overnight. You have to change it through your actions and words and by gaining respect.

Articulate your value added.
Even though women do a fantastic job selling their organizations, they do not always do a great job explaining their successes. We need to get women to think about their jobs and translate them into skills used at the board level. You do not need to exaggerate, but you do need to articulate what you are bringing to the boardroom. For a lot of hugely successful women, it has been a long time since they had to sell themselves. You need to think of yourself as a brand, and this brand is reflected in how you look, act, and communicate.

Something that I've also come across is some women are long-winded in how they explain things. In the boardroom, you listen more than you talk. I have heard several people who did not necessarily do well in the board interview because they talked too much and did not listen enough. You need to give succinct answers and move on.

For instance, we were interviewing a woman for a senior executive job. I thought she was incredibly impressive with the right criteria. However, she took a long time to answer questions. The CEO didn't want to hire her. When I asked him why, he said she rambled and went through everything. In his opinion she did not seem confident. I thought it was interesting because it seemed to me that she told us her line of thinking, where she started out, the different options she considered, and why she ended up where she did. He did not like that. He wanted to go from the problem directly to the solution.

That was a perfect example of how we were different. He just wanted to have an executive walk in the room and say s/he solved the problem. I, on the other hand, wanted to know what assumptions were made, the risks and opportunities, and why management came to its conclusions.

Get P&L experience.
Women can do some things to make it more likely they will be considered for board opportunities. One is to network outside their company and, if possible, outside their industry. You have to network starting in your twenties. You cannot begin in your fifties or sixties when you are ready to join a board.

The second thing is that women need to be more aggressive about getting line jobs where you have profit and loss responsibility. Think about the people who typically get on a board of directors. Often those people have run large organizations, either as a CEO, division president, or general manager, or as a partner at a professional services firm. These people have been in high-level positions making money for the organization. They typically do not come from support positions.

Become a life-long learner.
I tell young people coming out of college who like people and want to go into human resources that they should go into sales. You meet a lot of people in sales, and you can have a P&L and show you have contributed to the organization's revenue. While human resources is an important area, at some point it would be good to show you have had P&L responsibility. At the least, you

have to be comfortable with numbers and budgets because all boards talk about numbers a lot.

The easiest way to get on a board of directors is to go in through the audit committee, and you don't need to be an accountant. One of the best audit committee members I ever had didn't come through banking or accounting. He was an engineer who had run the software divisions at several large technology firms. However, he had done a lot of budgeting, and he understood numbers. He probably wasn't the person to turn to for accounting regulations. However, he realized the numbers reflect the business, and he understood business. So always be willing to join the audit committee once you have worked on budgeting, strategic planning, and revenue-generating projects.

I tell people these days we are all life-long learners, and we need to set our own curriculum. You need to start thinking now about what skills you need to join a board and start educating yourself. Do not wait for someone else to do it for you, and don't believe someone can do it better than you. A study showed men apply for a job when they have 50 percent of the qualifications, and women only apply when they have 90 percent of the qualifications. It is clear women don't always pursue board opportunities where they could add value.

Another important issue to consider is that you have the time to devote to board service and still be control your schedule. I have often said that I would be much happier with a thirty-five-year-old director who had control of her schedule, who was an entrepreneur, or who had the support of her organization for board meetings, compared to a sixty-year-old fantastic expert who reported to someone, who was not supportive and, therefore did not control her schedule. You need that dedication and time commitment.

Board meetings normally are set a year in advance, However, when companies are making an acquisition, are in the middle of a business crisis, have an emergency CEO succession problem, or are dealing with an activist, directors need to have flexibility and time. A board needs to make sure that, regardless of age, directors are available when needed.

More boards are moving in the right direction and, for the first time, I can imagine being on a corporate board that is half women, with rich ethnic diversity. The movement and energy continue to accelerate with you, the next generation of women board leaders. It's about time. Let's make it happen.

Best of luck in your board journey,

Pam

Pam has 18 years of experience as a public company director, serving on seven public company boards where she has been Chairwoman, presiding director, and chaired audit and compensation committees. She has been involved in IPOs, equity and debt financings, acquisitions, divestitures, restructurings, auditor changes, sale of the company, cyber breaches, and planned and unplanned CEO succession. Pam is currently a member of the audit committees of New Residential Investment (NRZ) and ATN International (ATNI). Previously she was on the boards of Monotype Imaging, Civitas Solutions, American Superconductor, Spartech Corporation, and Avid Technology.

Pam spent more than 20 years on Wall Street as a managing director in Investment Banking at Credit Suisse First Boston doing mergers and acquisitions and financings for technology companies. She was also an officer of Oak Industries until it was acquired by Corning, and CFO of a high-tech start-up. She is on the boards of directors of the Center for Women & Enterprise and NACD's New England chapter. Pam is co-chair of the Boston chapter of Women Corporate Directors and a member of the Boston Women Leaders Network, Massachusetts Women's Forum and the Boston Club. She has a BA in mathematical economics and MA in economics, both from Brown University.

GENEVIEVE SHIROMA

Commissioner: CA Public Utility Commission

Former Chairwoman: State of CA Agricultural Labor Relations Board

"You reach a point where you can get too comfortable, and it's time for a change."

Dear Women Leaders of Tomorrow:

As I reflect on my journey, I have achieved the distinction of having been appointed by four California governors—Gray Davis, Arnold Schwarzenegger, Jerry Brown, and Gavin Newsom—to top-level state government board roles at the Agricultural Labor Relations Board and the California Public Utilities Commission. Along the way, I ran for office and the voters chose me to represent them on our local customer-owned electric utility, the Sacramento Municipal Utility District (SMUD), for five terms spanning twenty years. My career started at the California Air Resources Board as an entry-level air-quality engineer, and I spent fourteen of twenty years as a supervisor and manager there. How did I do it?

I was born in Lodi, California. My father was a farmworker, and my mother and he would bring four children into the world. My parents, who were children of Okinawan and Japanese immigrants, were born and raised in Hawaii. They moved to California in the early 1950s with high school degrees and a bit of college education. My father was also a United States army veteran, having been drafted into the U.S. Military Intelligence Service in 1945. When they arrived in California almost a decade after WWII, they found a land full of promise but still recovering from the unconstitutional incarceration of 120,000 West Coast Japanese Americans in concentration camps, most losing everything they had worked for. As a newborn, my parents brought me to their home, a converted barn. We led a humble and impoverished existence in the 1950s and '60s.

With family, teachers, and community mentors, I felt valued at an early age. I was given the freedom and opportunity to figure out my passion and choose my path, taught how to communicate to advance initiatives and points of views, counseled on the importance of research, and guided on the organizational skills necessary to meet deadlines and get things done. Further, my parents had a strong sense of right and wrong and tended to speak up, especially my mother. My father, who is still with us at ninety-four, shared with me recently that, from the time I was a small child, I had strong opinions and also spoke up.

For those who came from Okinawa and Japan during the Meiji era, leaving home was a significant and courageous undertaking. An adventurous spirit went along with that and was passed on to the next generation. My grandmother was a "picture bride" who,

34

in 1913 at the age of twenty-one, traveled from Hiroshima to Kobe and boarded a ship to Hawaii to meet her new husband having exchanged pictures. Years later, she encouraged my mother to go to college. My mother would say to us:

"The U.S. is a big open place, so go out and explore it and decide how you fit into it."

That was important because in the Japanese culture, there is a stigma around family embarrassment or failure. My family was already breaking the mold by being impoverished. Further, my mother made the difficult decision to separate from my father because he could not walk away from the poker table. Gambling is a common struggle in the Asia Pacific community. Thanks to our community's help, state programs for families in need, and my mother's inner strength and grit, she raised her four children by herself.

I must point out here that throughout my life, opportunities have crossed my path where I learned quickly to decide to take them or not. These occurred talking to a teacher, walking down a hallway or down the street and having a conversation, sitting next to someone who shares an idea, or taking a phone call as I did before I decided to run for office. It is important to recognize opportunity, size yourself up quickly, do not be afraid to fail, and grab the ring.

With help from scholarship funds, I was able to attend San Joaquin Delta Community College in Stockton and then the University of California at Davis, receiving a degree in Materials Science and Engineering. I matriculated during the Vietnam War, the civil rights movement and women rights movement—a time of activism and volunteerism. I got involved in my neighborhood association, took up causes, and phone banked for local candidates.

My first full-time job was as an entry-level engineer at the California Air Resources Board. There, I had the opportunity to work with remarkable people who had built the California Water Project, the big aqueduct system that carries water from Northern to Southern California. These people knew how to get things done. My mentors knew how to take a law approved by the legislature and signed by the governor and turn it into tangible results, such as the reduction of air pollution in Los Angeles, the curtailing of toxic air contaminants around refineries, and the analysis of whether a proposed power plant would meet all air pollution control requirements.

I was fortunate to work with supervisors who saw my potential and gave me leadership opportunities. I took the next step in becoming a supervisor encouraged by simple "Go for it" words of encouragement from a division chief. In any endeavor, it is important to earn the reputation for delivering well-researched, well-written, credible products on time. It is important to know how to work collaboratively and inclusively with staff, colleagues, and managers who may have diverse viewpoints and approaches to problem solving.

Some people have potential but may not know how to get to that next step. In my case, I was coasting along in a successful career in middle management. I felt respected and worked with the top management in my organization. I was getting "aye" votes on the proposed regulations my team took to the board; yet at some point, I thought:

"Maybe I need to challenge myself and do something different."

36

You reach a point where you can get too comfortable, and it is time for a change.

I ran for Sacramento city council in the mid-1990s. The person who encouraged me to run for office was a Latinx woman already In elected office. She had watched me in my neighborhood volunteer roles and told me it was time to step forward. After a twenty-year career spent successfully working at the Air Resources Board and in middle management, I was suddenly thrown into a completely different environment; walking precincts; and talking to people about safety, potholes, union contracts, and garbage service. I must admit, I thought:

"What have I done?"

I had willfully decided to put myself in the scrutinizing public eye and to start anew.

I lost the city council election by less than two hundred votes to another woman of color. That could have been it for me in terms of deciding not to run again and going back to what I was comfortable with. In fact, I did go back to my role at the California Air Resources Board but continued to be active in the community. Barely a year later, in 1998, a friend informed me of a public office vacancy, the Ward 4 elected director position on the Sacramento Municipal Utility District (SMUD) Board. He encouraged me to stand for election for the vacancy because I had the qualifications as a neighborhood activist and my experience reviewing power plant proposals. I was hesitant because I had lost the previous election.

However, I decided to go for it because I decided it would be an opportunity to do more for the community. I knew from my roots what it was like to be poor and a person of color, and my community had helped me succeed. I carried aspirations from my mother, the community, my teachers, and those who made it possible for me to garner the scholarships that had made all the difference for me. I now had an opportunity to give back and serve on a board to help customers with their bills and essential services and advance clean energy and innovation. I was going to take that opportunity. I won and served on the board of SMUD for twenty years through five elections, including serving as the president of the board, chosen by my colleagues several times.

The SMUD Board of Directors is like a corporate governing board insofar as you are not an employee. You meet several times each month to vote on budgets, initiatives, and policies. Hence, I also continued my full-time job at the Air Resources Board while contemplating my need to challenge myself even further and do something different in terms of my career.

While I was attending an art reception at our local museum, another Latinx woman shared there were vacancies at the Agricultural Labor Relations Board, the farmworker collective-bargaining board. She thought I would be a good candidate as a farmworker's daughter and my knowledge of government and the legal processes. I sized myself up (it would be labor law not air pollution law), talked with friends and mentors, and decided to apply with the support of my state senator (who had been the one to encourage me to run for City Council), state assembly member, and many others. Governor Gray Davis interviewed me, liked my credentials, and appointed me, and designated me as chair of the board. I was reappointed by Governor Arnold Schwarzenegger and Governor Jerry Brown, who signed the original law creating the board. Each time, I also stood for confirmation by the California State Senate after a hearing by its Rules Committee. Having grabbed the ring, I had a rewarding second twenty-year career.

At the age of sixty-five, I am now in what I call my third incarnation, the Air Resources Board being my first, and my time on the SMUD Board and serving simultaneously on the Agricultural Labor Relations Board as my second. After deciding not to run for election to a sixth term on the SMUD Board in 2018 and looking ahead to retirement, in early January 2019, I learned about a vacancy on the California Public Utilities Commission. I quickly sized myself up, concluding I had more to offer the people of California with my forty-plus years of experience, including twenty years serving on the SMUD electric utility board, and applied for the position. Governor Gavin Newsom liked my credentials and appointed me later that month. The Senate confirmed me a few months later to a six-year term.

I do not think I am unique, although I realize my life experiences have set me apart. When I encounter a woman with potential who may not recognize it, I want to say to her:

"If I could do it, so can you. Let's talk about our experiences and commonalities."

That is to say:

" Don't be afraid to fail. You bring something valuable to the table."

Being unafraid to fail is hard because reputation is a big factor in success. In the end, it is the substance you bring to the table that matters.

You build your successes and earn your reputation. You raise your hand and speak up, break into a conversation, and add valuable insight. Even if it may feel awkward at first, do it anyway, and then deliver well-written, well-researched, well-thought-out products on time. The ability to write and communicate is essential, so seek training, mentorship, and observe those who are successful. I do that to this day. There is always something new to learn.

The U.S. does not rank high in female board representation. Germany and Great Britain have had women occupy the highest roles, which the U.S. has yet to achieve. California's new law requiring female representation on corporate boards is an important step. The benefit is that it jumpstarts inclusion. When I became a supervisor in 1984, affirmative action was the law of the land. When we interviewed candidates for a position, there was a heavy push to casting a wide net. We interviewed women and people of color. I saw tangible results in that qualified people, who would not have been given a chance otherwise, had the opportunity to interview and accept a job. This, in my view, produced outstanding teamwork, innovation, and productivity. With the adoption of California's Proposition 209 in 1996, which outlawed affirmative action, these proactive efforts went away.

I believe the grassroots approach is also an effective approach. Some nonprofits train women for board roles. Alternatively, there are opportunities for women to speak on panels or conduct brown-bag lunch hour talks. Many of us are looking at the talent around us to see who displays potential. If I can, I reach out to share my story and hopefully put a spark in someone to challenge themselves. We are not born with the ability to share our story with a group, speak in front of an audience, raise our hands, and weigh in on a subject. It takes practice, nurturing, and training.

I'm always scanning the room and wondering:

Could she run for office?

Could she serve in my place on a board?

Could she take over a seat on a corporate or nonprofit board?

Mentoring is an important obligation given the support and opportunities I have received. It is important to build the bench for those who will be ready to take your place. I am a firm believer in Malcolm Gladwell's book "The Tipping Point" in that one thing can make a difference. Again, recognizing opportunities, knowing when to seize the moment, whether it is for yourself or your community, putting aside your fear of failing—the journey is boundless.

Many did that for me, which inspires me to do so for others. I leave you with the advice to take the time walking down the hallway or sitting next to someone to have a conversation and discover new opportunities for yourself.

Yours truly,

Genevieve

Genevieve Shiroma was appointed to the CPUC by Governor Newsom on Jan. 22, 2019. Prior to joining the CPUC, Commissioner Shiroma served as a member of the Agricultural

Labor Relations Board from 1999 to 2019, serving as chair 1999 to 2006, 2011 to 2014, and 2017 to 2019. Previously, she was Chief of the Air Quality Branch at the California Air Resources Board from 1990 to 1999, an air quality supervisor from 1984 to 1990, and an air quality engineer from 1978 to 1984. For five terms, from 1999 to 2018, Commissioner Shiroma was the elected director of Ward 4 of the Sacramento Municipal Utility District (SMUD).

Commissioner Shiroma is presently the lead Commissioner for approximately 65 formal proceedings spanning the regulated electricity, gas, telecommunications, transportation, and water industries. She leads the Microgrids and Resiliency proceeding established pursuant to Senate Bill 1339, the rulemakings over Transportation Network Companies, the Lifeline discount phone and broadband Program, the California Alternate Rates for Energy and Energy Savings Assistance Program, the customer energy investment financing rulemaking, and major general rate cases including for Southern California Edison Company and California American Water Company.

Commissioner Shiroma serves as the Commission's representative on the Low-Income Oversight Board, is Co-Chair of the Commission's Emerging Trends, Finance & Administration, and Internal Audits Committees. In 2020, Commissioner Shiroma was selected as the Secretary/Treasurer of the Western Conference of Public Service Commissioners of the National Association of Regulatory Utility Commissioners (NARUC) and appointed to serve on the NARUC Emergency Preparedness, Recovery and Resiliency Task Force and Subcommittee on State and National Response to COVID-19.

Commissioner Shiroma resides in Sacramento and holds a Bachelor of Science degree in Materials Science and Engineering from University of California, Davis. She was born and raised as a farm worker's daughter in the Acampo-Lodi area of San Joaquin County.

PHYLLIS CAMPBELL

Chairwoman: Pacific Northwest Region, JPMorgan Chase

Board of Directors: Alaska Airlines, Nordstrom

"Stereotypically, we Asian Americans are known for our work and disciplines. But we're not always known for creating the networks and relationships that, in the long run, count toward opening those doors to board opportunities."

Dear Chairwomen of Tomorrow:

I grew up in Spokane, Washington. I was fortunate enough to be a part of my father's dry-cleaning business, which taught me about each aspect of business. We had the opportunity to wait on the counter, learn customer service skills, work on bookkeeping, manage the cash registers, learn people's orders, clean the restrooms, and work with my dad's small employee team. We experienced what it's like to be a small business owner. It seemed hard at the time, but when I look back on it, I'm so grateful we were exposed to what it takes to run a business.

I was the oldest of five siblings. My two younger brothers worked in the business with me. We grew up with modest means. My father ran the business, and my mother was a medical tech at a hospital. She worked long hours and graveyard shifts. I ended up with a lot of the surrogate parenting duties with my brothers. I learned management skills early, not only in the household but in the business. I learned about delegation, organization, and how to make sure things got done. We were a close family and supported each other. With our parents gone a lot of the time, we had to fend for ourselves.

When I decided to go to college, I didn't know what I wanted to major in. I started out in political science, thinking I would get a law degree eventually. But once I took a few business classes, I realized I wanted to go back to my love of business, which I considered to be my roots. I transitioned out of political science and into business administration. I relished business finance, marketing and accounting. I got my business degree and that was the start of my interest in the corporate arena. I thought I could apply my skills after graduating because at that point I was interested in working for a larger business, although I didn't know where to focus.

As I emerged from school with my bright, shiny business degree, I actually got rejected more than I got calls back. I was shocked. I got so many messages from companies saying they didn't hire women, didn't want women, or had only ever hired one woman who hadn't worked out, or that I wasn't mobile enough. I heard everything in the book. I tell this story as a lesson about persistence. I called a bank I wanted to work for that told me no many times. In fact, I called them thirty-six business days straight. They eventually got tired of me and hired me. I'm not sure if they really wanted to hire me, but they wanted me to stop pestering them. However, they were skeptical, saying that they had not had good "luck with women." I hung in there, rolled up my sleeves, and did things other people weren't willing to do. I learned the business from the ground up.

Hiring managers had many excuses at the time. One person specifically said women, in general, didn't like working for the woman in charge. I found the notion women not necessarily liking to work for other women absurd. I asked this hiring manager if this one woman was unpleasant or whether there was some other problem. But he believed that women don't like to work with other women. He mentioned backbiting and all these stereotypical things. I found it interesting there were so many stereotypes formed just because one woman didn't work out. I remember saying that, and I got this "you don't understand" stare.

Another excuse I faced was that company invested a lot of money training the last woman they hired, but then she got pregnant and quit. In this way, a single example became an unfortunate prologue. They didn't want to take that risk. I told them I was going to get in there, show them what I could do, and prove I could do it. I wanted the chance. They finally gave me a chance, but I believe it was more to get rid of an annoyance and less because they believed I could do it.

I didn't have a mentor back then. I relied on my own internal resilience, which was hard. As a recent college graduate, I thought I was marketable. But I had thought that a lot of companies would love to hire me, so running into a brick wall was hard. I didn't have anyone to talk to except my husband, who wasn't in the field but a great support. Culturally, as Japanese Americans, we learn to be pretty independent, self-sufficient, and to not bother other people with our personal issues because others have issues too. I had all these cultural messages to gut it out and do it on my own. Obviously, I reached a point in my career when I realized I needed to reach out to people. There are people who are helpful and willing, but I had to ask.

Eventually I engaged a mentor. He told me I was one of the hardest workers he knew, and I would be successful because of it. But that's only about 30-40% of my success. I needed to lift my head up, get out there, meet people in the community, and work my network. Your contacts will serve you for the rest of your life. If you just sit at your desk and run the best branch the company has ever had, you're never going to build the relationships you will need to expand. I tell that to a lot of people of color because we're taught that hard work is everything. You need a lot more to get you to the next level.

Once I had a mentor, I really began to work my networks and talk about my community. I became chair of the Spokane Valley Chamber of Commerce Board. I really worked the network as my mentor suggested. In the long run, he was right. Long story short, my first board opportunity came when a woman who was the HR manager at my old bank told the CEO I would be a great board member. I didn't even know what a board member was, but she opened the door for me. I had coffee with the CEO, and we really hit it off. He asked me to meet some other board members and I did. In effect, that was my network working for me. He opened the door to other board members, and we found we had a lot of common interests.

That's how I joined my first board at the energy company. That leads to the advice that, stereotypically, Asian Americans are known for our work and discipline. But we're not known for creating the networks and relationships that, in the long run, open doors to board opportunities.

The surprises along the way were mostly on the upside. I had to learn quickly what a board is about. In my first board meeting, I had to listen and observe what made an effective board member: what they actually talked about, how the meeting actually goes, and how to get ready for the committees. Luckily, another woman on the board took me under her wing and was a tremendous resource for me.

I asked her if we could have coffee after a board meeting one day. She was the mentor who would tell me about the dynamics that go along with this board, including the different personalities, the tensions, and how I could make a difference. She encouraged me to speak up in different areas. She gave me my sea legs. That was really important, and something I would encourage others to do. If you're not assigned a board buddy, find one and admit that you need their advice on what you could have done or said differently. She became that for me.

I was surprised by how much I didn't know—especially on the difference between what the board was supposed to do and what management was supposed to do. You could effectively weigh in on certain issues and at certain times. It's essential you understand the personal dynamics in the room. There's always someone who speaks first and has a more prominent voice because of their tenure or stature, and other people follow. If I disagreed, how was I supposed to get into this conversation without seeming to be the outlier all the time? Those were all the dynamics I had to learn. My board mentor really helped me understand that.

Women and people of color obviously bring diverse perspectives to the table. Because these perspectives are different, they are often ignored or not taken as seriously as they should be. I brought something up about this in terms of layoffs. The questions I asked at the table were about fairness in letting employees know. They were questions about culture that aren't often seen by men at the table.

Not that they don't think about those issues. However, I think people get caught up in the business matters and don't look at the human factors and the ethics and culture questions. As women, we tend to call out those questions more often. I remember saying something about the implications of a layoff decision and asked if the company could take a pause. I got cold stares, and others said we needed to make this decision quickly. Another woman at the table also said she wanted to pause on the question because she thought it was important.

I still wasn't heard. I was told I didn't understand that layoffs supported the best interests of the stakeholders in the company, and that it was part of the company's business model. This was about survival, and not about "soft" stuff. If a third woman had been on that board, the conversation would have gone differently because basically we got rolled. Unfortunately, the outcome didn't turn out well, and there was a lot of backlash. I knew that would happen. I think that, because of our life experiences, women ask more questions about culture, human experience, and other issues that may not come to the floor of mainstream boards.

I'm excited to see so much attention and focus recently on bringing more diversity to boards, both private and public. I say the glass is half full and half empty. I am disappointed we are not farther along as we should be. We all had this vision in our minds of at least 30%, especially in the U.S. and with at least 50 percent, being people of color. We're not nearly there. We are in some countries where there are quotas.

I suppose we can look like a glass-half-full to the countries that are more progressive and have put a stake in the ground. They have achieved gender and other types of diversity by making it a mandate. In the U.S., I don't support hard mandates. However, I do support targets, transparency, disclosure, and emphasis by institutional investors. Otherwise, I don't think things are going to move as quickly as we think it's going to move.

So my glass-half-empty is that we haven't made nearly as much progress as I thought we could have. But my glass half full represents the fact that institutional investors are making this a priority, and it's come up in every conversation I've had. I'm encouraged by that. Every institutional investor is saying that when you add diversity, you get better long-term shareholder outcomes. The value outcome is from having diversity on the table. People are talking that way, and it will be a needle mover in the next few years.

Intergenerational leaders are another form of diversity with which boards are going to need to get comfortable. Let's face it, if you're in a consumer-facing company, this is your current and near-future customer base. For example, the Nordstrom board has embraced millennials on the board who bring that perspective. But just like with any other diversity, the board has to listen and help this board member who, by definition, doesn't have a lot of experience. It is a two-way street.

The younger generation has to work hard to understand the dynamics and style of older board members. On the other hand, the board has to listen carefully and mine the wisdom of the younger generation's perspective. At the end of the day, if you're a consumer-facing company, it's really important to understand that perspective and what the younger generation brings to the table. To me, the best boards welcome this challenge and work hard both ways to make this happen.

The Starbucks board was one of the first within the top 200 companies in the country to appoint a younger woman to their board. She's still there, and I remember talking to another who said they had to work hard to onboard her. But once she got onboarded, the board learned to work with her, and she has added so much value to the company. This is another type of diversity we need to consider. Boards need to rethink how they bring folks on who are different.

Another thing we need to think about is how we refresh our boards. That includes tenure, evaluation, and determination as to whether particular board members are relevant for the future of the company. Let's face it, some board members were great when they were brought on ten or fifteen years ago. However, when you think about the future of the company, would you choose these board members because of what they bring to the table?

Boards will have to become much more rigorous in terms of what they bring to the table. It's critical to evaluate skill sets, criteria, and relevance of the company going forward. The turnover and the refreshment will open up a lot more spots for diverse people. Without turnover, we could be talking about the same problem in the year 2040 because there will not have been open slots.

If I could be on any board, I would choose Unilever as they are a truly global company with a reputation for corporate responsibility. They think about all their packaging, and their sustainability strategies. Everything is done in terms of being sustainable. I admire their culture which seems to think about the planet and the people, not just profits. That's something to think about. Look for companies that you personally admire, that you'd like to be associated with, and that is in sync with your values.

Here is my advice for younger people, the next generation of board leaders. First of all, look at a board that stretches you and is in harmony with your values and culture. If those things are there, you know you're going to contribute. It is important you believe in the mission, values, and culture of the company.

I'm excited to see how you'll forge your path. I look forward to working with you on boards soon.

Yours truly,

Phyllis

Phyllis Campbell is the Chairman, Pacific Northwest for JPMorgan Chase & Co. She is the firm's senior executive in Washington,

Oregon, and Idaho across businesses, representing JPMorgan Chase & Co. at the most senior level to clients.

Previously, Phyllis served as the President/CEO of The Seattle Foundation, the largest community foundation in Washington. During her tenure, the Foundation doubled in charitable assets, to $600 million. Prior to that, Phyllis was the President/CEO of U.S. Bank of Washington for over six years. Under her leadership, the Bank doubled in size, through customer-focused growth initiatives and acquisitions. Phyllis has an extensive career of board service, both in the for profit and not-for-profit sectors. She was elected to ATSG (NASDAQ) in January 2021 as an independent board member. She has served as an independent director for Alaska Air Group from 2003- 2020. She previously served on the Nordstrom board of directors from 2005-2016 and chaired the Audit Committee for seven years. She currently serves on the Diversity Advisory Board (DAB) of Toyota and is a board member of SanMar and the Allen Institute. Phyllis is on the board of the U.S.-Japan Council and is the immediate past board chair.

Her awards have included the following: In 2016, she was recognized as the "First Citizen" of Seattle/King County. In 2015, she was awarded the Lifetime Achievement Award by Seattle Business Magazine and the Rev. Dr. Martin Luther King Jr. Vision from the Mountaintop Award. She also was the Pinnacle Award recipient of the 2015 Outstanding 50 Asian Americans in Business Awards. In 2014, she was recognized by the National Association of Corporate Directors (NACD) as a "Top 100" Director, as chosen by a committee of her peers and *The Ascend/Deloitte Inspirational Award*. She was the inaugural NACD Director of the Year Award from the Pacific Northwest chapter, *Top Women in Finance Award* from Women of Color Magazine in 2010 and *Woman Who Makes A Difference Award* from the International Women's Forum. She was also awarded the 36th Regents' *Distinguished Alumnus Award* from Washington State University.

Phyllis holds an M.B.A. from the University of Washington's Executive MBA Program, a B.A. in Business Administration from Washington State University, and is a graduate of the Pacific Coast Banking School at the University of Washington, as well as Stanford University's Executive Management Program. Phyllis also holds honorary doctorates from Whitworth University and Gonzaga University.

GILLIAN MUESSIG

Chairwoman: Trip.me

Former Board of Directors: World Affairs Council

"This is our moment of opportunity and our obligation as citizens of the world.
Women are desperately needed to balance the masculine energy already present in boardrooms."

Dear Chairwoman of Tomorrow:

Like voting in elections, filling a board seat is a privilege, and it takes work to do the job well. The foundation lies in education. Attaining the seat lies in the hands of champions. Success in the position lies in your ability and willingness to spend the time required to remain up to date in the company's affairs, its competitive landscape and your field of expertise.

My path to the boardroom of private companies was slow. I hope letters like mine will help you arrive in the boardroom of both private and public companies more quickly than I did.

I was born and raised in New York City, the second of five children. When my father passed away, my family depended on welfare to make ends meet. My sister and I worked after school. I was fortunate that the family pediatrician, who owned her own private practice, took a liking to me. She was one of few women doctors at the time and provided my first exposure to the idea women could break out of the conventional mold of the 1950s.

At the time, New York had five specialized public high schools. They admitted students by entrance exam. These schools are famous for having graduated many of the movers and shakers of the twentieth century in the U.S. Fortunately, my mother valued education and understood an excellent education was our bridge to a better life. As a result, I had the privilege of attending one of those high schools and then Barnard College, Columbia University. I was admitted to Barnard based on my effort—decent grades and entrance exam scores. However, because we lived in poverty, I was able to obtain financial aid scholarships to supplement my academic scholarships to make my attendance possible. However non-intuitive it may be, our poverty was my good fortune.

My counsel: If you don't have one, get a university degree. It doesn't have to come from an Ivy League college, as long as it is accredited. If money is tight, take as many courses as possible at low-cost community colleges and transfer to a university. Add credits only as you can afford them. Do not go into debt to obtain a degree. Therein lies a can of worms that can take decades to pay off.

Upon graduation, I followed my spouse to the Seattle area where I remain today and began working. My spouse held a rigorous position in the militaristic corporate culture of an aerospace company, where failure was never an option, and redundancy and oversight were the norm. There was no margin for error. As a result, our family was traditional in that my spouse adhered to a rigid work schedule while I raised three children and ran my consulting business "on the side."

At that time, deciding to have children wasn't necessarily a mindful choice. I loved my children, and my husband and I planned for them. But it did not occur to me that I could choose to not have children. The effect of having children without childcare support was substantive. Aside from a few home- or school-based daycare centers, there were no resources for childcare. Today, if you elect to have a family, you'll have significantly better choices. My children were five years apart in age, so when my rather long child-rearing-induced hiatus was over and all the kids were all in school, I finally started a consultancy.

My counsel: Ask yourself whether you wish to have children in an already overpopulated world. If you do, think about whether you plan on using au pair help, a nanny, family, or private or public childcare, or whether you'll be able to share caregiving duties with your spouse.

In 1994, the World Wide Web exploded like the crack in the universe and changed everything. I joined a group of people who founded Market Link International. We were the "first international commerce center on the World Wide Web." Nothing came of it. However, I learned a lot about start-up teams and operations.

In 1997, while still attending college, my eldest son joined my consulting company. He was looking to build the next big thing on the Web. I introduced him to the basics of a working company. We quite literally cannibalized my consultancy to co-found the company that became the world's most popular provider of search marketing software, SEOmoz. It was a difficult journey, the kind most entrepreneurs don't talk about.

When SEOmoz (now known as Moz) became a C corporation and took venture capital seed funding, I took my first board of director seat. Subsequently, because Moz had a large brand in the industry, many start-up entrepreneurs asked me to serve on their boards of advisors. A few asked me to serve on their boards of directors. Had Moz not enjoyed large brand awareness, I would not have been asked to serve. Your path may also begin with a seat on your own company's board and your entrepreneurial success may lead to board seats on more private and eventually public companies.

Luck has a great deal to do with entrepreneurial success and should not be underestimated. It's true about the importance of being at the right place at the right time with the right person. The same can be said for finding and succeeding at getting board of director seats.

My counsel: Be mindful about your desire to serve as a board director. Begin with service on an advisory board. It has a lower bar to entry, puts you in touch with other board members and jumpstarts your network of people you want to become your peers. Foster your ability to recognize people who can take your message that you wish to serve as a board director to people and places that matter. Search for board opportunities. LinkedIn is a powerful tool. Conferences, venture capital firms, and peer groups of CEOs of early-stage companies are good places to find your first board opportunities. Successful private board and not-for-profit board service can lead to public board service.

In 2009, I launched a podcast called CEOcoach. The show focused on the business rigor required to make a company move from an idea to a product to a viable corporation. I shared all the mistakes I'd made in my time, so others didn't have to repeat them. WMR.fm produced that podcast for eleven years, I retired that show in May 2020 and continue publishing through a new podcast called VC Confidential, also produced by WMR.fm.

My counsel: Having a public presence has helped me garner the attention of investors, advisors, founders, and venture capitalists. Those are paths that can lead to board director opportunities. But it will not happen without your active input. Consider writing a regular blog post or podcast demonstrating your strategic capabilities, perspectives, and insights. Leverage that "personal marketing" asset when letting people know you are interested in a board seat. They can learn more about you through your published content.

When I left Moz in 2012, I continued advising other companies. In 2018, my business partner Anne Kennedy and I formed the Sybilla Masters Fund, a venture capital firm based in Seattle. We get a board seat in each portfolio company in which we invest. Since we can't serve on every board, we have venture partners. We find great satisfaction in this work. If I help one hundred more women launch their own funds and serve on boards of directors, we can begin to make a dent in the gender imbalance of both private and public boards.

At one point, I was serving on four boards around the world. I currently sit on boards in three continents. All my board governance roles have been for private sector companies, nominally all in technology. I serve and have served companies engaged in sectors such as fintech, travel, big data, marcommtech, health sciences and smart cities. I've served on nonprofit boards. What I bring to the table is thirty-plus years of business experience and acumen.

My counsel: Do not limit yourself to your professional industry. Find a common thread of expertise and serve companies across a wide spectrum of industries.

Governance is significantly different in the private and public sectors. To learn more about it, I took a course, which also covered board readiness, at the University of Washington. Although it lasted only a few days, I learned a great deal. Both public and private boards have governance, legal, and fiduciary responsibility to their companies. But in their earlier stages, private boards are much smaller than public ones. They are typically a tightly knit three-to-five-person group that includes an investor, a founder, and perhaps an outside, independent board member who joins the board at a later stage. In contrast, public boards tend to be larger, and their governance follows a rigorous public reporting structure.

My counsel: Whether you serve on a public or private board, never lose sight of the fact that your first obligation is the governance of the company. Make sure you know what's going on inside the company as best you can. If something does not seem right, say so. Press the issue. If you are asked to be silent on an issue, dig deeper. Honesty in business is your primary focus.

There is so much more discussion of female board governance today than before, as evidenced in our language, support systems, books, podcasts, conversations with women who want to become board members, and the like. No such ecosystem existed in my day. These are the markers I look at when I say that women are making progress, although we aren't getting there fast enough. We are inching forward as we have for generations. I am hopeful we've turned a corner over the last months. California passed a Women on Boards law stipulating board of directors of publicly held companies located in California must have at least one female director on their boards by December 31, 2021. Germany has already applied such a law countrywide. The U.S. is slow and will probably implement the same thing state by state. Hopefully, gender-balanced boards will be the norm before my days are over.

My counsel: Do not be patient. Do not wait for others to ask you to serve. Propose your service. Be clear about what you can offer. Put others forward to serve as well. Make a concerted effort to improve diversity.

If your goal is to become a public director, first consider directorships for a private company. Begin with advisory boards. Listen and learn, then become a guest on the board of directors. You'll then be qualified to move onto the next role. Because a directorship role has fiduciary and legal responsibilities for the health of that organization, it is a serious responsibility that should not be taken lightly. Many folks can push forward and figure it out. However, this isn't a good time to wing it. It is a perfect time to listen, lurk, learn, and then figure it out.

On the flip side, women are far more qualified to do this work than they think. What they must know before serving on a board should be codified. To that end, the course I took at University of Washington proved quite useful. It illuminated what was expected of board members, which conversations took place in the boardroom, how to negotiate prior to getting there, and what to expect in regard to reporting. Board training helps you understand you are fully qualified. Women are often surprised to find they are already qualified to serve. This is our moment of opportunity and our obligation as citizens of the world. Women are desperately needed to balance the masculine energy already present in boardrooms.

I leave you with this story. When I named the Mastersfund®, I was visiting my colleague in Philadelphia. We went to the Union League of Philadelphia, which was founded in 1862. There I saw a photo display of the story of some of Philadelphia's historically prominent women. As I took in the exhibit, I came upon Sybilla Masters' story.

In 1712, Sybilla Masters sailed to London to pursue a patent for her invention of a machine that would pound and cure corn into what was then known as Tuscarora rice and is today known as grits. Sybilla lived in London for three years, opening a millinery shop to support herself. During her absence, her husband, Thomas Masters, cared for their four children in Philadelphia and regularly corresponded with England's King George I in support of his wife's patent. In 1715, the patent for the machine, as well as a second patent for the creation of straw hats made of palmetto leaves, was awarded to Thomas Masters as women were forbidden by law to hold patents. Had Sybilla's husband Thomas not insisted in writing that the requested patent was ". . . for an invention found out by his wife, Sybilla Righton Masters," Sybilla's name would have been lost to history.

Sybilla Righton Masters received the first patent of any inventor, male or female, in the Americas. In the process, she greatly benefited both herself and her husband. While history (which means quite literally his story) often ignores women's contributions, the message here is this: It takes both men and women to make things right. And it is to both their benefit that we do so. The Mastersfund is named after Sybilla Masters.

To those who aspire to become Madam Chairwoman, I say, you are far more qualified than you might think. The boardroom is a powerful place to be, not just in the public sector but also in the private sector. Remember that you stand on the shoulders of giants, and the generations that follow will stand on yours.

Sincerely yours,

Gillian

Gillian Muessig is the CEO of Outlines Venture Group and Managing Director of the Mastersfund, a global gender-lens venture capital fund. She is a co-founder of Moz, the world's most popular provider of digital marketing software and has served on dozens of Boards of Directors and Advisors worldwide. Gillian has supported governments and organizations as a business and investment advisor, including the Bill & Melinda Gates Foundation, U.S. State Department, German Marshall Fund, and SwissContact.

Her radio podcast, VC Confidential, focuses on the expanding capitalization options for early-stage technology companies. Over more than three decades, Gillian has helped thousands of companies to launch, grow, pivot and thrive.

ROYANNE DOI

Board of Directors: Gojo & Company

*"Don't be caught climbing the ladder of success
only to find that it was leaning against the wrong wall."*

Dear Future Women Leaders:

I am honored to share some lessons with you based on my work experience.

"Success is a journey, not a destination."

Sage words from my life mentor and the basic tenet upon which I mapped out my professional career/life. So I thought I would organize my advice to you based on four life stages in my own journey.

#1 HARD WORK AND CONSISTENT PERFORMANCE (Growing up)

I am a fourth-generation American of Japanese ancestry. My great-grandfather left Hiroshima, Japan, before the turn of the twentieth century to chase the American dream as an immigrant. While my parents were relatively poor growing up, they were not interned (like my husband's parents in California) during WWII. I was born and raised in Hawaii for the first eighteen years of my life, and I was lucky enough to grow up as a middle-class daughter of a teacher and an engineer.

When I was thirteen, I decided that I wanted to be a judge. Back then, judges in the civil rights cases were changing the world. I have a soft spot in my heart for underdogs. I told my father I needed to go to law school after getting my undergraduate degree. He told me he would pay for my college degree, but I was on my own for graduate school. I ended up graduating Magna Cum Laude from Washington University in St. Louis. I never cut class. My mom was working three jobs and my dad took a second mortgage on the house to pay for my college tuition. I felt fortunate to be able to go to the mainland for my education.

I attended UCLA School of Law on a full scholarship my first year. I then worked part-time as a law clerk while going to law school full time, and also worked full-time summer jobs to pay for my second and third years of law school. After we graduated from law school and taking the bar exam, many of my friends went on vacation to Europe or even home for a visit. But I went to work immediately after taking the bar exam because I was running out of money to pay rent.

I am the first lawyer in my extended family. My dad was the only one of his siblings who attended university. After law school, I was the only Asian-American lawyer in my "white shoe" law firm. I often describe myself as a person with an "immigrant mindset," which for me means my family had to work hard for everything they got in life. There was no sense of entitlement. We know life can change in a moment, and that we could lose everything for reasons that might or might not be fair. (Having said that, I recognize that as an Asian-American woman, I enjoy a myriad of invisible privileges based on where and when I was born.) But, in my youth, I learned it was important to work hard—give everything a 102% effort, ask for help when I need it and persist until I succeed. These lessons served me well in my youth. However, as I got older, I learned how to work smarter, not just work harder.

#2 Surviving AND Thriving Through Change (Thirty-two years old)

Growing up, I was an intense teenager with a life purpose, a personal creed of core values, and a ten-year plan—another nugget of pure wisdom from my life mentor, George. By the time I was thirty-two years old, I was on my second ten-year plan (twenty-five to thirty-four years old).

The plan had evolved into one with annual goals covering seven areas: physical, mental, spiritual, educational/professional, financial, social, and community. Initially, my plan was to become a trial lawyer and a law firm partner in California. However, I couldn't because, in 1994, my husband and I moved to Japan for his job.

Before relocating to Japan, I had been a litigation attorney, but I had no hope of ever becoming a Japanese lawyer litigating in Japanese court. I would need to be fluent in Japanese, go back to school to study Japanese law, and pass the Japan bar exam. It was clear I would not be a trial lawyer in Japan. No amount of grit or persistency was going to get me there. I was miserable. I studied Japanese but had no friends, no work, and no money of my own. I gained weight, sat in my pajamas all day, and contemplated divorcing my husband. My ten-year plan was obsolete. I was stuck and I needed to get unstuck.

> A 10-year plan is like a batter's box. It is just a place to stand when you are swinging for home runs.
>
> Don't be caught climbing the ladder of success only to find that it was leaning against the wrong wall.
>
> Each of us guards a gate of change that can only be opened from the inside.

I let go of my ten-year plan of becoming a Los Angeles trial lawyer, and I adjusted my career plan for my new life in Japan. I got a job as a lawyer and government affairs representative for a non-life-insurance company. Eventually, I made and followed my third ten-year plan (thirty-five to forty-four years old) and moved from insurance to banking, asset management, and securities.

#3 SUCCESS IN JAPAN AT THE BOARD LEVEL (forty-seven years old)

Fast forward to my fourth ten-year plan (forty-five to fifty-four years old). I was promoted to Senior VP when I was forty-two years old. I had become an experienced financial services in-house lawyer. I had served on a for-profit board for a software development subsidiary in HangZhou. I had been nominated for the International Law Office/Lexology Global Counsel Award and was one of five finalists in the category of financial services and regulatory lawyer.

I started learning about corporate governance. This made me realize the importance of the corporate secretary function:

namely, what was presented to the board, what the directors knew or didn't know, and what role directors should play in an organization. I was a senior regional counsel for Asia Pacific, managing a fifteen-member law team in Tokyo, Hong Kong and Australia, covering institutional investor clients in thirteen countries. But I somehow missed the corporate secretary role. How would I get that missing piece of legal governance experience?

I changed jobs.

For most women, career plans are not escalators. An escalator career is when you get on at the bottom floor of a company, stay with the same company forever and slowly rising up the ranks until you make it to a C-suite corner office. For most women, a career is more like a career lattice or jungle gym. You climb as high as you can go and move to the left or right when you need to. When I changed jobs, I went to a company that needed me to build their corporate secretary team, and I became a chief legal officer in Japan.

My natural tendency is to be a relationship-oriented person, but I flexed and became a "process queen." First, I focused on the board schedule. I created a board of directors meeting schedule based on the Japan regulator's inspection manual.

(i)   I added anything the examiner would want to see to a list of mandatory agenda items.

(ii)   I considered the appropriate frequency of reports from finance, audit, sales, compliance, and risk.

(iii)   I worked backwards from the board approval date at least a month for the report to be presented at committee, and at least two months for the report to be generated by the relevant division.

(iv)   I added a tickler system to remind important business divisions it was time to gather information for the report to the board within three months.

Second, I focused on organizing the content of agenda items. We created summary templates so that the board members could understand the purpose of an agenda item in a single glance:

(i)   whether the agenda item was only to report information or required board approval;

(ii)   what business division generated the agenda material and is responsible for implementing action; and

(iii)   an executive summary of the information to be considered by the board members for better context.

We also established a tracking system for "homework" so that any task discussed during the board meeting was assigned to a responsible person and put in a queue for tracking until its successful completion.

As a young lawyer, I had dismissed administration stuff as boring. As a mature lawyer, I appreciated the bigger picture of director responsibility and liability. I paid attention to the board role of oversight and monitoring with the appropriate granularity of details—enough to make a good decision but not too much to diminish the authority of senior management.

Potential Liability: As a board director, you need to know your obligations.

Legal Inventory: Prioritize risk assessment of the most relevant laws from every country in which you do business. Saying you didn't know is not a legitimate defense.

Joint and Several Liability: You can't rely only on someone else's expertise to rubber-stamp a board decision.

#4 GLOBAL ETHICS & COMPLIANCE (fifty-four years old)

My dream job wasn't even in my fifth ten-year plan (fifty-five to sixty-four). When I was nineteen years old and declaring my philosophy major, I met a man who had a business card with the title "Corporate Philosopher." I was intrigued by the idea a company would pay someone to think about the right way to do things. Fast forward thirty-five years, and I was lucky enough to be appointed as a chief corporate ethics officer for a Fortune 500 company. When they initially offered me that job, I declined, explaining I couldn't leave my husband in Japan and work at the company's corporate headquarters in New Jersey. They said they would let me do this global role while remaining in Japan. How wonderful is that?! I traveled to Europe, North and South America, and Asia helping my company "penetrate" corporate values and integrity into international subsidiaries and domestic middle management.

Some people say working long hours for something you don't care about is stress. But working long hours for something you do care about is passion. This brings me to a brief anecdote about how I got this job: The prior chief corporate ethic officer had seen me ask a question from Japan at a regional legal meeting, and she remembered me as being proactive enough to ask the question and the quality of the question. When they were considering a slate of possible internal candidates, she brought up my name to her boss, the chief ethics and compliance officer. He agreed I might be good for the job. Little did he know that global ethics officer was my dream job at nineteen years old, or that I have had a lifelong passion for ethics.

I often recommend women speak up or ask questions at meetings or conferences. If you say nothing, you are adding value like a potted plant in the corner. If you have a voice and a seat at the table, use it.

Not everyone needs a series of ten-year plans for their life. Some people manage to have a fabulous life without it. But I was just a local girl from a public school in Hawaii. I needed all the help I could get. My ten-year plans gave me courage when I was unsure, discernment when I had difficult choices to make, flexibility and stability when things changed, and a place to stand when I was swinging for a homerun. So I encourage you to take the time and do the due diligence of planning where you're going to apply your talents and skills. Best wishes for your continued success.

Sincerely yours,

Royanne

Royanne Doi is currently serving as a Global Legal, Ethics & Compliance Adviser at Yamaha Corporation. She is a corporate governance specialist with past positions as Chief Legal Officer, Corporate Chief Ethics Officer, Chief Compliance Officer, Head of corporate secretary team, Regional Director of Government Affairs. She has work experience in life and non-life insurance, banking, asset management, securities and construction industries. During her tenure as a global ethics officer, Royanne's company received Ethisphere's designation as one of the World's Most Ethical Companies for the first time in 2015, and multiple times thereafter.

Royanne has an undergraduate degree in Philosophy, from Washington University in St. Louis, graduating Magna Cum Laude, Phi Beta Kappa. She earned her Juris Doctorate from UCLA School of Law and is a member of the California bar. She has also lived in Japan since 1994 and has three passions: economic empowerment for women, the cross-study of behavioral ethics & neuroscience, and forever learning.

SUSAN ST. AMAND

Past Chairwoman: Ottawa Community Foundation

Past Chairwoman: Ottawa International Airport Authority

"Don't be afraid to step in and step up. Do what you say you are going to do. Show up on time. Be grateful for the abilities that you have. Say thank you. These essential, humble things can take you a long way."

Dear Chairwomen of Tomorrow:

In the past, I would always say the term "chairperson" should not be gendered as we tried to find a balance against the term "chairman." However, in using the word "chairwoman," the gender role becomes evident, visible, and hopefully more acceptable as a term and as a role. I hope my story will inspire you to take on this position in the future.

I grew up in a tiny town in Northwestern Ontario Canada, as one of four children, with two sisters and a brother. My grandmother was a powerful role model, in that she was brilliant, always learning, and contributed to her community. My grandfather was the first mayor of the town in which I was born. He was a business owner and started his business before the town was incorporated.

I did not see him much outside of dinners and family events. He always respected my grandmother, and I felt she was the force, and possibly the brains, behind the mayor. Back then, it was unacceptable to see a woman leading anything, especially in a small town. However, she was a leader, and he respected her leadership. Although he was the visible one, she was the invisible force supporting him and every bit as engaged in community discussions, except at the township council table or in the "Gentlemen's Club." She was one of my earliest role models.

After growing up in this and neighboring small towns, I moved away at an early age to attend college because there were none nearby. Some of my professors were quite capable and willing to support young women in their endeavors while others were less inclined to do so.

My father owned a small gas station business, and my brother and I worked for him for many years. My father and I were close and worked together in the business. He never treated me as if my gender mattered, other than not being able to clean the men's washroom when men were inside.

In my last year of college, my father offered his business to my brother, and not to me. When my brother expressed no interest in it and did not want to work there seven days a week, my father sold the business. Interestingly, I never took the fact that he did not want me to own it as a slight. I felt he wanted me to pursue my dreams to their fullest, which was not that business. He encouraged me when I started in my next role in banking and when I went through my management training program. In 1982, few women worked in that field. It was a tough job market and interest rates were close to 20 percent. People were going bankrupt and having a difficult time.

At first, the senior bank management team was surprised I'd agreed to start in management training and to move every year or two to a new location. Moving was the only way to progress in a banking career in 1982, and few women were offered or accepted such opportunities. I did not think about it too much at the time. I did what I had to do to get the job done and earned respect all along the way. It was not until much later I discovered I was being paid much less than my male counterparts. I focused on myself, my career path, and where I wanted to go. I carved a lot of that out by myself.

I left banking to go into life insurance and start my own business. Few women held leadership roles in that sector as well. Sadly, this is still the case. I shifted careers partly because I wanted to do volunteer work and get on boards to learn and contribute more from a social and financial/economic standpoint. I am an extrovert who loves meeting people and discussing their perspectives and experiences.

In the area of social capital, my role models growing up had been my father and grandfather because they were well-networked and respected in their communities. My mother and grandmother were also well-networked and respected in other ways. At the time, I did not think much about these commonalities and differences. My two sisters had no interest in moving up the corporate ladder or getting involved in board work and pursued other interests and activities.

When you run your own business, you have to keep developing your leadership skills. I always kept learning and was never afraid to ask. One of my closest mentors was a phenomenal individual, who recently passed away at the age of ninety. He was instrumental in that he encouraged me to pursue opportunities when they presented themselves. What I needed most when moving forward was the confidence my mentors instilled in me, particularly in regard to board work.

After one of my first board meetings, a man told me that he was disappointed that I had not said much during the meeting, and that he'd expected more from me. I walked out of the meeting realizing he was right. Despite being the only woman around the table, my voice needed to be heard. I have often been the only female on a board. I read the material, do my research and always come prepared. I check my ego at the door. I know what I'm talking about and ask questions. Asking questions reveals a lot. When you do, you often voice what others are afraid to say. My mentors greatly encouraged me to ask questions, learn, and speak up at the table.

My first Board Chair role was on a psychiatric hospital foundation board. I had been volunteering and assisting the board in building a program specific to their endowment funds and giving plan. A lawyer client of mine, who served on the board, told me I was good at what I did, and my expertise was needed on the board. He asked me if I'd help out on the committee. Once I was on the committee, he asked me to join the board. I did, and before I knew it, held the vice-chair seat and later became the chair.

Throughout my board service experience, I've been surprised by how few women are represented on boards and how seldom boards have female chairs. Over the years, I have always been amazed when I become the first female chair of a board. Though that has been my biggest surprise, I have been fortunate in always feeling support from fellow board members.

My second biggest surprise, when initially serving on boards, was how many board members showed up unprepared. When you lead by example, however, and are as prepared and diligent as you can be, others follow. If you are the only women at the table, come prepared and ask thoughtful and important questions. This, in turn, will raise the bar for everyone else because no one wants to look like they are not pulling their weight.

On the boards I sit on today, and certainly those I've served on in the last ten years, I find the level of preparedness has improved. I have served on thirty-some boards and found their professionalism partly stems from the number of board-specific training programs available. Learning and understanding fiduciary responsibility is more accessible to everyone now than it was ten to twenty years ago. Twenty-five years ago, the scarcity of educational opportunities on boards surprised me. Now, there are numerous sources one can tap into for education, which is fabulous.

I believe board-training programs are essential because so much is happening today. Our world and organizations are complex and complicated. Those at the top of their field are presented with questions that haven't been asked before. Board-training courses center on social capital and relationships. People you meet in training have different learning experiences than you do, which may not be covered in the course curriculum. They can provide you with valuable opportunities to ask questions and discuss topics you might not have previously thought about. This an important side bar to training programs that will enhance your knowledge.

I had expected the number of women networking and taking board-training courses to rise more rapidly in the recent years. However, there has been backlash from male individuals who felt boards did not consider them for a position because they planned to fill the seat with a woman. The situation has become adversarial. In my opinion, that is not the right approach. If I could do one thing, I'd change it so we can all be stronger together, and include males, females, gay, lesbian, transgender, and other groups to represent the communities we serve.

Socializing at a bar after the board meeting can sometimes be just as important as the board meeting itself. I've often been the only women to attend social board gatherings after formal board meetings. Board social gatherings open up the opportunity for informal conversations even if you don't consume alcohol. Conversations occur both inside and outside the formal board setting, so one can potentially miss a lot of information if you don't take part in casual outings. Sometimes, you need to be present more than you might think.

When important discussions take place, including your voice requires self-confidence and a certain comfort level, no matter what your gender. Both genders must feel equally accepted. If you are the only woman in the room, you cannot assume the rest of the room is against you. You have to feel you are there for the right reasons, are part of the leadership equation, and are accepted.

On one of the boards I served on, the CEO pressured the nominating committee to select someone other than me as chair because he did not want a woman to fill the role. The nominating committee members, to their credit, argued this board would cease being relevant if they didn't step into the twenty-first century and become inclusive. The CEO was not with the organization for much longer.

We should have people saying women need to be at the table. History is a remarkable teacher, especially when it shows women being represented on boards. Teaching this history and making it visible is critical for future generations. I don't think either of my two daughters ever thought being male or female made any difference. I remember when one of them told me she thought every mother served on boards, as I did. She had no idea this wasn't the case until she attended university. She wouldn't think twice about getting involved and engaged in something.

I hope young and middle-aged women are like this and are willing to step up the corporate ladder. I was sitting on a board during my first pregnancy, and my daughter turned twenty-five earlier this year. I was reasonably young, raising a family, and running a business. I didn't see it as being extraordinary. It was just something I did because it was meaningful to me. It continues to be important to me that my daughters see me contribute regardless of my work-life situation. I wanted them to see they could have a life as a mother, make a living as a businessperson or an executive, and contribute to the community. I wanted to show them they can decide on their own priorities based on what is going on in their lives and in their community.

There is less emphasis on gender diversity on boards today than there was a few years ago. The needle isn't moving as quickly as it could or should. Perhaps it's because those of us who've served or chaired on boards aren't visible to younger generations, so they don't know what's possible. They often fear board members are unreachable and don't know how to reach out to them. Unfortunately, gender parity on boards is not taking place at the speed it should. I believe that, unfortunately, some form of quota system must be instituted to rectify this situation.

Achieving board parity would be easier if for-profit and not-for-profit companies had to publicly disclose their board matrix and composition. I am a big believer that when a for-profit company exports to other countries, it's essential for it to know and understand the cultures of those countries. Its board needs to understand those cultures. The same applies to gender. If your clients are 50 percent male and 50 percent female, you need to assess whether you represent their community and take action if you don't. You can demonstrate what you are doing through a report card checklist.

Boards nowadays are challenged because they require professionals with experience in cyber and technology risk, HR, cultural understanding, finance and taxation, all of which add up to a large matrix of board members. However, boards also need to remain workable. A thirty-person board is difficult to manage. These boards need to have visible yardsticks and opportunities in place to move toward gender equity. In other words, more opportunities for learning should exist, not only pertaining to risk and what it means, but also to what it means to be a fiduciary and to serve on a board. These opportunities should be available to all gender types. And different gender types should be included in a qualified list, and boards should have a certain number represented to move things forward.

Why don't we compare historical examples? Sweden, which has more gender balance, seems to be in a relatively good economic state. When comparing different cultures and economies, one needs to consider whether gender balance positively impacts the economy. You'd probably find that it does. Although plenty of data supports this finding, it is not easy to illustrate. I don't have compelling, concise documentation. If companies had a clear picture of the variance in having a gender-balanced versus a non-gender-balanced board, it wouldn't take long for them to change in order to honor their fiduciary responsibility to act in the best interest of their organization. When I think of the unfortunate economic circumstances Japan has suffered over the past thirty years, I wonder if a more gender-balanced workplace would have made a difference.

To all the young women out there—don't be afraid to step in and step up. Do what you say you are going to do. Show up on time. Be grateful for the abilities you have. Say "thank you." Be prepared and don't be afraid to stand up. These essential, humble things can take you a long way. Don't think you have to choose between being a mother or a leader in business because you can be both. When you are both, you lead by example for the next generations.

Sincerely,

Susan

Susan St. Amand is the Founder and President of The Sirius Group Inc. and Sirius Financial Services in Ottawa, Ontario, Canada.

Susan has over 30 years of experience in finance, governance, strategy, risk management and philanthropy. As a member of a business family and an entrepreneur she built her firm on a foundation of trust and mutual respect. Susan's integrity, passion, 'big picture' view, intense listening, communication skills, and comprehensive approach make her uniquely skilled.

Susan is a member of The Family Enterprise XChange, the Institute of Corporate Directors (ICD), The International Women's Forum, The Society for Trust and Estate Practitioners (STEP), The Purposeful Planning Institute, ADVOCIS, Conference for Advanced Life Underwriting (CALU).

Susan is the immediate Past Chair of the board for the Ottawa Community Foundation, Director on the National Board of the Family Enterprise Xchange, Past co-chair of the Institute of Corporate Directors (ICD) Ottawa Chapter, Past Chair of the Board of the Ottawa International Airport Authority, Past Chair of CALU, Past Chair of the Ottawa STEP Chapter, Past Chair of PEMCO a private steel company, and one of twenty founders of the Women for Mental Health campaign. Over the last 30 years Susan has been a director on over 25 boards.

CLAIRE CHINO

President and CEO: Itochu International

Advisory Board: Cornell Law School

"When women realize the power of their own voice, within a board setting or elsewhere, it allows for truly positive changes in our society."

Dear Women Leaders of Tomorrow:

First, a little background . . . My name is Claire Chino. I was born in the Netherlands, grew up in Japan, and later moved to Los Angeles. I credit the LA public high school system for teaching me English. My father was an auto company executive at a time when the U.S. and Japan were embroiled in a trade war.

I came to know that litigation in the U.S. is an everyday event. My father testified in several lawsuits as witness on behalf of the company for which he worked. This inspired me to pursue a legal degree and to become a lawyer. I initially worked for a law firm, but then I moved to a company in Tokyo to become its in-house lawyer. The company later offered me an assignment in New York to be President and CEO of the U.S. operation (ITOCHU

International). This was my first time in a position outside of the legal world.

Transitioning from a lawyer to CEO

Initially, I was worried about this new position because I had never been trained as a businessperson. In order to be a good CEO, I thought I had to be a math wizard or an expert on Excel spreadsheets, neither of which I am good at. But to my pleasant surprise, I soon found out the skills required of a CEO are not just math. As CEO, you have to know the business and understand the people really well. You also have to spot issues, prioritize issues, and solve problems. I had been trained on this as a lawyer, and these skills are now serving me well in my decision-making as a CEO.

How a diverse environment can make you less self-conscious

Japan is a homogeneous country. Many people (especially non-Asian people) who traveled to Japan for the first time tell me how much they stood out in that environment. I am sure you can imagine how self-conscious you might be if you are the only White person in a sea of Japanese people. When you are in an environment where everybody else other than you is alike, you become more aware of the fact you (alone) are different.

New York City is the polar opposite of Japan, full of diversity. And I mean diversity not just in terms of race but ethnicity, language, religion, body type, and so much more. In that setting, it is impossible to compare yourself to others because everybody is so different! Here in NYC, I never think of my gender, race, or physical attributes because everybody is different. Here, I can focus on myself, my individuality. Here, I am just me.

The importance of focusing on the individual and the individual talent

You are an individual with different layers of identities. All of these make up who you are. In my case, I am a woman, Japanese, Asian, bi-cultural, etc. While I am all of these, any one of these is not the entire "me." Most importantly for the purpose of this letter, my gender is not the only thing that defines me.

But in an environment where you are the only woman, it is easy for your gender to play a bigger role for you and for the others. This can happen, for example, in a Japanese company setting where you are the only woman in the business meeting. You may feel you need to represent the female view. Or the others may turn to you for the women's perspective.

Because your gender is certainly an important aspect of who you are, this is understandable. But the crucial thing to remember is your voice is the voice of you as an individual. Your voice should matter to others because of who you are rather than because it represents the female voice.

How mentors can help you do better

I believe it is important for any person to have a "mentor." A mentor is someone who can show you the way forward. She is somebody you aspire to be. Studies have shown one who has a mentor tends to do better in the organization than one who does not have a mentor. This is because one with a mentor learns from the mentor's successes and failures, while one without a mentor has to learn from her own trial and error.

I frequently meet younger women who say they cannot find a mentor who has all the qualities they seek. I tell them they may never find that one person. You should look for qualities or skills you find important and combine them to create your own super mentor. For example, the barista I used to order from in Tokyo always remembered my order and would proactively ask:

"Same thing today?"

That kind of attitude was inspiring to me and taught me to proactively ask questions and remember details in my role as a lawyer. I think there are qualities in everybody from which you can learn.

It is important for women to have mentors and to become mentors themselves. You have so many qualities that younger women can learn from.

How sponsors can help with your promotion

A "sponsor" is different from a mentor, although it could be the same person. A sponsor is someone who can promote you up in an organization. I have had both mentors and sponsors, although more mentors than sponsors. My first sponsor promoted me to the position of General Counsel within the Legal Division. My second sponsor is another person who promoted me to the present position. I believe it is important to have both mentors and sponsors, but especially sponsors as you become more senior in an organization.

Why is diversity important for the board?

There is a big movement in the U.S. as well as in Japan to see more board diversity. Traditionally in Japan, the board consisted of people who were "promoted" from within the company. Until recently, boards only consisted of these inside directors who were all men, Japanese, and above a certain age. In the U.S., it was historically men, Caucasian, and senior in age.

So why are investors and shareholders seeking more board diversity (including gender and race) in recent years? In order to answer this, let me turn to a book called *Wisdom of Crowds* by James Surowiecki. The book describes an incident whereby the

U.S. Navy "lost" a submarine. It initially tasked its routine experts to come up with a hypothesis as to where the submarine might be. The experts came up with a hypothesis, but the submarine was not found. The Navy then gathered experts from different specialty areas. They came up with a different hypothesis, which ultimately led to the discovery of the submarine. The moral of the story is that experts in certain fields tend to think alike and have trouble thinking outside the box. On the other hand, people with different backgrounds (diversity) can shed new light on a matter.

In this day and age, where it is vital for companies to stay competitive, it is important their boards stay broad-minded and visionary. Because people with similar backgrounds tend to think more alike than those with different backgrounds, board diversity is crucial in order for companies to stay nimble and forward-looking, ahead of the game.

Networking is so important

There is an organization called the Women Corporate Directors (WCD). It is a group of women who are also members of the board. I have been a member of this organization for some years, and I find it important to have a network such as this. Through networking, you learn about current topics and best practices. You may also find out about new professional opportunities. But at the end of the day, it is nice to have a network where you feel safe bouncing off ideas in order to gain new perspectives from people who are in similar positions. As a board member, you have to broaden your horizon in order to fully contribute to the board.

Be aware of unconscious bias

There is still unconscious bias against girls and women, and we have to work hard to eliminate bias and gender roles, which can be implanted in us at an early age. When I was attending kindergarten, a four-year-old boy came up to me and snatched away the pair of scissors I was using. He said, "Boys first." He could not have come up with that idea by himself at such a young age. Who instilled that notion in him? Is it society? Is it his parents? Are girls also conditioned in the same way to think of their "roles?" I truly hope our society can become free of gender bias (among other biases). In that respect, education plays a crucial role.

Your voice matters

Please remember how important your voice is. Your voice should never be given less value because of your gender. When women realize the power of their own voice, within a board setting or elsewhere, it allows for truly positive changes in our society. I am counting on you as the Leader of Tomorrow to not box yourself in (or have others box you in) in order to create a world where the focus is on individual talent - and where individuals shine because of who they are.

Yours truly,

Claire

Claire is Managing Executive Officer of ITOCHU Corporation ("Itochu"), a Fortune Global 500company headquartered in Japan, and President & CEO of ITOCHU International Inc., a subsidiary of Itochu in New York, overseeing North America. Before assuming her position in New York, she was General Counsel of Itochu, and prior to that, a partner with an international law firm.

In 2013, she became the first female executive officer of any major trading company in Japan. Claire has received several recognitions, including from the World Economic Forum (Young Global Leader), Yale University (Yale World Fellow), Asia Society (Asia 21) and the U.S. Japan Foundation (USJLP Fellow). She has also been recognized in the legal community as a "Top 25In-House Counsel in Asia" (Asia Legal Business), "Asia Pacific's Innovative Lawyer" (Financial Times), and "FT Global General Counsel 30" (Financial Times) and has received a "Transformative Leader" award (Inside Counsel). In 2018, the California Lawyers Association recognized her as the 8th Annual Warren M. Christopher International Lawyer of the Year. Most recently, she became the recipient of the Smith Medal from Smith College. She is a graduate of Smith College (B.A. cum laude) and Cornell Law School (J.D.), where she serves on the advisory board. She is a classically trained singer and gives solo performances from time to time.

GAVRIELLA SCHUSTER

Board of Directors: ChinaSoft International

"I'd done almost everything I'd wanted to do. I wanted to learn about all aspects of the business so that I could walk away and run any business. I learned about operations, marketing, services, licensing, product development, and sales . . . I started thinking about where else I could go. Board service seemed like an attractive option."

Dear Future Chairwomen:

I grew up in Boston, Massachusetts. As a teen, some of my friends who owned computers exposed me to technology. They'd lug large computers over to my house in big carrying cases, and we'd play around with them. Meanwhile, I cultivated my work ethic early, starting my first job as a waitress when I was fourteen, and then consistently held one, if not two, odd jobs throughout high school, in tele-sales, at a farm stand, and at a Hallmark store.

My aspiration to become a genetics engineer influenced my choice of universities. I went to the University of Michigan, which at the time was one of the few schools with a genetics curriculum.

91

Moving to Michigan from Massachusetts was a great learning experience and spurred my independence. I had to learn how to navigate a forty-thousand-student school, where everything involved standing in line. Two of the major things I learned were how to stand in line and how to creatively find the resources, support, and help I needed. When I went home after my freshman year, I interned in a hospital's HR department, primarily handling administrative duties. The woman who headed our department gave me great guidance, and said:

"You're doing a great job here, but after you graduate, never, ever take a job like this. Follow the path to accomplishing much bigger things and never settle."

I didn't think much of it at the time, but it actually turned out to be amazing advice. During my junior year of college, my dad lost his job as a hospital department head. It was crushing for him, and he had a hard time finding another job because his field was so specialized. I realized I was headed in the same direction by majoring in such a specialized domain as genetic engineering. I could envision myself twenty to thirty years into my career with no runway left due to my specialization, and thought:

"I don't want to do that."

I took a step back, went to the university's counseling office to consider my options, and decided to change my major to social psychology. This enabled me to no longer solely study science but to take a much broader course load, including political science and business. I earned a social psychology degree, which provided me with the general experience and knowledge I needed to navigate the job market.

Since I didn't have enough money for graduate school and needed to secure a job right away, I asked the school's counseling office which type of job I should apply for. I took a career placement test and its results indicated management, which was ironic to me. What twenty-one-year-old walks into a company as a manager? I nonetheless started applying for job listings promoting management-training programs, such as those from Merrill Lynch, Anderson Consulting, Procter and Gamble, and Cigna Health Insurance. Many companies offered management training programs to recent graduates. Sometimes they were internal two-year MBA programs training graduates to do whatever it was the company did. I accepted a job at Cigna Health Insurance because it was described as hands-on and experiential.

My first day on the job, I was tasked with leading a team, which suited me well. I worked for Cigna for the first five years of my career and was promoted four times. I lived in Connecticut, had both a day and night shift, and handled New York and national accounts. When I left, I'd been leading a team of about six hundred people who processed healthcare claims, and my customers were the HR departments of our big accounts. It was a great experience for me, both in learning to be a manager and learning the business.

During that time, I started an MBA but didn't finish it. Halfway through, I met my husband. He and I decided to move to Seattle, where Cigna offered me a sales job. Working in the healthcare field during my first year in Seattle was a great experience, especially as it pertained to gender balance. I experienced more gender balance in the healthcare industry than I experienced working in tech.

I left Cigna to work at Aldus, a small, early-version desktop-publishing-software company. Although I had no experience in the software business, I was hired for my people-management skills and tasked with managing a combination of operations, customer service, and tech support teams. It was a great company. I became knowledgeable about the software industry and about our cycles from engineering to launch.

Three years into working there, Adobe acquired Aldus, and I remained with the company for another year or so. I learned a lot but eventually decided to leave Adobe because, even though it had an office in Seattle, I felt that to further evolve I'd need to work at its headquarters in Mountain View, California.

Since I didn't want to relocate, I started applying for jobs at Microsoft. I was hired in 1995, primarily thanks to my experience outsourcing Adobe's customer service. The outsourcing model was nascent, and Microsoft was just starting to implement it. I was brought on to manage the outsourcing of its customer service and fulfillment centers.

For about a year, I developed four different programs at five locations around the world, selecting outsourcers and setting up fulfillment centers. I then became a global operations manager, working with corporate vice presidents in the business, taking their requirements, and figuring out how to implement them. The company was looking for someone to figure out the bigger picture of what we were trying to do, so I offered to fill that role.

After about a year, I moved from operations to marketing, which was a new field for me. I started defining programs and figuring out Microsoft's broader opportunities in the market. In those early days, we just knew we had a product to take to market but didn't know where its market would be. The work was really fun because it provided me a lot of freedom.

I started creating go-to market plans and platforms and holding end-to-end responsibility with our global strategy and execution arms. From there, I kept moving. I took over and built up a Microsoft-created training and certification program, which served as a core foundation for Microsoft's Certified Professional program. I then built out Microsoft's Global Training Providers Network, including the process and infrastructure underpinnings.

Microsoft had products coming out that needed an IT Pro ecosystem. In response, we launched SQL 7, which required we competitively recruit Oracle DBAs (Database Administrators), so I created a specific program and training for them. Microsoft then launched Windows 2000 for which Active Directory specialists were needed. We had to pull them from Novell, so I created another compete-recruit program to bring those specialists into Microsoft.

After that incredible ride, I moved into enterprise services, Microsoft's small consulting service arm, which at the time was even smaller than it is today. There, we tried to structure the program to have more repeatability through packaging our consultants 'output and scaling business through our partners. I helped our consultants create a knowledge base by documenting and packaging what they did. Many of them were programmers, so they'd create code stitching as systems integrators did. We'd package it up into the solution accelerators we shared with our partners.

Microsoft isn't so much one company as it is a group of little start-ups that exist within a larger frame of shared services. This is less true now but was the way we operated back in the nineties. I've always found that each one of these groups feels like a different company because group general managers set the tone for their teams.

Diversity and inclusion weren't even a thing when I started at Microsoft. Bill Gates ran the show, and everything in the organization went either from someone at a low level up to Bill or from Bill down. Either ideas rose up organically because someone saw an opportunity and asked for funding to do it, or Bill just decided something had to happen and everyone did it. I have no idea what it must have felt like to be a manager in the midst of that because I wasn't in that role. I can't imagine it was empowering as managers were "in the middle."

Within that framework, Microsoft's culture was definitely male-centric. To be heard, one had to be aggressive, bossy, loud, and prepared to take heat in every meeting. Back then, the company culture valued conflict, and it felt like only good things came from it. Looking back, it was really hard. I'd jumped right into this difficult situation after working for Aldus and Adobe, which had an opposite, almost overly nurturing, corporate culture.

Microsoft has changed a lot since then. It had to grow up and implement more governance. After my time in consulting services, Microsoft created a U.S. subsidiary, which was a big turning point for the company. Instead of trying to run everything from Redmond, Washington, dedicated global regions became governed by general managers. Microsoft's culture evolved quite a bit because employees had to learn to work more collaboratively and work through others.

In those early days, the newly minted president of Microsoft North America pulled me out of consulting services to work in licensing. I worked there for a while in enterprise licensing starting up the Enterprise Agreements and Software Assurance Departments. From there, I moved over into the business group and became a product manager and planner.

I created a product called the Microsoft Desktop Optimization Pack. Windows Client was releasing Vista, which had a poor end-user value proposition to the enterprise. So, I developed a way to sell Windows focusing instead on security and manageability. I developed the value proposition of the "optimized desktop," which needed the Windows Client and Desktop Optimization Pack together in an enterprise agreement. As a result of the success we had, I was promoted to lead the whole Windows Client commercial business.

Eventually I moved back into the U.S. subsidiary to lead our cloud and enterprise business, at a time when Azure was a low, single-digit, million-dollar incubation product. I had to figure out how to build an ecosystem around it and go-to markets for both our direct and commercial licensing businesses. I led that challenging initiative for several years. After that, I joined the partner business to help build a cloud-based ecosystem.

While on the Windows Client team, I realized how difficult it was to be a woman at Microsoft. This was a period of great awareness for me as I had finally entered into the realm of general manager, which brings with it a whole different operating sphere in the company. The president of that division had a "my-way-or-the-highway" management style. If a team member didn't conform to what he asked, it was a problem, so working there was hard.

The team produced Windows 8, which wasn't great for IT pros, making it difficult to sell in the commercial enterprise, so we came into conflict quite a bit. By then, I'd become a Microsoft partner and general manager and understood that working wasn't just about doing a good job, doing what one thought was right, or even running a business. It was also about playing a game and that there were a lot of unwritten rules to the game.

It was hard for me to know my limits or how much I was willing to compromise or change myself for the job I had to do. I wasn't willing to make a dramatic shift from who I was, which was ultimately why I decided to move back into the U.S. subsidiary. As part of the sales organization instead of engineering, this was a more respectful and balanced work environment. In contrast to the lack of gender balance found on engineering teams, where I was usually the only woman in a meeting, the sales and marketing division was more inclusive and collaborative.

While I'd gravitated toward leadership roles from early in my career, the thought of serving on a board occurred to me while running Microsoft's Cloud and Enterprise business, which was about a $6.5 billion business in the U.S. alone. I'd originally thought I'd work at Microsoft for five years, given my tenure at previous companies. At that point, I'd been at Microsoft for fifteen years. I thought:

"How much longer am I going to stay here?"

I'd done almost everything I'd wanted to do. I'd wanted to learn about all aspects of the business so that I could walk away and run any business. I'd learned about operations, marketing, services, licensing, product development, and sales. What else could Microsoft offer me? I started thinking about where else I could go.

Board service seemed like an attractive option. I possessed a big-picture view. I understood my industry and how to build businesses to scale. Work was still busy while I was thinking about this, so although I started networking, I didn't really do anything about getting on a board.

One of my former bosses asked me to join Microsoft's partner team to help reboot the company's ecosystem to become cloud-based. Until then, 99 percent of Microsoft's programs had been built for partners to execute on-premises and didn't leverage the cloud. The thought of building a rebooted partner ecosystem sounded like fun, so I decided to remain at Microsoft to see it through while keeping board governance in mind. My thinking was that I'd be working with all of the partners who ran tech industry businesses, which would give me opportunities to network and find interesting companies to influence and grow.

This job also gave me a good view of the market to better understand where I might want to go with board membership. I sponsored the Athena Alliance, run by Coco Brown, to come to Microsoft and set up a Seattle chapter and recruited a bunch of my peers to join. From my engagement with Coco, I learned to write a board bio, optimize my LinkedIn profile, and think differently about my resumé and Job. I started to get a sense of what it would mean to sit on a board.

I took a great two-day class about "Women on Boards" taught at the University of Washington, which had about six women serving on its large, high-profile board of directors. The class taught me not to be intimidated by the idea of board governance, since I already exercised those responsibilities every day in my role at Microsoft. Sitting on a board of directors would be like sitting through the frequent meetings I held with partners, during which I went through their business plan and guided them on making investments to grow their business. I couldn't be hands-on working with our partners. All I could do was to say:

"When I look at your business, here's what I think and here's where I would go."

A number of partners who'd changed their businesses based on our conversations had been wildly successful. They'd returned and provided me with an update, saying,

"Here's what we did and here's the way we're thinking about it. What should we do next?"

These gratifying successes reinforced my penchant to hold an advisory role going forward.

When I leave Microsoft, I want to help more companies scale. I like the idea of being a guide and advisor without being in it every day. There's absolute value in being able to step back and listen to what various members of a leadership team are saying, look at what they're doing, and offer alternative points of view or insights. They may not see the places where they are stuck.

One of the things that's made Microsoft so successful is its ability to question its past actions and assumptions about its business, customers, or partners. I've gotten good at driving that transformation of understanding how to unpack this work and get down to the root of questions such as:

"Why do you think what you think?"

"What may have changed between the time that was successful and now?"

This has enabled me to move forward on this vision of myself doing something different. Microsoft employees can only sit on one public board at a time, so they need to be selective. The board governance opportunity I found came about thanks to one of the things I learned in the University of Washington class. I learned that it typically takes three to five years for those serious about obtaining a board role to land one, so people should start looking as soon as they can, even if they don't want to serve for some time.

To heed this advice, I started sharing my board governance aspirations with those in my network. I told headhunters I wasn't interested in other jobs but to let me know if they had a board position. When I'd meet with a partner, I'd ask them to let me know if they knew of anyone looking for a board member. My opportunity came out of one such conversation.

One of our partners 'CEO shared a gentleman he worked with in China was looking for an American to serve on his board to provide a different tech-industry perspective because his company, Chinasoft, planned to expand geographically. I thought that sitting on a Chinese board would be interesting. Being able to understand the business from the inside out seemed like a great opportunity.

I accepted the board position at Chinasoft a few years ago. It's been rewarding to help the company transform its business, grow geographically, and consider expanding outside China. It led me to better understand their business inside China. I give a lot of credit to Henry Chen, Chinasoft's chairman and CEO, for being so forward-thinking as to include an American on his board. By the way, I am not the only woman on that board. The other is a China-based professor.

Overall, I don't think we in the U.S. are doing well as it pertains to female or minority representation in corporate governance. I am a founding sponsor of both the Women in Cloud Network and Women in Technology organizations. Under the leadership of Satya Nadella, Microsoft's current CEO, I am also responsible for a new initiative focused on enabling Black-owned tech businesses in the U.S. accelerate their growth. By any measure, however, we're not making enough progress.

Studies show it isn't enough to have one woman or minority on a board. It doesn't shift anything, and they still get talked over. When two or three gender or racially diverse members join, there are allies—someone who can support and repeat what the other person says when he or she is not being heard. An alliance can form so that one person doesn't stick out. When you're the only person from a diverse background, you don't know if you're representing more than yourself. When you have at least one ally, you know you can get somewhere together. The impetus right now may be for boards to include one diverse board member only, but two or three are needed to effect change.

I think that people of color face even more barriers in their aspiration to board governance than are those faced by women. I can only speak from my own experiences, which I know carry white privilege. From speaking to some of my racially diverse peers, I have come to understand that they need to overcome even more biases than I have had to, and it becomes an exhausting exercise every day.

There are more white women than people of color in corporate executive ranks. Despite the small numbers, I recognize that white women have an advantage because more white women already hold positions of management authority within organizations. So the urgency of this challenge extends beyond white women out to black men and women, and any group that is of a minority in a white male-dominated workforce. We have work to do, and I hope we reverse the trend and take on this challenge.

At Microsoft, we've found slight process changes can make a big difference to increase diversity. Teams that go beyond hiring for expediency and focus on having both diverse and external candidate pools for any open job end up with more diverse hires. When diversity becomes a focus in this way, hiring goes further than pulling from friend-of-friend networks. Many hand-select their successors or groom them over years of mentorship. We need to break away from that pre-selection system and require external hiring instead so that, ultimately, the best people are hired. The same goes for boards of directors, which are close-knit communities. Those that require board candidates to have been CEOs before considering them for a role are limiting it to white men.

A lot of focus right now is on the boards of Fortune 500 companies, but honestly, I'd love to join a boardroom of an already established company that is still growing but hasn't hit that point of scale. I think it's the most enjoyable stage. Companies in the $100 million to $1 billion growth stage have the most upside. How does one retool to hit that point of scale?

I'd also selectively serve on boards that aren't driven just by making more money but are purpose-driven by the UN's

Sustainable Development Goals and by doing more for the planet. Honestly, I haven't yet found the company that meets this criterion. However, I will know when I do. Many such companies exist but are already too large.

One company I love and enjoyed working closely with is EcoLab. It's that kind of company at an earlier stage. I appreciate where a company is in its journey. The great news is that Microsoft is a great networking bed. I plan on leveraging its ex-employee alumni network to help me find the next company or set of companies to help grow.

So my advice to you, to the future generation, is to think about where you want to go with your career. Really consider:

What kind of impact do you want to have?

When you look back on your career, what do you want to be known for?

This will help guide you in your decisions and job choices. When first starting out, one often lacks a grand master plan or road map. In my case, I didn't want to become a subject-matter expert. I wanted to learn about all parts of a business. I wanted to be able to build, grow, and scale as much equity in myself as I did for the companies I worked for. I didn't want to find myself thirty years down the road stranded in an outdated job. Knowing where I wanted to go helped guide me in all the decisions I made, in pushing me forward, inspiring me to think differently and take risks.

When I'd hit a roadblock and didn't know what to do next, I gravitated toward a job that would help me learn new skills, have new experiences, and connect with a different network. I eventually have decided to serve on a board to go broader and get a new scale of experience. It gave me additional goals to work toward and network for. When you know your purpose, what you want to achieve, and the impact you want to have, you'll recognize opportunities, as opposed to waiting for them to find you.

I wish you all the best—there are a lot of challenges ahead, but therein lie the seeds of great opportunities!

Yours Truly,

Gavriella

Gavriella is the Corporate Vice President of the Microsoft Commercial Partner team leading a global portfolio of channel partners that has influenced over $1 trillion in ecosystem revenues through Microsoft's fastest growing ecosystem. She has over 30 years of leadership in digital and cloud transformation roles, driving strategy and execution spanning all aspects of business model and product development, launch, marketing, sales and partner development. As a builder and change agent, she specializes in building new businesses and has grown a P&L to over $6.5B and 30% YOY growth.

Last fall she was awarded the ATHENA global leadership award for her advocacy on behalf of women in IT. She is also a founding sponsor of both the Women in Cloud and Women in Technology Networks. She sits on the board of directors for Chinasoft International and the University of Washington Bothell. She most recently gave a TEDx talk on gender equity.

Gavriella specializes in starting up and turning around businesses by inspiring a vision for future customer relevance and engaging the team in developing the roadmap.

PAULA LUPRIORE

Board of Directors: Semtech Corporation, WujiTech Inc.

"When opportunities pop up, say yes."

Dear Future Chairwoman:

I've had an exciting journey as I think back.

I grew up on the East Coast and spent most of my time in Rhode Island. I went to college there and graduated with a degree in applied mathematics. I wanted to go into actuarial work, and never thought I would venture into computer science until a friend of mine mentioned an opportunity one day:

"IBM is visiting the campus and we should practice interviewing."

The two of us were the only women in our engineering classes throughout college, so we became good friends. We were both interviewed, invited back for on-site interviews shortly after, and received job offers. Hence my twenty-three-year career with IBM began. I started as a software programmer and spent eight years in the technical ranks. I advanced into management and then the executive ranks and became a Vice President. I also was a

107

member of IBM's Corporate Technology Council and the Chairman's Senior Leadership Group.

It was an exciting and extremely rewarding journey filled with great experiences and great memories.

When you talk about people who have inspired me along the way, a president I worked for was a mentor for me. He retired from IBM and joined the board of a public company in California. He was a great influencer, which is how I relocated to the West Coast. This public company was in the semiconductor industry, an industry that would be new for me but one to which I would bring my hardware, software, and systems experience, so I joined. As a senior executive for this company, I led product business units with P&L responsibility, then advanced to Chief Operating Officer and then to Interim CEO.

That was an interesting venture for me. Due to unexpected changes overnight, I was handed the keys as Interim CEO. I worked with the board, bankers, and investors to lead through a restructure and sale process that ended successfully for the company and the employees.

I had a long and successful career and had never taken substantial time to travel and visit family in different regions. This felt like the right time to do some of those things. My travels were short-lived when the phone rang one day, and my mentor said he was going to invest in a new start-up on condition that I became its CEO. I agreed to meet the founder, was intrigued by his venture in health-tech, and signed on.

As part of my journey, I was an inside board member at the public semiconductor company as CEO. I was also asked to join a public company board in the education sector as an independent director. Most recently, I have also been appointed as an independent director of the Semtech Corp. public board.

Regarding gender diversity, I did not feel a difference being the only woman on a board versus being on a gender-diverse board. Advancing at IBM, I was considered more second- to third-generation female in terms of achieving the executive ranks and being promoted. When I was in my first vice presidential role, I was the only female senior executive leader in a multi-billion-dollar division in a male-dominated industry.

The good news is that today, we have more women in the technology space, although still not as many as we need. I never let that make me feel like it was a male/female type of thing. As I look back from a career perspective, it was all about results and being driven by strong performance, not necessarily about gender or political biases. When I walked into the room, I did not walk in feeling as if I was the only female. It felt like I was just one member of the team.

It was culturally what I had become used to after so many years at IBM. It is a perspective shift, not so much a male-female agenda—it is an equity advancement agenda.

At IBM, I was asked to be a lead executive for advancing women in the company. We held a women's leadership conference and, while thinking about potential speakers for the conference, I knew I knew I wanted to make the presentations more gender-equal and invite some male executives too. One of the male executives who supported me walked up to the podium and suddenly hesitated uncharacteristically. I was surprised because he was an experienced and confident man. After the conference, he pulled me aside, thanked me, and asked:

"Is that how you and other females have felt over the years after walking into a room with all men?"

I told him I often look right and left and hope to find someone who looks like me, but there has not been a lot of that. He replied,

"I now understand."

Gender diversity in the boardroom is changing. Do I think it is moving fast enough? No. When you think about it, we have had female CEOs of public companies for many years. Why, then, has it taken so long to get more parity in the boardroom? I say it is moving slower than it should. Why? I think there are a lot of reasons for that.

Men network: and women have not always felt as comfortable working the territory. Sometimes it takes that networking aspect to become known. At IBM, when I was in corporate headquarters in a strategy role, I remember my boss—who was one step away from the chairman's office—asked me to go to lunch. He asked if I liked sports. I told him I did. I enjoyed playing volleyball, going to basketball games. I also took dance class from when I was young and competed in gymnastics.

He said:

"What about golf? What about sailing?

"You need to learn to like it. IBM thinks you have potential, and you have achieved so much, but you need to keep this momentum

going. You will get to a point where that will be important to you, to nurture professional relationships."

I heard him, although I did not really understand what he really meant. If I had, it may have made a difference when working toward advancing to the boardroom. I was younger and advancing at IBM, so in my mind, everything was progressing at a meaningful rate. I really did not understand what this white-haired, top corporate executive told me about the importance of building these relationships and networks outside of work.

Finally, I want to say—when opportunities pop up, say yes. When you are still in an executive role in the broader corporate environment, it is easier to make the leap onto a public company board. Some of those opportunities out there are critical, so say "yes." Nurture your relationships early on, socialize them, and stay in touch.

Thinking back, a lot of the executives you work with leave the company and get on other boards. When you are working with them, you may have these great relationships. However, if ten years goes by and you have not stayed in touch, it is more difficult to reestablish those connections. Nurture those relationships you value and that value you. One needs professional relationships but, more importantly, we need sponsors who will put your name out there and help find suitable opportunities for you.

It is often difficult to even hear of the opportunities. If you have long-term goals, then nurturing relationships you have cultivated throughout your career may eventually help sponsor you into the boardroom. Also, sometimes you just need to call these contacts, even if you have not spoken to them for five or six years. Call and let them know you are interested in board opportunities. They may not be thinking of you because time has passed, so you may not otherwise come to mind.

Just as important, of course, is staying focused on performing well in all your leadership roles, being a team player, and keeping a conscious balance between the business and the team that is making you and the business a success.

Good luck, and enjoy the journey!

Truly yours,

Paula

Paula currently serves as a Board Director of Semtech Corp. (NASDAQ:SMTC), a technology company serving consumer, enterprise computing, communications, and industrial end-markets. She is CEO and Board Member of WujiTech, Inc., a private company developing bio-analytic software solutions. Prior to that, Paula was Interim CEO of a publicly traded robotic automation technology and manufacturing company, where she also held positions as EVP and COO. During a sharp economic downturn, she successfully led the company through a successful restructuring and sale of the company. Paula has also served as an Independent Board Director of PCS Edventures, Inc. a publicly traded company that designs and develops education products for the science, technology, engineering, and mathematics (STEM) market, where she served on the audit and compensation committees.

Paula began her career as a software engineer at IBM, and spent 23 years leading product engineering, strategy, marketing, and technical sales, achieving extensive experience in Enterprise software and hardware, large systems, and consulting services across various industry verticals. She was Vice President at IBM, member of the Corporate Technology Council and the Chairman's Senior Leadership Group. Paula's expertise in digital technologies and business performance at the senior executive levels helps to strategically transform companies and contributes technical and business acumen to the Boardroom.

PENNY HERSCHER

Chairwoman: Lumentum

Board of Directors: Modern Health, Delphix, Verint, Faurecia

"We need more diversity, and encouraging the women around you
to pursue those bigger jobs is essential."

Dear Chairwomen of Tomorrow:

My name is Penny Herscher. I graduated with a degree in mathematics in Cambridge, England in 1982. I was fairly unemployable with a math degree, so I went to the Cambridge career counselor. who suggested I could be either a bank teller or a teacher. I wanted more.

Eventually, I got a job as a computer programmer with Texas Instruments. However, I had to teach myself how to program before I started the job. I then became a self-taught computer software engineer in the semiconductor industry.

At the end of 1983, I moved to California where I worked as a software engineer for a young company until I moved into marketing after four years out of college.

From there, I went to a start-up called Synopsys, and that's where my career really took off. As Synopsys grew, I moved from business development to marketing and finally to VP before becoming a general manager. I was then the CEO of a start-up from '96 to 2002. I took the company public in 2001, sold it in 2002, and took 2003 off. By 2005, I decided to do another start-up, which I ran until 2015 and which was then was sold in 2017.

The first public board I joined was a difficult situation, given that I've never had any formal board training. I actually thought I knew what I was doing because I had taken my own company public and, at Synopsys, I had interacted with the board quite a lot. Nonetheless, if I had taken a one-week class or used more resources to help define what it means to be on a board, I probably would have made fewer mistakes.

In addition to my lack of real board experience, it was 2006. The company had gone through a difficult stock-option back-dating issue and had to let half the board and the CEO go. This was a somewhat broken situation, and the board was "clubby." Most of the directors had worked together before. And, of course, I was the only woman, which didn't help.

It's something to consider when going on a board. Being on someone else's board is completely different than being on your own. When you're the CEO and Chair, you're effectively organizing and running board meetings. Most importantly, you're the decision maker, and you're looking to the board for input and advice. In contrast, your role on someone else's board is to give support and advice, but you're never the decision maker.

My career has been a whirlwind of experiences and, luckily, I did not have to face them alone or without mentorship. Two people made a huge difference in my career.

The first person was Bob Dahlberg. When I was an engineer, he came to me and said:

> "I think you're in the wrong job. I think you should be in marketing and not in engineering."

Though that came as a huge shock for me, he was absolutely right.

The second person was one of the company founders and then CEO, Harvey Jones. He saw me in action at twenty-three years old and mentored me for about seventeen years. He sponsored me and gave me opportunities to grow. At the time when he was helping a start-up with engineers he knew, he pulled me in with them and said, "You guys need a CEO, and this person could be your CEO." He continued to mentor me through that whole experience. I think that, without Bob and Harvey, I'd probably still be an engineer.

One of the challenging issues you face is that you have to be in a senior position before you can get on a board. You need to have board-level scope of responsibility, either reporting to a CEO or being a CEO yourself. I have had many conversations with women where I say, "You need a bigger job." If your goal is to be on board, you need to have a big job. You won't get it if you're three levels down in the organization.

We need more diversity at the executive and board levels and encouraging the women around you to pursue those bigger jobs is essential. Too many boards right now are pale, male, and stale (although this is changing in 2021). Age diversity on boards is good within reason, because you need to have a certain level of maturity to be on a board, which is not related to age. You can be twenty and be good or you can be fifty and not be good at all. However, you still need to have the big job. If you built a company and took it public at twenty and retired at thirty, that's great. Boards want experience and maturity and wisdom. It doesn't matter what age you are, provided you have those qualities.

Diversity on boards is changing slowly. One solution is to force board refreshes quicker by introducing term limits. In France, for instance, you're considered an insider after nine years. The board I joined in France has two four-year terms. At the end of eight years, you're out. It is all clear upfront. You don't get these eighty-year-old board members who sleep in meetings. It's frustrating to me how unbelievably slow it is here in the U.S.

I've been shouting into the void for ten years—women get to the top and get on boards! You have to swing for the fence in your career. Take on big jobs and take big risks. I think balance is a myth. We are in a highly competitive world across gender, race, and countries. Human beings are competitive. If you want to get to the top, you have to make sacrifices to get there.

I'm not a good person to talk to if someone wants to be home with their children every night and have a balanced life and a big career. Now if you are someone who wants a successful career as a senior executive and you are willing to sacrifice to make that happen, absolutely talk to me. You're competing in a dog-eat-dog world, whether you're competing with China or with the guy who wants your job. It's competing. I know it's not a popular message for some millennials, but in life, not everyone gets a prize at the end of the game.

More than ever, you have to reach for the prize, to trailblaze in new ways. It's a real turning point for women. You need to take king action. I can't wait to see what you do!

Yours truly,

Penny

Penny serves on three public company boards: Lumentum, Faurecia SA and Verint Systems and two private company boards, Delphix and Modern Health. She was President & CEO of two technology companies, Simplex and FirstRain, over the last 25 years. She is an experienced technology CEO, based in Silicon Valley, who took her first company, Simplex Solutions, public and then sold it to Cadence Design Systems in 2002. She sold her second company, FirstRain, to Ignite Technologies in 2017. Prior to Simplex, Penny was a member of the executive leadership team at Synopsys, through the IPO, on the way to becoming the #1 EDA company. She started her career writing code at Texas Instruments and then at Daisy Systems. She holds a BA Hons, MA in Mathematics from Cambridge University in England.

ALISON DAVIS
Board of Directors: Fiserv, Silicon Valley Bank, Collibra

"We are transitioning into a fully digital world, and companies need their boards to help them bridge to the future. I love working with teams leaning into this challenge."

Dear Future Women Leaders of Tomorrow:

Let me start by saying I love board service. I see it as important work that makes an essential, but not always well-understood, contribution to society. As a board member, I help the organizations I work with stay relevant, be sustainable, and contribute to society by shaping purpose, strategy, culture, and execution over time. I really enjoy the work and highly recommend board service to other women leaders around the world as a great way to leverage your skills and experiences to have an important impact.

I was one of the first in my network to join a board, so I didn't have many role models in the early days. I have always tried to be as helpful as possible to others as they think about board service and how to navigate the process. Early on, I was often the only woman in the boardroom. These days, there are often two or three women on most of the boards I serve—in one case five—as the gender diversity of boards is fortunately increasing.

I agree with the view that once there are three or more women on a board, there is often a subtle shift in board focus and discussion. It is hard to generalize. However, I have noticed women often bring attention to different issues. For example, they can be more focused on cultural issues, employee health and wellness, product-safety issues, and risk issues. Women may pick up on subtle body language in the boardroom highlighting interpersonal conflict, defensiveness, or motivation issues among the executive team. As a result, these important topics get more focus—a clear benefit of diverse lenses and perspectives in the boardroom.

I spent most of my career in financial services. After my undergraduate studies, I worked for McKinsey & Company for nine years in London and New York, then seven years with AT Kearney. I became well-versed in business strategy. I got to work with CEOs and their teams at major global financial services companies in banking, insurance, asset management, and payments. We often presented to the board to get their approval on strategy.

Later, I moved into a corporate executive role and became the Chief Financial Officer at Barclays Global Investors, now BlackRock, which managed trillions of dollars of pension fund assets and was a major investor in most large public companies globally as a result of their focus on index positions. While in this role, I started receiving calls about joining boards.

My first major board role was almost twenty years ago at First Data Corporation. The board was impressive with many CEOs and former CEOs of major companies like American Express, McDonalds, Raytheon, and Visa. The board had a high standard of corporate governance. It was initially quite intimidating.

Ric Duques, the Chairman at the time, was supportive and welcoming of me. He made me feel my perspective was valuable and encouraged me to speak up. Another board director, the CEO of a Fortune 100 company, encouraged me to put my name in the hat for the audit-committee-chair position early in my tenure. I felt I wasn't ready, but he insisted I would do a good job and offered to support me. This type of support made a big difference and helped build my confidence as a board member. I learned a tremendous amount about good governance and the important work of the board from this first experience.

While at BGI, I only had the bandwidth to serve on one corporate board given the demands of my CFO role. By the early 2000s, I had shifted careers and become a partner at a private equity firm focused on investing in banks and financial services companies. It became part of my job to serve on the boards of our portfolio companies to support our management teams and help ensure the success of our investments. It was also part of my role to recruit other board members and make sure the board had the right skills and worked well together.

I learned what an important difference a strong and well-functioning board can make, especially when managing leadership succession or dealing with turbulent times and challenges in the business. I also learned how easy it was for good governance to be derailed—for example by the lack of diverse views leading to group think, by small interpersonal tensions between board members that escalated over time, and by one or two people dominating the discussions and/or others not feeling their views were respected.

For the last decade, as the financial services sector globally has been transformed by new technologies and the digital economy, I have shifted to investing in early-stage fintech through my company Fifth Era. I also write and speak about the importance of innovation and new technologies and have coauthored three books on how to be a good early-stage investor, corporate innovation best practices, and blockchain.

I now serve on the boards of large, public financial-services companies that are transforming their business models for a digital future (such as Fiserv, RBS and Silicon Valley Bank). I am also on the boards of high-growth, new-technology companies passionately bringing new and better offerings to market (such as Xoom, Ooma, and Collibra). I feel privileged to be helping companies on both sides of the transformation—the incumbents and the disruptors—and believe the insights from serving each make me be a better director.

At this point in my career, after more than twenty years of governance experience and service on over twenty boards, I am increasingly taking on board leadership roles. I have most often served as the Audit Committee Chairman because of my finance background (at Xoom, Ooma, Collibra, Gamefly, LECG, and others). I have also been the Board Chairman (at LECG), Compensation Committee Chairman (at Diamond Foods), and Technology and Innovation Committee Chairman (at RBS).

As board or committee chairman I get to work more closely with management and determine the agenda to maximize the impact of our meetings and make sure we focus on the most important topics. I also get to make sure all board or committee members feel comfortable sharing their diverse views and wisdom and have a transparent and respectful relationship with management, which is both supportive and appropriately challenging. A healthy board culture is particularly important when faced with big challenges.

While board work can be incredibly rewarding, it is not for the faint-hearted. I have had many challenging board experiences. One was a near bankruptcy resulting from an unexpected event. Another was an accusation of fraud against management team members resulting in an accounting restatement, SEC, and Department of Justice investigations, and shareholder lawsuits. Another, early on, was the complete meltdown of the company after missing earnings and a breakout of internal conflict and political strife causing great damage to the operations. Another was in the financial crisis, when one of the banks my private equity firm owned and where I was on the board experienced some distress, which took more than two years to resolve.

RBS, where I served on the board for nine years, was another casualty of the financial crisis. In 2007, it was the world's biggest bank and would have collapsed had it not been bailed out by the UK government and UK taxpayers. I joined that board several years after the crisis in 2011. However, it was 2020 before the bank was fully restored to health after much heavy lifting by several consecutive CEOs and leadership teams. It was a great lesson in how long it can take a company to come back after losing its way and a great reminder of the important role of the board in long-term stewardship, rather than short-term earnings maximization.

Sometimes difficult times and challenges can bring out the worst in people as they become stressed and afraid, and the workload of the board increases exponentially. A fragile or poorly functioning board during good times will likely really struggle during times of crisis. These days, before joining a board, I pay a lot of attention to the board and board-management dynamics. These are a huge factor in whether a company can manage the inevitable storms when they hit.

I have been through a dozen or more CEO successions—a particularly important time for a board to come together and lead a successful transition. Many board directors believe it is the role of the CEO to determine the purpose, vision, strategy and culture of the company. I disagree and think the board ultimately needs to take full responsibility on these things. I have been on the boards of many companies where several CEOs have come and gone. (The median tenure of a CEO in the U.S. is about five years.) It can be damaging to a company to change its strategy, reinvent its purpose, and shift cultures every few years. I believe it is an important responsibility of the board to lead on these dimensions and ensure smooth transitions as leadership changes.

Most large companies are being disrupted by new technologies in this timeframe. We are transitioning into a fully digital world, and companies need their boards to help them bridge to the future. I love working with teams leaning into this challenge. Many boards responding to disruption are seeking directors with skills and experience in digital and emerging technologies and leaders in companies powered by modern technology stacks using agile processes, cloud-based, customer-experience driven, data-driven, etc. So it is a good time for a younger set of executives with experience in these areas to consider and be considered for board service.

Boards are also finally fully embracing the importance of diversity. As part of this, executives from HR, marketing, cybersecurity, risk, and other functional areas are more likely to be considered for board service. I wholeheartedly encourage the next generation of women leaders to consider serving on a board and to be proactive in looking for good opportunities.

In summary, board work is incredibly important, enjoyable, and fulfilling. It can also be challenging. Boards can play a powerful and important role in reshaping global capitalism to be more sustainable and to contribute positively to the world and to human life on the planet. Boards are finally welcoming and seeking out women, minorities, and candidates with diverse backgrounds. Your time has come! Don't miss the opportunity to serve.

Yours truly,

Alison

Alison Davis is Managing Partner of Fifth Era (www.fifthera.com). She is an experienced corporate executive, public company board director, an active investor in growth companies and a best-selling author on the topics of technology and innovation.

Alison is currently a non-executive director of Silicon Valley Bank ("SIVB"), Fiserv ("FISV"), Janus Henderson Group ("JHG") and Collibra ("COLLIBRA"). She is the Chairwoman of the Advisory Board for Blockchain Capital, and an advisor to Bitwise.

She is a former director of RBS ("RBS"), City National Bank ("CYC"), Diamond Foods ("DMND"), First Data Corporation ("FDC"), Ooma ("OOMA"), Unisys ("UIS") Xoom ("XOOM"), and many private companies and was the Chairman of LECG ("XPRT") until its sale in 2011. Alison is a frequent speaker on corporate governance.

Alison was previously the Managing Partner of Belvedere Capital, a regulated bank holding company and private equity firm focused on investing in US banks and financial services firms where she worked closely with the Federal Reserve, The OCC, the FDIC and various state banking regulators. Prior to this, Alison was the Chief Financial Officer of Barclays Global Investors (now BlackRock), the world's largest institutional investment firm with more than $1.5 trillion of assets under management. Earlier in her career, Alison spent 14 years as a strategy consultant and advisor to Fortune 500 CEOs, boards and executive teams with McKinsey & Company, and as a practice leader with A.T. Kearney where she built and led the global Financial Services Practice. She is a bestselling author (*The Intelligent Investor – Silicon Valley*, *Blockchain Competitive Advantage*, *Corporate Innovation in the Fifth Era*, *Build your Fortune in the Fifth Era*).

Alison is active in the community supporting non-profits and social enterprises as a board director, fundraiser and volunteer. She has been frequently named a "Most Influential Women in

Business" by the San Francisco Business Times. She received a B.A. Honors and a Master's in Economics from Cambridge University in England, and an MBA from the Stanford Graduate School of Business. She was born in Sheffield, England, is now a dual US/UK citizen and has lived for the last 25 years in the San Francisco Bay Area where she raised her family with her husband, Matthew C. Le Merle.

LISA SHALETT

Board of Directors: PennyMac, Accuweather, Bully Pulpit Interactive

"The concept of leadership was not just extended to those who were called leaders, or who had a title of some senior position or managing director. There was a concept that everyone had the capacity for leadership."

Dear Future Chairwoman:

When I think about early influences, I think in terms of people and lessons. Four people in particular were role models and/or invested in me and affected the paths I took. Some important lessons that have really stayed with me are the work ethic, work-life balance, and the power of creativity and positive energy in creating possibilities.

A big influence for me early on was my mother. In addition to being a great mom, she was an entrepreneur. She had an amazing talent for interior design. When I was little, she started a business in architectural interior design with a friend. They were really good at it and easily won clients and did some spectacular things. That meant she would often be away working all day. We lived in the suburbs, and she would be working in the city. This was before Uber and Lyft, and moms would carpool for after-school activities and take turns doing the driving. My mom was never home in time for her shift in the carpool.

To still contribute, she hired the local taxi company to take her shift in the carpool. Now as I look at Uber, I think she was onto something! This whole experience was my first exposure to the concept of work-life balance and finding ways to make things work. This is still a big theme in my life. Whenever it was my mother's turn to drive, the taxi company showed up to take her shift. The other mothers would complain, and the other kids would make fun of us and give us a hard time.

On the one hand, there was a lot of creativity and ingenuity in trying to find solutions, and that was such a great example. On the other hand, there was stress caused by someone doing something out of the box. That was a really formative experience for me, as well as growing up with a mom who worked.

My dad was also an early influence and had such a strong work ethic. As an OBGYN, his schedule was always at the mercy of whenever a baby decided to show up. He would need to drop everything and rush to the city. Both parents were tremendously dedicated to their careers. These were my formative memories and experiences in pursuing an ambitious career as a woman. It was through watching my parents embrace opportunity and take on challenges that my sister and I learned how to thrive.

Fast forward to when I had my first child and was getting ready to go back to work. I thought I'd get some good feedback from my mother, given she had set such a great example that a woman could have both work and family.

But she said to me:

"You're going back to work?"

I replied:

"Of course, I'm going back to work."

She then said:

"No, no, I know you're going back to work, but you're going back to work so soon?"

It stopped me in my tracks—was there criticism there, no way to win? Long story short, I went back to work, and all was just fine. But it was just so interesting to have that backdrop and the experience was a great inspiration. When you get older, you really appreciate those kinds of examples, especially when you might not have understood them when you were young and in the moment. I've seen the same cycle of appreciation with my sons now, who are twenty and twenty-three. They've really started to appreciate the career I've had, and they seem to have turned out okay despite my crazy hours and such.

Another memorable influence early on was the vice principal at my high school (who happened to be a woman and, as such, a great role model of a woman in a leadership role). I went to a public high school on Long Island. I remember her profoundly because she called me into her office one day and said out of the blue:

"Lisa, I'd like you to compete on behalf of our high school and try to get this scholarship to go live with a Japanese family for a summer."

That really meant a lot to me, to even be considered, much less selected for an experience that hadn't been on my radar. (And, if it had, I probably wouldn't have thought I was a fit for it.) That was an early lesson that has continued to guide me: don't limit your own thinking and don't limit your possibilities. Anything is truly possible. Subsequently, winning the scholarship created an incredible experience I could never have imagined in a million years, which became a cornerstone of many of the choices I made in my educational and career journey.

Later in college, I studied Japanese. While I'd had all this exposure to Japan during the summer created by the scholarship, I had not learned much of the language. My host family didn't speak English and I didn't speak Japanese, so we mostly spoke in charades. But I wanted to learn Japanese. My college Japanese professor, a woman named Tazuko Monane (a.k.a. "Monane Sensei,") was truly incredible. She had boundless energy and passionately loved teaching Japanese. She infused a special energy and enthusiasm for my already emotional connection to language, which became a defining goal of mine.

Shortly after I graduated, she revealed she had ovarian cancer and passed away soon after. I was shocked. She had been suffering from cancer the whole time she was teaching with such incredible energy and devotion. I think about that often as she was such an inspiration. She exemplified loving what you do and the kind of difference you can make in other people's lives through that passion. I haven't really talked about these last two influences in my life as none of those necessarily defined my career in terms of developing specific skill sets. Rather, it was the lessons in perseverance and humanity I learned through these experiences that influenced how I showed up in various moments of my career and as a leader.

So, fast forward . . . I never would have imagined I would be on Wall Street. I didn't know anything about Wall Street and had a really narrow view that these jobs required you to be an accounting or economics major type. Thus, as a liberal arts person studying East Asian Studies, what business did I have to think about Wall Street? This was before the era of CNBC and the constant news flow about markets. People who knew the language of the markets followed them in the newspaper. I had no real role models who worked in Wall Street as LinkedIn wasn't around, and it was difficult to connect to people on Wall Street. I didn't see this as a relevant path for me.

After watching the movie *Wall Street,* it seemed like a place to avoid! After business school, I was working in a media company in a role that was supposed to be Japan-related, and then ended up being U.S. focused. Not doing a Japan-related role made me realize how much doing something related to Japan meant to me—more than I had realized. So I wanted a change. I stumbled across a listing in the Harvard Business School career alumni newsletter—in those days an actual physical newsletter—that mentioned Wall Street in the context of a job called Japanese Equity Sales. That is how I ended up on Wall Street: an opportunity created by my Japan background.

My first experience on Wall Street was at a firm called Barclays de Zoete Wedd or BZW, which was the securities arm of Barclays. Barclays at the time was very much a UK bank, not the global entity it is today. Working in New York for a UK bank was like working in a small regional office. For the most part, it was about sales and trading in the equities business. I worked on a small team, serving clients who were mutual funds, hedge funds, and pension funds that were investing in Japan. My background in Japan was valuable to them. Then the opportunity emerged to go over to Goldman Sachs when they were restructuring their desk. I happened to hear about that from someone who has become an incredible mentor, friend, and peer of mine—Kathy Matsui.

Kathy was a few years ahead of me in college and had started working at BZW. When I went to Tokyo for my interview, I was delighted to see her name on my interview schedule—but that didn't happen. It turned out that the day of my interview was the day she left to go to Goldman Sachs. We kept in touch and literally wrote physical letters to each other. (Email existed by this time, but our messages couldn't go through firewalls across different companies.) I still have those letters.

One day, I got a letter from Kathy saying:

"Hey, we're restructuring Goldman's Japan desk. I've heard enough about you to know that you're exactly what we need. Figure out a way to get into Goldman Sachs."

That was the prompt to make the move. And I was lucky to get the job of associate in Japanese Equity Sales in New York at Goldman Sachs. There, I was like a kid in a candy store. This was the quintessential Wall Street. It was a massive trading floor the size of a football field. It was noisy, busy, and full of constant

133

activity. It was very different from that small trading floor at Barclays.

New York was the headquarters of Goldman and it was such a jolt of energy. That was a pleasant surprise, and it felt incredibly comfortable. I knew it would be a great home because there was always something to learn; there was always motion and activity; and there were always ways to help clients. I had terrific colleagues who were team oriented. The privilege of working with such smart people in a role where markets would restart every day and give you a fresh sheet of paper to work with and a whole new host of things to learn and new ways to add value. It was incredibly exciting in ways I really hadn't imagined before and very different from the movie *Wall Street*.

As I look back on the early days of that journey into Wall Street, one profound theme for me was empathy. When I had that first experience in Japan, I home-stayed with a family who spoke no English. And I spoke no Japanese. There were a lot of cross-cultural experiences that, when I was fifteen or sixteen, I had to learn and process without being able to communicate. The thing I learned was this tremendous sense of empathy and what it feels like to be in another person's shoes. That has stayed with me as I started managing people. That, combined with wanting to be honest and transparent, and to support people in their own growth and in the team's growth, have been defining characteristics of leadership for me.

In those early days of my career, pre-Goldman, I had some examples of people I didn't think were good bosses. Those examples stayed with me because what's really important in those situations is, through exercising empathy, you learn what leaders should NOT do and what it feels like to be treated poorly. It's really important to learn the power leaders hold to inspire, to motivate, to engage, to challenge, and to support. If these qualities are absent, bad leaders can easily demotivate people or not get the best out of them. When you're in those situations (and probably everyone will be in a situation like that at some point or another), it's important to remember "how NOT to be" and "how NOT to make people feel." To paraphrase Maya Angelou, people remember how you make them feel. As a result, you become a better leader for it. I had many examples of great leaders throughout my career at Goldman. It was amazing how much leadership was so core to the culture there.

At Goldman, the concept of leadership was not just extended to those who were called leaders or who had a title of some senior position. There was a concept that everyone had the capacity for leadership, and that really stayed with me. When I was technically "junior," I took that to heart and took the initiative to do things. And by doing those things, I differentiated myself at an early part of my career, which led to accelerated promotions and opportunities. I was fortunate to be in a culture that started with integrity. That was so important.

Goldman had business principles we all had to learn. They made sense to me and resonated, and I took them seriously. Most importantly, I saw behavior around leadership, culture, mentorship, role modeling, and excellence exemplified around me all the time. That was a great environment. Before long, you have an opportunity to start being those things yourself, whether you're a junior person running the summer program, or whether you are gaining more responsibility and managing a small team.

In a regulated industry like Goldman, where I spent twenty years, you definitely get a sense of the importance of integrity, rules, regulations, discipline, and the right way of doing things. Is that outright a discussion of governance? Not really. We need to consider questions like:

- *What's it like to be a board director?*

- *Is there still too little discussion about all the different stakeholders of a given business?*

You can put your head down and focus on your clients and the strategy of your given business, but no one's really talking to you about different stakeholders. You have a sense of shareholders and who they are, and perhaps fiduciary responsibility and what that is, but not the broader sense of what is now called stakeholder and stakeholder capitalism. It's interesting these days that younger folk naturally gravitate towards environmental, social, governance types of topics. As a result, there'll be a greater connection and opportunity to learn more about the types of things related to stewardship, stakeholder management, and board work.

During my career, I didn't have a lot of guidance or teaching on those issues. Apart from trying to do the right thing for my clients, it wasn't until I was the chief operating officer in Compliance, Legal, and Audit that I really had exposure to different aspects of governance. Those functions needed to report to the board and the management committee. That enabled me to be on various committees, like the business practices committee and the commitments committee. That experience with discipline, practices, judgment, and rules prepared me well for board work. When you're working in those kinds of areas, which are fundamentally about anticipating and mitigating risk, you learn from smart people how to ask good questions. That is one of the most important roles of a board director, and I'm grateful to have had that experience.

I moved from the role in Global Compliance to leading Goldman's brand (during the financial crisis no less). That's where there was a tremendous focus on different stakeholders and how to communicate with them and what their issues might be. The board was one of those stakeholders, which helped. In that role, I presented to the board. This was the first time I really tried to imagine what they might want to hear, what they might need to hear, and what might help them do their roles. I did not get a lot of mentorship and guidance around being a board director, nor was I told it was even anything to aspire to. My path to the boardroom was not designed to the extent you might think, from the outside looking in.

When I left Goldman Sachs, I was most focused on leaving well, because a twenty-year career is an incredible and precious thing. I wasn't necessarily focused on getting on a board. At Goldman and most investment banks, you cannot be an employee at the bank and be on a board at the same time, due to potential conflicts of interest. That's another reason I had little exposure to the boardroom. Had I been in the investment banking division, I would have had greater exposure to board service, as investment bankers often present to and work with the directors of their corporate clients.

As I was leaving Goldman Sachs, I reconnected with my section mate from business school. He worked at an asset management firm and was a shareholder in a lot of companies. He had a strong understanding of fiduciary responsibilities and cared a lot about diversity on the company boards where he was a shareholder. He said:

"Now that you're available to serve on boards, I would love it if you were a board director."

We had been through business school together, and he obviously knew a lot about me, my reputation, and my integrity. He said:

" I would like to find ways for you to be a board director in a company I'm invested in. I'm going to go through my portfolio and look for the CEOs and companies I think most highly of and the boardrooms of those that need more diversity. I'm then going to start making introductions. Is that okay with you?"

That was pretty much my introduction to the possibility of being a board director. And I was fortunate and took that vote of confidence seriously.

I first met with the CEO of Brookfield Asset Management. There was no board seat available at that time. Regardless, we had a great discussion. A few weeks later, there was a board opening, and he asked me to interview for it. I reminded him I had never served on a board before because often the requirement for getting on a board is that you must have served on another board. Getting on your first board is usually difficult and can be a major hurdle. Nevertheless, his reply was:

"I don't care whether you've been on a board before. You've been a partner at Goldman Sachs. That's good enough for me."

The board happened to be a real estate board. I told him I don't know much about real estate. I certainly couldn't hold a candle to the rest of the board. And he replied:

"No, we don't want another person who knows about real estate. We know about real estate. We'd like someone who brings other skills like you."

I was lucky to have had the chance to interact with someone who was that open-minded, maybe even contrarian. That was my first opportunity to sit on a public company board. Usually, it is difficult to get on your first board. It was a wonderful experience.

I was the only woman on the Brookfield board. The company had moved another woman from that board to another board within the parent company. However, at this point, there were no other women on the board, which was one of the reasons why my friend introduced me into that situation. The board was not huge, but I learned a lot. The company was domiciled in Bermuda where there are certain rules as to geographic diversity represented on boards. As a result, this board was incredibly diverse geographically. There was someone from Sweden, South Korea, the Middle East, Canada, and several people from South America. I represented the U.S. It was fascinating. In some ways, as far as gender diversity goes, it did feel like after I joined the board, the "woman box" was checked, and there really wasn't the need to go for further diversity. I think that still happens a lot across the landscape of board governance to this day.

That board experience sharpened a lot of the skills I already had, and I learned how those skills could be applied to the boardroom. To some degree, you learn on the job, and I was lucky to have great board directors with whom I could discuss lots of things and learn. When I joined that board, I had to learn the language of real estate, which was a completely new language.

I got on my second board relatively quickly because I raised my hand in the context of leaving Goldman and spoke to the leaders of the merchant bank at Goldman Sachs. Goldman had invested in a portfolio of private companies. I told them I had these skills; I was a known quantity to them, certainly as a partner and as a culture carrier. I'd be helpful to them and their companies as an advisor or as a board director. So would they introduce me to some of the companies? They hadn't really thought of things that way. They weren't necessarily looking to fill a board seat among their portfolio companies.

One of the members of the merchant bank called me not long after that conversation and said:

"You know, there's a really interesting company on my watch list. We haven't invested in them yet. They're not of the right size for us to invest, but they're the leader in marketing compliance. As far as I know, you might be the only person on the planet who's done both marketing and compliance. Would you be open to meeting the CEO?"

I replied:

"Of course."

I thought I would just find ways to be helpful. And it turned out he also was excited to have a person who had both marketing and compliance experience. After we got to know each other, he invited me to be the independent board director on his VC-backed private company board. I joined that board because I really couldn't resist putting my skills to use, and I saw so many ways to be helpful. In the case of a private board, often there's more opportunity to be helpful with business development, introductions and a variety of other things. Public boards tend to be more about governance with less direct involvement in the company. So that was the way I got on my first boards.

Thankfully, more women are getting on boards, due in part to the pressure from different stakeholders such as institutional investors, activists, ESG-focused entities, the markets, the business community, and the companies' customers. It's always interesting to look at sources of pressure for change as clearly investors are paying more attention to board diversity. And I'm hopeful the needle will continue to move as the light gets brighter and the scrutiny gets greater.

It is still difficult for women to get on boards, and then to get on more boards after that initial hurdle. I think it's largely an issue of the way most people get on boards. There's a whole search industry. Despite a lot of technology being introduced to identify potential members of pipelines, that work isn't being done well enough. Sometimes it's the boards themselves because the specifications or job listing for a board director stipulate the candidate needs to have been on a board before. That rules out a lot of diverse candidates who have never been on a board, so it becomes a massive obstacle. I would love to see those specifications change.

Goldman Sachs announced last year that it won't bring a company public unless there's at least one diverse board director. This year, that number goes to two directors. That's a clear source of pressure, creating a lot of focus from shareholders, proxy voting,

ESG, and things like that. In private companies, the LPs (investors) are starting to ask questions about board diversity. And guess what? If you don't have a good answer, that LP might withdraw its money. As a result, there are all kinds of sources of pressure that get us closer to the goal, and I'm all for it.

And who you know and who you have the ability to reach out to and get to know is important. The data I've seen shows that anywhere from 60 to 80 percent of board seats come from relationships, rather than search firms. My own experience provides several examples of that. All of my boards have come through my own network, as opposed to search professionals.

Think about it—boards are mostly male, and older, and they tend to know people like themselves. When you have a seat to fill, you're likely to bring someone in from your circle. That doesn't favor diverse candidates. It'll be interesting for women to get on more of the nominating committees and drive that change to help fill the pipeline.

Everybody has a responsibility to broaden their networks so that they're not using the networks they're comfortable with, especially because recent conversations on diversity mandates for boardrooms call for directors who are persons of color. White people are realizing they typically don't have so many relationships with executives from under-represented groups in their networks. We all need to do a lot better with respect to that.

Technology can help. There are tons of lists being created now that help identify diverse candidates. The specifications need to change; the search professionals need to do better; and individuals hoping to be candidates for board seats need to make themselves better known. Board directors need to ask themselves:

"Is my personal and professional network diverse enough?"

You can really start out early to build those pipelines before the seat needs to be filled, giving you a chance to get to know people who might become candidates. Another opportunity I feel strongly about would be to create board-observer positions. You don't necessarily have to be a board director, but you have the opportunity to get experience with a board that prepares you to be on a board later. There's a lot of room for simple improvements. I don't necessarily see all of this happening, although there's a lot of talk about those things.

Ultimately, the concept of governance and putting yourself into situations where you can observe would be helpful. I've noticed that over the past decade, junior people have a lot of entrepreneurial friends who are starting companies. Maybe they are creating a board. You could be a corporate secretary and get exposed to a board that way. Perhaps you have people in your network who are on boards, so you'll could talk with them about their experiences. Do this particularly if you're still in school or have access to an academic institution. You can ask about courses or find things to read with respect to governance, board work, and case studies. Get in the flow of information and conversations about board work.

When you see situations involving management and companies having issues, pay attention to shareholder meetings and listen to what's being discussed. If you're working at a company, try to meet the general counsel or the corporate secretary who works with the board and ask them about what they do and how they suggest you learn about board work. There are so many ways to put yourself in the flow of exposure around those things. You have to make that an objective of yours. Over time, you'll build up a lot of great relationships and experiences that make you an excellent candidate for boards.

But don't forget—enjoy the journey as much as you would relish getting to the destination. You'll want to be able to look back on your career trajectory, as I do through this letter, and feel so grateful for every moment of friendship, inspiration, and experiences that were beyond even your wildest dreams when you first started on your path.

Wishing you the best of luck,

Lisa

Lisa Shalett is a retired Goldman Sachs Partner, advisor to growth companies and independent board director, with a remarkable breadth of leadership and operational experience, over her 25+ year career. At Goldman, Lisa held senior leadership roles in 5 divisions, worked in 2 regions, led revenue-producing and revenue-supporting businesses, managed global P&Ls and important client relationships, and helped transform the way Goldman communicates with its key stakeholders. Most recently, she was Global Head of Brand Marketing & Digital Strategy, managing Goldman's brand during the financial crisis, as a change agent and innovator. Having served on boards of every type (public, private equity-backed, venture capital-backed, family-owned, and non-profit), Lisa brings a deep understanding of stakeholder priorities and long-term value creation.

Lisa currently serves on the boards of PennyMac Financial (NASDAQ: PFSI), on the Audit and Nominating/Governance Committees, AccuWeather, where she leads the Marketing Committee, digital agency Bully Pulpit Interactive, and Chairs the board of non-profit Generation W. In 2017, she founded Extraordinary Women on Boards, an influential peer-to-peer community of hundreds of women corporate directors focused on advancing board excellence, modernizing governance, and increasing board diversity. Lisa has an MBA from Harvard Business School and a BA, *summa cum laude,* in East Asian Studies (Japan) from Harvard.

ALICE KATWAN

Board of Directors: Cielo

"Having Board members that 'don't look like each other' can bring different viewpoints and perspectives. That's what some of the public boards need, as well. They need a different perspective to come on and diversify the thought process. If you look at the boards that have women on them, those are some of the most successful companies out there."

Dear future Chairwomen,

I am honored to write this letter to you. The women before me have stood together amongst all odds and because of them I have been afforded more opportunities. I hope that by sharing my story I turn the page to yours.

My father came to America when he was 14 years old with only the clothes on his back and his drive to attain the American dream. My father was a real estate broker, entrepreneur, SF District Supervisor and a Palestinian peace activist. Most of my memories growing up was watching my dad speak in public arenas, run numerous events, and lead various meetings in our crowded living room. I learned through my father's example. He built bridges between opposing sides, he raised awareness about marginalized people, and he did so with passion and dignity. I wanted to be like him.

I started my pursuit in elementary school by selling newspapers at the corner grocery store down the block from my home. From there I sought out jobs simply for the experience. From passing out advertisements for local businesses to babysitting all the kids in a ten-mile radius, I wanted to develop the same work ethic that my father possessed. I went to college during the rise of Oracle and at the rise of Silicon Valley. I watched as the Oracle Towers overtook the peninsula skyline and grew excited about a future in corporate America. With a BS in Marketing and Business I was ready to make my mark. My husband and I shared similar career goals and settled in a home in Silicon Valley.

I knew that I wanted to be in sales because in sales success is measured. However, as a woman in corporate America I faced many challenges. As a young college graduate and newlywed living in the Valley it seemed my dreams were coming together, but it took me a good few months before I found my first job. It was the late 90's during the "boom" and if you didn't have experience, or if you weren't part of the network, no one would hire you. Using my new family connections, my mother-in-law took it upon herself to do her own ground roots recruiting for me the old-fashioned way. At my brother-in-law's restaurant where most C-level execs dined, she took a coffee pot and went from table to table asking men in suits what jobs were open for me. With her sweet Middle Eastern charm, she got the attention of Ken Gardner, CEO at Sagent Technologies and I got my first job in technology.

Through much networking and coaching and support of my very social husband, I gained confidence to put myself among the masses and landed more job opportunities. As I was getting my feet wet and gaining momentum in my field, my father died suddenly while giving a speech at San Francisco's Grace Cathedral. It was the year 2000, I was in my second trimester with my second son and I lost my hero, my role model and my dreams felt dim. With the support of my wonderful husband and my two baby boys, I kept my head up and continued to do what my father taught me. I knew that my father wanted to see me doing what I loved and to be happy, so I stayed focused in my career and grew my family with a third son.

Trying to balance my ambitious career and be an amazing mom took a toll on me and I found myself in the hospital over stressed and overworked. The cure was to find my balance. I decided to only take promotions and bigger jobs when it's the right time for me – not just when they're available. Sounds crazy right? How could a woman in this industry turn down promotions? Trust me when I tell you it will be there for you when you are ready. I paced myself and believed in my goals enough to stay healthy and take care of my family for the ultimate work-life balance.

Once my kids grew older and were more independent, I was able to take on extracurricular career opportunities. I became a board member at the Club of Silicon Valley and participated in events that helped build confidence in other women. Soon after I was invited to speak and share my story in other corporate arenas. While I was at Genesys, I started a women's organization, and was invited to be an advisor at a start-up, Mesosphere. This was the time I began boosting up my desire to give back, do public speaking and be a champion for women in technology and business. Most recently at Salesforce, I sat on several panels where Karen Catlin, Jo Miller and a few other luminaries in the Valley shared their inspirational messages to the masses.

Representation of women is still an issue. Many companies say it is a priority, but there's a lot of women that get discouraged. I feel like it's more difficult for me than it is for my male counterparts to get those board positions. There's more scrutiny on women and the toughest part is the entrance of it. For a public board, you need to have someone take a chance on you; to give you that first position for you to make your name in that network. That has been the hardest thing for me, and I believe diversity will go a long way on boards. In my experience, the teams that are less diverse tend to perform lower than the teams that are more diverse. They need a different perspective to come on and diversify the thought process. Most boards that have women on them are some of the most successful companies out there. Be that woman!

To the young woman ready to embark on a career in technology don't be afraid and be confident. It's going to be the millennial generation who breaks the barriers more than ever before. You are going to be the change agents for all women. Raise your hand and make a difference. If you see something that doesn't seem right, speak up. You have more strength and power and we are here to support you.

Wishing you all the best,

Alice

Alice Katwan is a highly respected sales leader with over 24 years building and leading sales teams in enterprise sales at Salesforce, Genesys, Red Hat, BEA Systems, and Network Appliance.

In 2015, Alice was honored with the Silicon Valley Woman of Influence award. Alice is passionate about promoting women's leadership and regularly speaks about how women can succeed in non-traditional arenas such as sales in high tech and as executives.

Alice currently leads the North America GTM team at Twilio.

External Engagements
o Latest article: Thoughts during Covid-19, Family-In-Place
o Honored as a 'Woman of Influence' by the Silicon Valley Business Journal in 2015
o Written Articles: *You can have kids and a career too!* and 5 Ways to Make Your Quarterly Sales Review Meetings Memorable
o Delivered Commencement speech at SF State University
o Previously on the Board of The CLUB of Silicon Valley, helping to build female leaders

GINA TEDESCO

Board of Directors: Jumpstart NJ Angel Network

"People need to appreciate how necessary soft skills are to succeed in board governance or in leadership roles. The better one understands human dynamics, the more one can recognize and predict what can go wrong."

Dear Chairwomen of Tomorrow:

I started working as an engineer at a time when there were few women in that field. As a young child, I was drawn to toys that were considered "for boys" and gravitated to playing games with the guys. Later, I often found myself the only woman in the room. This started when I was in grade school. I excelled in math and was invited to participate in a gifted and talented program which gave me the opportunity to learn "programming" when I was twelve. I realized much later that, as a woman, I was one of the lucky ones.

After receiving my mechanical engineering degree, I worked for an engineering consulting firm in Washington, D.C. Its staff was mainly men. I cannot say there was a secret to my success. I just worked to the best of my ability, and my work spoke for itself.

151

Early on in my career, I wasn't conscious of the fact I was any different from the other newly minted male engineers or my gender somehow made me different. Perhaps my childhood experiences as that girl who hung out with the guys gave me an advantage. Perhaps it was that, during my college years, even if people told me I didn't look like the stereotypical engineer, I thought like one: if you encounter a problem, you work through it to find a solution.

I was promoted quickly when I switched engineering firms while earning an MBA. I was then hired by a French company, Rhone-Poulenc, for a program that sent young international executives from all over the globe with science, engineering, and business backgrounds to the French headquarters to be deployed around the world as "company and country ambassadors." I was chosen to participate as one of the Americans.

Interestingly, the cohort before ours had only one woman in it, whereas ours was split evenly. There were ten of us. I was one of three American women who participated with two other women from the Netherlands and Brazil. The concept was lofty and innovative at the time and created cultural diversity. Although I am not sure it worked the way the creators originally envisioned, I worked for the company for almost ten years and rose up through the ranks based first in France and then in Brazil experiencing diversity firsthand.

Just yesterday, I was mentoring a young woman about gender bias, and she was unaware how often people don't realize they are exhibiting biases. Unconscious bias is prevalent everywhere. It is founded in our upbringing, our history, and our personal experiences. One needs to recognize one's biases in order to overcome them.

When I joined Golden Seeds, an early-stage investment firm focusing on funding women-led ventures, much later in my career, I met many accomplished women who had, early on, worked in the financial sector and had experienced blatant and overt gender bias. I think I benefited from the fact that, at the time, although there were still biases, the pharmaceutical industry appeared more accepting to me as a woman than Wall Street had been to my colleagues.

In a sense, I was fortunate to have worked in France and Brazil, in addition to the U.S. I went from the engineering field to finance. My experiences in finance, and handling mergers and acquisitions at Rhodia, the Brazilian subsidiary of Rhone-Poulenc, were always on the company side in an industry with more female role models. This, coupled with my problem-solving mindset, gave me more opportunities for advancement. Looking back, I was once again one of the lucky ones.

I met my husband during my time in France and, after moving to Brazil, I worked at Rhodia while my husband took over his family business, which was also in the pharmaceutical industry. The business grew, and we decided to professionalize it and move to the U.S., where we started a complementary business together, a consulting and trading company connecting the Asia-Pacific Region, Brazil, and the U.S.

I began the transformation from employee of a big global corporation to a serial entrepreneur. I brought along the experience I had gained in the pharma industry in finance, although I had to reacquaint myself with working in the U.S. after so many years abroad, not to mention learning the differences between owning my own venture and working in the corporate world. It was trial by fire. I went back to Fairleigh Dickinson University in New Jersey for a refresher entrepreneurial certificate program. Today, I am teaching there as an adjunct professor in entrepreneurship so that the next generation may perhaps be spared from repeating the same mistakes I made on my journey.

New Jersey is often referred to as the nation's medicine chest with its plethora of pharmaceutical companies, so I was able to leverage my experience when I returned home. We had the opportunity to start another new business in the pharma sector with my husband's uncle. We began as consultants and, before we knew it, founded a biotech company and ultimately brought a product through Phase II clinical trials. And that was my first experience serving on a board.

In a twist of fate and financing structure, we reverse-merged into an already publicly listed company and raised money from family offices and a European pharma company. By pure happenstance, I became both the CFO of a publicly traded company and one of its board members. Looking back, I should have been terrified to take that leap. I did not know what I know now, so without hesitation, I leaped into the abyss.

My philosophy had always been to problem solve, execute successfully, and not play corporate politics. However, the boardroom was way more political than I could have ever imagined.

Soft skills are largely overlooked. Perhaps it is inherent to the start-up pharma industry since so many smart people come together to solve thorny scientific and technical issues, whose sheer size and intricacy seem insurmountable. Yet in reality, the people problems are much more complex and way more difficult to solve. They stem from preconceived notions, differing backgrounds, varying experiences, interpersonal skills, and ever-changing team dynamics

People need to appreciate how necessary soft skills are to succeed in board governance or in leadership roles. The better one understands human dynamics, the more one can recognize and predict what can go wrong. These dynamics come into play when interacting with employees and investors or when investors interact with a CEO. And they are ever-present in the interactions between board members because everyone has different motivations for serving on a board. Of course, expertise and intellect are important. However, awareness, diversity, and empathy are equally vital for a company to succeed and for a board to be effective. Being the only woman on the board, I believe I changed the dynamic for the better.

Bringing diversity into the boardroom makes a big difference, and I've tested this hypothesis in my classes. After selling both my businesses, I taught a course at Fairleigh Dickinson University in which teams of my MBA students consulted with start-up ventures, helping with market research and devising strategy. In the four years I taught the class, I gathered a lot of compelling data confirming my hypothesis regarding human and group interactions.

My co-professor and I even contemplated writing a book about the team dynamics we observed, with the aim to raise awareness about how, when different players come to the table, their different personalities and interactions matter more to the

155

success of a project than the problems posed by the project itself. The patterns in group dynamics, team interactions, and personality traits we kept seeing over and over in our simple, non-controlled and certainly not double-blind classroom experiments could certainly be extrapolated and applicable to any business. Our non-scientific conclusion was that diverse teams were more successful. Recent research and data now prove this is true for investment returns for companies as well.

On my first board, I was part of the "40 Under 40" because I had co-founded the company. When you are the co-founder of a company, you are automatically thrust into a role where you might not understand the magnitude of the responsibility. One of my esteemed professors, who was then in his seventies, served on my board because we needed his independent perspective. In addition, my husband's uncle, an older gentleman with vast global pharma experience who'd been on countless boards, was our Yoda. His wisdom and advice were instrumental to our success. Without him and the professor as our guides, we could not have accomplished what we did.

Although I had been around the world, so to speak, and advanced in the corporate world, I was still young, around the same age as the millennials who serve on start-up boards today. Diversity comes in many forms, and I am glad now I recognized my lack of life experience at the time. You cannot be stuck in your generation. Generations can harmoniously work together if they realize they need each other, and that different people excel at different things.

In our biotech company, we did not need more board members. We did, however, partner with more women in the business itself.

Many of the companies we worked with were women owned. Our outsourced FDA-approved filling laboratory was led by a woman. We hired women scientists and staff. Maybe because I was part of the leadership team, there was an unconscious understanding we needed more diversity, a reverse bias perhaps. Today, unconscious bias needs to be acknowledged, and diversity needs to be consciously deployed. This is the path to parity.

Being exposed to different cultures has helped me develop a mindset that sees differences as strengths. I would not say other countries are doing anything specific to incentivize gender diversity in boardrooms. Diversity is not about having a woman on a board per se. It's about having diversity, including diversity of experience. Europeans are more adept at this because they are geographically close to other countries. In the case of Brazil, I wouldn't say gender diversity is more prevalent than the U.S. More work is needed to reduce the gender gap and address racial discrimination.

The issues Brazil faces have led to creative solutions. For example, the Brazilian banking system is incredibly sophisticated in response to hyperinflation. Brazil's challenges have brought forth novel technology solutions and creative solutions. There is value in taking advantage of diverse experiences and looking at problems through a different lens. Corporations, no matter their nationality, are looking for a competitive edge because startups are disrupting them. The Brazilian corporations we consult with do not know the start-up lingo, so we teach them how to adopt a startup mentality, how to work with startups, how to act like a startup. Businesses need to stay on the cutting edge to survive. If you are only using 50 percent of the available brainpower, it makes sense to be open to diversity in all its forms. Diversity then becomes not just a nice to have, but a need to have.

I did not have a female mentor. As women, we are making progress leadership-wise. Unfortunately, we still have a long way to go. If you look at the Fortune and S&P 500, only 5 percent of the companies have women CEOs. Numbers are still skewed toward men in charge. We know women beget women, so if we do not recognize our biases and consciously strive to promote qualified women at all levels of the organization, the number of women at the top will not increase, and leadership parity will not happen. In 2018, of the $125 billion invested by venture capitalists, 88 percent went to all male teams. Only 10 percent went to gender-diverse teams and 2 percent went to all women teams. We have much more work to do.

At various times in my life, I held different roles. I have always felt comfortable changing directions. As an entrepreneur, I worked 24/7 while raising twins. When we sold the business, I had to decide what I wanted to do. Teaching came about by accident because, as I mentioned before, I'd gone back to Fairleigh Dickinson University after returning from working abroad to meet people and re-familiarize myself with what was going on in the U.S. One of the professors I met there conducted a case study on my company. I was invited to attend a seminar to learn more about teaching and loved it. At that time, I was between jobs and trying to decide my next move, whether I wanted to start another company or go back to the industry. Teaching was a new challenge and another novel learning experience for me. I became an adjunct professor, a guest lecturer, and then a mentor. I never had a female mentor, so mentoring was my way of paying it forward to help more young women become one of the lucky ones.

One of the hard lessons I learned as a professor is that, when teaching a class, you need to accept you will not reach everyone. You are not going to make everyone show up, do the work, and do it well, even for a grade. That is also the quandary with quotas. If you force people to do something, they won't necessarily comply. The question becomes whether we can all do our part to raise awareness and talk about issues of biases, lack of diversity, and systemic racism to solve the problems at their roots rather than forcing people to abide by arbitrary standards. You have to give people the data showing what is happening and what the outcome will be if nothing changes. You have to encourage them to think critically, be aware, and be part of the solution.

In business, if the competition is gaining a competitive advantage by employing a diverse team, sooner or later other companies will have to reform or go out of business. There is coercion. There is persuasion. And then there is survival. Hopefully, the people you do reach will change the mindset of others. We each need to do our part to bend the arc.

I'm hopeful for this generation. I feel the millennials and those coming up after them have more diversity in their DNA. There is something to be said about how they interact with each other despite their differences that will help spur more diversity. I see it in my classes today, the increased awareness and, most importantly, the openness to accept and embrace differences much more readily and fully than generations before.

Millennials started their careers at the beginning of the digital age when the kinks hadn't all been worked out. I find Generation Z a little more practical. My twins, who are on the cusp of Gen Z, don't remember not having the internet, and they always had mobile phones. There is a generational difference in how technology is perceived. Many kids in school now do not know what jobs they will take upon graduation because the world is changing so rapidly. I truly believe everyone has a superpower they need to discover for themselves. No matter where technology leads us, experiencing challenges firsthand and acquiring knowledge by doing will allow you to uncover your superpower.

My students are often eager to set out on their own right after graduation. In general, I don't think that is a good idea. Getting even a few years of experience is crucial. Starting a business and serving on a board involves taking on a lot of responsibility. It includes a fiduciary responsibility, taking actions which are sometimes unpopular, and holding a checks and balances role. People need to appreciate this before taking on a board governance role. Even if you are working for someone else for a couple of years, you will be learning and, more importantly, you will have the time to build a cadre of diverse people to guide you if you find yourself at the bottom of the abyss.

A few final words of wisdom: Find your superpower. Share your vision. Be authentic. Embrace experiences. And make your own luck by inviting all types of people into your tribe. Never try to be the smartest person in the room. Instead, be the person who ushers all those smart, diverse, exceptional people out of the room to accomplish something purposeful and grander than anyone could accomplish alone. Only then will you be a leader.

Yours truly,

Gina

Gina Tedesco is an active investor, serial entrepreneur, professor and mentor. Globally experienced, her career of 28 years includes co-founding 3 successful start-up ventures, overseas postings in finance and M&A with a global pharmaceutical company in Paris, France and Sao Paulo, Brazil and industry expertise in internet technology, software as a service technologies, biotech, pharmaceuticals, and education.

Currently, Gina is Managing Member of Amala Ventures, which invests in early-stage companies with diverse teams and innovative and disruptive technology in the USA and Brazil. She is also a Managing Director and NJ Chapter Lead of Golden Seeds, a national network of angel investors dedicated to investing in early-stage companies founded and led by women and a member and board trustee of Jumpstart NJ Angel Network, a private, member-lead, angel group that invests in early-stage technology companies in the Mid-Atlantic region.

Gina serves on the boards of a number of private companies and has served as a trustee of a non-profit education foundation. She is a member of the Advisory Board for the Rothman Institute of Entrepreneurship at Fairleigh Dickinson University where she also teaches on-line courses in Entrepreneurship as an Adjunct Professor.

Fluent in English, French and Portuguese, Gina earned a B.S. in Mechanical Engineering from the University of Massachusetts at Amherst (Pi Tau Sigma) and an MBA in International Business with a concentration in Finance from The George Washington University (Magna cum Laude) as well as an additional post-MBA concentration certificate in Entrepreneurial Studies from Fairleigh Dickinson University.

MELANIE BROCK

Board of Directors: SEGA Sammy Holdings
Chair Emeritus: Australia and New Zealand Chamber of Commerce in Japan

"Knowing when one possesses sufficient leadership skills to cut through the noise is another element that distinguishes terrific from poor chairmanship."

Dear Chairwomen of Tomorrow:

Thinking about what advice I would give the next generation of leaders is a great chance for me to reflect on my career and the amazing support and guidance I have received along the way. I consider myself lucky to have met some incredible people, and I hope to meet more too. I am only in my mid-fifties and certainly hope to be working and learning for a few more decades.

In saying that, my message to the next generation is to keep at it and be grateful and thankful. And when you are in your fifties, lend a hand and keep the support cycle going.

In my case, most of the governance roles and opportunities I have had have come through person-to-person introductions.

Sometimes, the opportunities popped up in the most unusual places. While happenstance is wonderful, these opportunities are best built upon when you are ready for them. It is essential to study, network, and learn as much as you can. Research, listen, and put yourself into circumstances where you are most likely to benefit. At the same time, be mindful that it is sometimes a chance meeting—an article you read, something you see on Twitter, or even something said on a podcast—that can offer you a hint of where to go. A feeling can turn into a trend or something you can focus on in your own business as well.

JAPAN

I first came to Japan from Australia in 1982 and have spent nearly thirty years there. I am grateful I was given the chance to come to Japan and live in Aomori as a young person. Studying Japanese and subsequently working as an interpreter, and now in my own business, I have witnessed a great shift in our engagement with Japan. Many Australians have good connections and a solid understanding of Asia-Pacific, and this has been built up over decades.

A lot of recent focus has been on China. However, I hope the Australia-Japan bilateral relationship, which is of significant importance and one I am committed to, will flourish and be refreshed. Being in Japan when I was so young and studying Japanese after that has certainly made me better, and it has helped me help others understand Japan too. The Japanese viewpoint and perspective I have developed has helped me inform those living outside of Japan how to conduct business, how to develop connections here, how to identify new opportunities in the marketplace, and how to learn more about Japan's culture, diversity, and trends.

It has been interesting to see how my view of Japan has crafted business opportunities for both myself and others.

CHAMBER OF COMMERCE

About fifteen years ago, I became more active in the Australia and New Zealand Chamber of Commerce in Japan. This was a great way for me to channel my great respect for Japan and the Japanese while supporting fellow Australians and Kiwis looking to develop business here.

My Chamber of Commerce experience reflected what I had witnessed growing up in Albany, Western Australia, where my dad had been an active member of the local rotary club and chamber of commerce. Through that, I developed a better understanding of what committees did and how they sought to be effective in a community. I learned the crucial part that philanthropy and community service play.

As my role at the Chamber in Japan developed, I came across opportunities to get more involved. I volunteered to be chair in 2010 and remained in that role until late 2016. As part of the role, I was afforded ex-officio status on the Australia Japan Business Cooperation Committee, a position I still have. As a result of my time on these boards/excos, I learned more about the structure of a meeting, how sometimes not saying anything is more important than speaking up, and that you can have a voice without demanding to be heard right there and then. I learned there are multiple ways of demonstrating and building influence. From a

Japanese perspective, I learned the importance of consensus and how to create it to achieve better outcomes.

Sitting through these meetings taught me how tricky it is to ensure debates take place, both in Australia and Japan, and that sometimes you learn as much from listening and watching. Perhaps I learned more as I was watching two different cultures at play.

Many of the groups and associations I have belonged to have been male dominated. The business world is a "man's world." I learned a lot about diversity, gender, and roles through observation. It certainly hasn't silenced me or changed who I am. However, these settings have been excellent "classrooms" where I have acquired better practice and knowledge on how to influence. In a macro sense, I tried to find my way in and around two different countries while operating in a male-dominated world. I've had to observe how gender played out in both countries and forge ahead.

BOARD

My role on a listed board in Japan started when I was nominated to sit on the Japan-based Sega Sammy Holdings Board, to which I was appointed in June 2019. I was a board member of the Australia Japan Foundation Board for five years until 2015 and, as I mentioned, I serve as an ex-officio member on the Australia-based Australia-Japan Business Cooperation Committee. I was appointed as chair of a privately run, Australian family council and appointed as a member of the Australia-Japan Research Centre Advisory Board in late 2019.

Getting more exposure, building on your own governance roles (whether for not-for-profit boards or for listed boards), and reading as much as you can about the experiences of other women will help you navigate what can be a difficult pathway. Many will counsel you to speak up, and often people will tell you to wait until you are asked for comment. There is often greater backlash toward women who comment. Somehow, you need to find the right time to say something and how.

I have found it essential to first observe the boards 'interplay and get a sense for that board's culture and style, and then contribute accordingly. Sometimes it will be related to where the board is based and where the meetings are held, as culture is relevant. For example, it's hard to simply apply lessons you might learn from a book, especially if that book is about leadership in the U.S. What works in the U.S. might not always work in Japan and could be counter-productive.

Respecting regional areas of influence is essential. Knowing your own space and skills is necessary to determine what is or is not appropriate for the country or culture in which you are working. Some of the advice I have received is simply not applicable in Japan. It is essential to know where your support comes from and know yourself enough not to feel the need to always follow advice, no matter how well meaning it might be.

GOOD CHAIRS

I have witnessed impressively led, well-chaired board meetings. A chair's capacity to consider a large number of diverse views is a key component of good chairmanship. Seeing this was essential to me when I served as chair of our chamber. Solid and empathetic leadership will help cut through the noise, and this is something that distinguishes terrific from poor chairmanship. I have held several board positions and got there by watching, listening, and learning. I like to think other women, women younger than me, are watching, listening, and learning and will also gain entry into organizations or onto boards. I hope these women will feel supported and know where to look to develop the necessary skills because sometimes it is hard to know where to find the right information.

TRAINING PROGRAMS

Training programs and seminars are an excellent way to learn. I believe some form of learning and formal training is essential. One of my friends served on a board and felt she did not possess a strong enough financial background. Her brother was an accountant, so she asked him if he would help her fully understand balance sheets and financial statements. It is a smart and a brave thing to recognize where your skill set needs supplementing and seek that training.

I wish there were greater focus on the importance of corporate governance training in Japan. This would both help women seek roles on boards and significantly improve the company's value. My son works with me, and I would love for him to take corporate governance training because he would better understand some of the issues I faced in my career. It would help him be a stronger manager and business owner too.

JAPAN AND WOMEN

Japan must focus on gender diversity. It then needs to grapple with how to incorporate younger people into its leadership ranks.

Japan's commitment is evident, but we need to move things forward. We need to support women and those who support women in the workforce. We need to protect and champion them, even if their approach and ideas might differ from our own. Until the government demonstrates true leadership, even with the efforts made by some forward-thinking leaders in corporate Japan, the shift to incorporate female leadership into the workforce in a meaningful way as an economic issue will remain a lofty goal.

In 2019, the World Economic Forum's Global Gender Gap Report had Japan sliding 11 places to 121st (out of 153 countries), which embarrasses and troubles many Japanese women I speak with. We all feel hopeful about the situation, and no one is giving up the fight yet. However, it is terribly disappointing and easy to become despondent. Now is the time to increase the pace of change and make a real difference. Demonstrating that women can work part-time is a fine achievement. What remains to be done is ensuring that those who want to work have access to childcare, and that societal biases in companies are broken down. In addition, there are pressing issues to deal with, such as providing support for women who suffer harassment, domestic, and sexual violence.

The basic argument for corporate Japan is gender diversity improves a company's financial position. Many reports and studies show increased diversity on boards and in upper management translate to better company results. Japan needs to start believing this and find ways to implement diversity. It is imperative women and men alike are supported through awareness raising and training to take up these opportunities. Without the support, women will continue to be sidelined and step aside from taking a chance on themselves, for fear they will be pushed back down or (even worse) still fail.

I saw a fascinating segment on TV regarding the newly opened Tokyo Olympic Stadium. A major complaint of the old facility was that there weren't enough restrooms. The new stadium not only includes more female restrooms but also LGBT+ and disabled patrons 'restrooms. Sometimes Japan looks stodgy and incapable of change but then it openly offers supportive bathroom facilities. Paradoxically, Japan might make progress faster than Australia on issues such as this. (Genderless bathrooms are still met with resistance in Australia.) Change in Japan takes place after consensus is reached and then often, more than it might seem, things move rapidly. In contrast, the West has a culture of debate which results in people raising issues early on. However, only too often, the debate becomes muddied and progress is slow.

I am not saying one system is better than the other. However, when Japan gets moving, it progresses quickly. If we can keep pressure on the national government to support corporate Japan and establish policies that help workers, increase wages, and ensure work-life balance for working families, then we should get there. Something has to give.

It is essential for the Japanese government to act as a role model for Japanese corporations. If the government includes more women in management roles, corporations will too. At the moment, there is still a lot of backlash in regard to quotas, even though I firmly believe that quotas or other quantitative numerical targets are the only way to bring about change. Investors will also increase the pressure as external shareholders make their voices heard to ensure that Japanese publicly listed companies take steps to ensure their board and management team are more gender balanced.

These shareholders would have more impact on gender parity than traditional Japanese shareholders. With private equity companies coming into Japan from the U.S. and gender-focused countries, for example, a shift may start happening. With private equity firms and shareholders calling for gender parity, Japanese corporations might argue that they would need to implement that parity.

When I was first appointed to Sega Sammy's Board in Japan, I was thrilled and a bit surprised to even be considered. There was a bit of press in Australia in regard to my being the first female and first non-Japanese on this publicly listed board. I was welcomed in a business-like manner, and it was made clear my global experience, my understanding of business outside of Japan and how it might impact Japan, were the reasons for my appointment.

I am grateful that my long history of working with political, governmental, and multilateral organizations in Japan—and not just my gender—was acknowledged. While the role itself is rewarding, I take the additional responsibility of ensuring future boards enhance their female representation and include someone who is older, younger, or of a different nationality. Japan has helped me understand that sometimes things are not as they appear and consider consensus-based approach. My biggest and ongoing effort is to ensure people understand that.

There are terrible stories about the pressure Japanese schools and Parent Teacher Associations (PTA) put on mothers, in particular, to sew bags for library books or sports shoes rather than to buy them. I know of women who stay up until two o'clock in the morning sewing things or getting something ready for a Halloween display. Then they are expected to create magnificent *obentos* (Japanese for lunchbox) before the children leave for school and then do their own work. That is where Japan is so different from the U.S. In Japan, the pressure to conform and perform, and the shame placed on Japanese women, make me so angry. There is too much pressure on Japanese women.

In some ways, I think Japan is coming to a tipping point in terms of gender diversity. Many people complain about Japan's slow pace of change. Often I am the person complaining. However, I believe that this country's history of changing and changing quickly once consensus is achieved provides hope.

While the pressure on Japanese women, the inequity and the lack of fair and equal opportunity in Japan is troubling and warrants immediate change and action, my country of birth, Australia, still struggles and faces its own challenges in achieving gender parity. We all have a lot to do to support women and their families.

FUTURE

At some stage in my career, I look forward to a governance board role on a company or entity based outside of Japan. A role such as this would allow me to provide Japan-based insights and, hopefully, help and guide that organization through its engagement with Japan. Likewise, the opportunity to learn about countries other than Japan would be fascinating. As investment by Japanese companies in Australia continues to expand, the American-Japanese relationship will strengthen, creating potential opportunities there too.

My #CelebratingWomeninJapan project remains committed to supporting women in Japan. We will continue to celebrate women in Japan and raise their profile and awareness about issues women face in Japan. Hopefully, through my board roles, I can help Japanese companies grapple with the issue of diversity and a more flexible working style.

Be bold and be strong.

Best wishes to you all,

Melanie

Melanie Brock is long-term Australian resident of Japan. Melanie uniquely combines practical commercial business leadership and language skills to consistently deliver on business, regulatory and partnership outcomes for Japanese and global companies. She has an excellent network in Japan's corporate, political and government sectors.

Melanie is a well-known advocate for Japanese women and diversity. Celebrating Women in Japan (CWJ) is a social media project she developed in 2017. The main objective of the CWJ initiative was to raise the profile of women in Japan and to break down commonly-held stereotypes. CWJ founder, Melanie Brock, is committed to diversity and inclusion, gender equality and

173

women's leadership. Her long-term goal, both personally and through this project, is to support Japan in its quest to reach greater gender equality.

Melanie is Chair Emeritus of the Australian and New Zealand Chamber of Commerce in Japan having completed over six years as Chair. She is a member of the 'Australia Japan Business Co-operation Committee' (AJBCC) and is the Advance Global Ambassador for Japan. Ms. Brock was appointed as a non-executive director to the board of Sega Sammy Holdings in June 2019

In 2020, Melanie was awarded a Commendation by the Japanese Foreign Minister for services to Australia and Japan. She is a single mum to two wonderful young men and a grandmother to three amazing little people.

TARA SINGH

Board of Trustees & Board of Governors: Mills College

Founding Chair: Nexus India & South Asia

"The best advice I can give you before you sit on a board is to know your self-worth and leadership style. When you're firmly rooted in both, you can duck every flying plate that comes at you while remaining calm and composed."

Dear Future Women Leaders of Tomorrow:

My name is Tara Singh. I was born in New York to a Sikh Punjabi father and an Anglo-German mother and now live in New Zealand. After earning my undergraduate and graduate degree at Mills College in Oakland, California, I worked in the FDIC's risk-management sector during the 2008 banking crisis, and then decided my passion was in the sustainable business field. Unfortunately, my education pigeonholed me into traditional finance, so I decided, against my family's advice, to return to New York to pursue my area of interest in Environmental Policy at Bard College.

What I did with my life had nothing to do with my degrees. Looking back, each part of my journey equipped me with the skills I use in my everyday life. The takeaway is when you follow your passion and interests, you'll be amazed at what you can accomplish and how well prepared you will be.

I took an unconventional path by attending business school right after my undergraduate degree. It provided me with a basic level of confidence and a vision for what I wanted to do early on. People typically wait eight to ten years before earning a business degree. I'd be a different person if I'd waited to go back to school. My philosophy is, as long as you are learning, you are living.

The first board I sat on was the Oakland, California-based Operation Dignity, a not-for-profit organization that services Oakland's homeless, including its veterans. A friend of mine had served on its board and had introduced me to the founder, a former homeless veteran himself. I joined that board primarily because I was inspired by this amazing man and his mission. I could see, because the founder had been a homeless veteran himself, Operation Dignity was different from other community-focused organizations doing work in similar areas. The passion and commitment from the board was palpable.

The best advice I can give you before you sit on a board is to know your self-worth and leadership style. When you're firmly rooted in both, you can duck every flying plate that comes at you while remaining calm and composed.

Formal decision-making has traditionally been relegated to men. I consider myself a feminine woman, and my ladylike leadership style has rubbed both male and female leaders the wrong way. As a woman, you have to know yourself and anticipate your reactions. When women who are comfortable with their femininity engage, male board members might become uneasy, primarily due to gender bias. You can be both soft and strong, compassionate and decisive.

One of the things I took for granted (from having earned my undergraduate and business degree at a women's college) was that sisterhood was prevalent. It is crucial! When you look across a boardroom, you are lucky if there is one other woman there. Instead of seeing other women as competitors, instinctively consider them sisters and gauge whether they're friendly or not. Women can benefit from being allies with the other women across the table and gain the advantage men already have in their comradery and alliance.

The role model I always go back to is that of my mother. I am grateful for her instilling her passion for volunteering and service into us children when we were young. The compassion she imparted in us for the marginalized and voiceless continues to be a driving force in my life today.

Serving in governance teaches you a lot about yourself. Every board has its own culture, and it's interesting to observe how we adapt to it. It provides an unparalleled opportunity to expand and grow.

My board training consisted of taking several business-administration classes while I put together my first business plan. Before that, I think I would have just jumped in. Board preparedness is akin to learning a new language or skill set. My classes were held at an all-women's college, which made for an enjoyable experience. The camaraderie and team-oriented spirit were beneficial and helped me own my power.

I wish I'd known prior to serving on boards how important it is to find one's niche. In order for a board to be successful, its members need to possess a broad range of expertise. It's crucial for board members to have skill sets they can broaden and also areas they can speak to from a position of mastery. It is paramount to identify and develop your area of focus early on. Not only does it help you succeed on a board but, more importantly, it helps the entire board succeed.

Throughout my tenure serving on boards, I've learned a lot about governance processes and vernacular. It sometimes reminds me of a game of chess. I encourage young women to familiarize themselves with the bylaws, the tasks of making a motion, passing a resolution, and the like. Feeling confident in how you address the board gives you a tremendous advantage.

Throughout history, a natural human tendency is to pair up the young with the old, which, for many reasons, has a nice way of working out organically. In terms of intergenerational leadership, the magic lies in bringing together seasoned board members who possess wisdom of experience and younger people with bright ideas, energy, and a finger on the pulse of the world. It's not just about youth or age. It's about how the two interact to add value to each other and enhance their effectiveness. The question is whether older board members will hesitate in giving younger candidates a chance, and whether younger candidates will respect the older generation's wisdom and experience. Powerful and dynamic boards will come about when all generations can collaborate with a spirit of respect and cooperation.

I think boards should have term limits because changing the guard is in the best interest of both the board and the organization. It's also good for board members to know they have a fixed amount of time to contribute as much as they can. Reaching their term limit doesn't mean they stop being a supporter, an ally, or adding value to the organization. It means everything should flow and not be static. There is a season for all things, boards included.

One of my hardest board experiences came about in the process of hiring a new executive director. The board decided to make a conservative choice, but I felt strongly the organization should hire a visionary instead. While I fully understand the risk-adverse place they were coming from, I'd hoped my preferred candidate could've been selected and helped us to grow in ways we had been unable to in the past. In retrospect, the organization flourished under the new leadership, and the hire proved to successfully deepen the organization's mission and vision.

Disagreeing with other board members on that fundamental level forced me to really consider their perspectives. Part of being on a board is working with people who come from different backgrounds and viewpoints, sometimes opposing to your own. It is helpful to start with the premise everyone has valuable points to impart and knows they can teach you.

I've held different roles on each of the boards I've served on from founding chair to treasurer. A board chair has the goal of directing their board. However, the aim of all board members is to bring out the best leadership in those around them, enhance one another, and develop a phenomenal group of leaders to push their agenda forward. What I've observed across all boards is that inspiring leaders sit firmly in their leadership, express themselves clearly, and encourage those around them to rise to their own potential, adding the most value to both the board members and the organization.

The number of women gaining access to boardrooms is growing in a positive and exciting way. One of my life goals is to increase female representation on boards and in positions of leadership. There's still quite a bit of work to be done, and women need more mentorship. Men naturally mentor other men.

It's usually a tap on the shoulder that gets women placed in board governance. It happens through individuals who respect them, mentor them, and with whom they have a reciprocal relationship with respect to growing and advancing in their careers. Getting into that abundant mindset can shift everything.

As you become more experienced and respected in your board leadership, always remember you can pass along your mentorship to another young woman. I cannot think of a more powerful gift you can give than believing in someone. Someone believed in you for you to get where you are, and your belief in another can be life changing. I love the word chairwoman—it is brilliant. Ladies, we've got to start owning it! #ChairWomenChangetheWorld :)

Sincerely,

Tara

Tara's philanthropic work and leadership has positioned her as a public advocate for women and girl child issues, sustainability in business and the environment. As a repeat delegate to the White House and United Nations, the essence of Tara's professional life's mission is to support women and youth and to empower our next generation of global leaders. Working with the support of the United Nations, Tara is a regular forum and session participant, having served on working groups and committees including the UN's Inter-Agency Network on Youth Development's (IANYD) Youth and Gender Equality and UN Women's Business and Philanthropy Leaders' Forum. Tara currently serves on the Executive Board of UN Women Aotearoa New Zealand and is their Auckland Representative, as well as on the New Zealand Women's Empowerment Principles (WEPs) Committee, a joint initiative of UN Global Compact and UN Women and a primary vehicle for the corporate the delivery of Sustainable Development Goal 5.

As a Founding Member of NEXUS, comprising 5000+ Next Gen of the world's most influential families from over 70 countries, Tara Chairs the India & South Asia and New Zealand & Pasifika Regions with a goal of galvanizing the next generation of ultra-high net worth philanthropists to catalyze new leadership and accelerate global solutions. Tara is a Trustee and Governor for her alma mater Mills College, an all-women private liberal arts college founded in 1852 in Oakland, California. She has used her background to work in financial risk management for the FDIC and to create and pilot environmental and entrepreneurial programs to assist women in developing financial self-sufficiency and entrepreneurial skills with micro lending cooperatives and factory workers in both India and Nepal. A long-time student of medical botany and ethno pharmacy, she was granted entrée to both H.H.

Dalai Lama's Tibetan Medical and Astro. Institute and its archives and the global Ayurveda authority, The Arya Vaidya Pharmacy, in order to conduct research on Traditional Tibetan Medicine and Ayurveda. Tara has also served on the Board of the Ik Onkar Peace Foundation, a United Religions Initiative Cooperation Circle, aiming to promote peaceful conflict resolution without the use of unnecessary violence, encourage economic and social justice while preserving planetary beauty and resources.

Cheemin Bo-Linn

Board of Directors: Blackline Safety, BMCH

"We have the responsibility to help young women rise to C-suite leadership and Board of Directors roles and also embrace public policy and community service."

Dear Chairwoman of Tomorrow:

I was born and raised in Houston, where I earned a bachelor's and master's degree. Then I took my first of many international assignments before returning to the U.S. to finish my doctorate degree in computer-based information systems and organizational change from the University of Houston. I also completed Stanford University's EMBA certificate program.

I mentor young women to dream big and build a portfolio of experiences. For me, during college, I aspired to be a CEO of a global company and I achieved this in my current role as CEO and President of Peritus Partners, Inc. My career goal was to build and scale a company that was customer focused, valued a diverse culture as a corporate asset, and operated within an ESG (environmental, social, and corporate governance) framework.

So during my career I held various functional executive roles as product development and finance manager, chief marketing officer, chief revenue officer, M&A partner, and supply chain lead. I have led growth from start-ups to Fortune 100 companies, including IBM Vice President where I managed a fast-growth, multi-billion-dollar P&L of IT products and consulting services. Since technology—especially digital technologies—plays a key role in every company and industry, I leveraged my ability to apply technology in my C-suite roles. I have worked in various sectors from internet, mobile, and energy to the financial services to consumer and industrial sectors. I was also selected to teach digital technologies (such as data analytics, artificial intelligence and cybersecurity) and digital marketing as visiting professor of the joint EMBA/MBA program with Columbia University, London School of Business and the University of Hong Kong.

Such a diverse portfolio of academic and corporate skills and experiences opens opportunities for me, and I encourage more young women to join me in the technology field and focus on innovation. My induction into the "Hall of Fame for Women in Technology," a program supported since U.S. Presidents Bush through Obama, gave me an opportunity to further support the vital role of innovation.

Since 2013, I have been CEO of Peritus Partners, a global valuation accelerator with a backend data-analytics platform. Also, I currently serve on two public company boards with prior election to five other private and public boards. One of my board roles is at a global leader in IoT gas detection and connected safety solutions enabled with artificial intelligence. The other company is a leading manufacturing, distribution, and e-commerce company where I serve as the Tech Committee lead focused on digital technologies such as e-commerce, cybersecurity, and supply chain and also the Audit Committee.

I am fortunate to have been elected to company boards in Canada, Europe, and the U.S. ranging from $40 million to $3.7 billion in net sales and more than $8 billion in market capitalization. I have served on all board committees including Audit Chair of two public companies. In 2019, I was honored to be named one of the "Top 50" directors in the United States by the National Association of Corporate Directors, the leading authority on boardroom governance with more than 21,000 members.

As I work with future leaders, I encourage young women to have a corporate voice and serve in C-suite roles and as board of directors. We need more men and women to join our volunteer work providing training, visibility, and board opportunities. Let's not lose such talent. As a board member, I and my peer board members leverage our operations expertise with probing questions as we fulfill our fiduciary responsibilities related to strategy, risk oversight, and governance. Your credible board performance will outshine any doubt as to why you have a seat at the table. All board members bring their own domain expertise, so we learn from each other, a great multiplier effect that benefits shareholders.

Also, I encourage more women to engage in politics and reciprocate with community service. In addition to my corporate boards, I also served on a Washington-based national advocacy group representing all segments of technology and the largest private equity organization, both focused on capital access as well as regulatory policy. Seeing the power to "moving the needle," I am also actively involved in promoting diversity including gender, ethnic, and experiences from awareness to building a pipeline to legislation. Since one of my pillars is my technology background, there are many opportunities I have been engaged in over the last ten years, such as YWCA techGYRLS, which empowers girls to study STEM (Science, Technology, Engineering, and Mathematics). When the "Top 100 CEO Leaders in STEM" Award was announced, we—as award recipients—took the next challenge to encourage more CEOs to establish mentoring programs with STEM investments, resulting in marked progress in the Fortune 1000.

Today's markets and technology are changing at an ever-increasing rate. We should think of this disruption as opportunities for us to seize. It's important for future young women to develop their own personal brand of courage and take risks (and for me being Asian, I had to get out of my comfort zone.) As I mentor others, we focus on preparing them for the next ten years, so you are not just surviving but thriving, then helping others.

We all have an extraordinary journey ahead of us, and it doesn't matter where you begin, just as long as you at least start and bring others with you. For me, it was innovative technology leadership, board service, policy, and community engagement all focused on positioning the next generation. Thank you for the opportunity to share my perspectives and I wish you all the best.

Sincerely yours,

Cheemin

Dr. Cheemin Bo-Linn has served as Board of Director for companies in Canada, US, and Europe, from Lead Director to Chair of Audit, Compensation, Governance, and Digital Technology. In 2019, she was named "Top 50 Board of Directors," (by the National Association of Corporate Directors which represents over 21,000 board members.) Currently, she is CEO and President of Peritus Partners Inc., a leading valuation accelerator with two divisions, an analytic platform and business IT/marketing consultancy. Leveraging her expertise in digital technologies (e-Commerce, artificial intelligence, block chain, cybersecurity, data analytics, and supply chain) she was IBM Vice-President running a fast growth, major billion-dollar P&L, and CRO/ Digital CMO at e-commerce, mobile, finance, and software companies.

Cheemin was inducted to the "Hall of Fame for Women in Technology", (a program supported since U.S Presidents Bush through Obama), "Most Influential Silicon Valley Exec" Awardee, named "Top 100 CEOS in STEM," and invited speaker to the United Nations, Dow Jones, and British Chamber. She earned a Doctorate degree in Computer Information Systems and Organizational Change from the University of Houston and completed Stanford University's EMBA Cert program. Also, through 2019, she was appointed Visiting Professor on digital tech (AI, big data, cyber security) and marketing at the joint EMBA/MBA program of Columbia University, London School of Business, and the University of Hong Kong.

LILA TRETIKOV

Board of Directors: Volvo Cars, Xylem Inc, nam.R, Onfido

"Every great leader looks for diversity. It's not just in our color and gender but diversity in thought. If you have a room full of engineers, bring in an artist, a biologist, an economist, someone who thinks differently and will challenge the dominant mindset. Then, do it again."

Dear Chairwoman:

I was born in what seems like a galaxy far-far-away in a country that no longer exists, the Soviet Union, amid the fall of the Berlin Wall, the end of the Cold War, and the sudden shock of geopolitical, economic, and cultural revolution. Almost overnight freedom of speech, free-market economy, and Western democratic values swept through the land like a tsunami. The ecstasy and perils of new freedoms created unprecedented collisions, deep-rooted rifts, and the ultimate reaction and return to origin. For those of us who could never live without the taste of independence again—these times forever shaped our lives. They made me who I am.

I grew up in a family split between the sciences and the arts. My mother was a filmmaker. My father is a mathematician. (I was still a young child when he became the youngest professor at Moscow State.) My young parents inspired me to dive deeply into both disciplines and challenged me to reconcile them throughout my life. I was young when I started university in Moscow so, by the time I was fifteen, I realized I could predict my path twenty years forward. Except that I didn't want to know the future. I wanted to make it.

I moved to New York. Alone. From the top of my class, I now dropped below toddler level in my ability to express myself. I enrolled in high school just to learn the language and culture. I started my day at 4 a.m. so that I could work all day after school. To support myself, I taught kids to play musical instruments, translated, waitressed and tutored. A year later, I applied to universities to continue my studies. While it was incredibly rewarding to receive letters of acceptance from top U.S. schools, the reality of the tuition costs quickly hit home. I was a poor immigrant and didn't have the means to earn $30,000 in tuition. The only school I could even dream of was UC Berkeley. Fortunately, it was one of the best in computer science.

Yet, I did not go there to study computer science. In my attempt to fuse art and science, I enrolled in architecture. One day, a new friend challenged me, saying that if I had "half a brain," I would dare take a computer science course. As it turned out, computer science was extremely competitive and required an entrance test just to get into the introductory class. I would be competing against kids who had a computer from the time they were in elementary school. I was glad to see a math-proof question on the test. In the end, I became one of a handful of girls in the five-hundred-student class. By the time I was seventeen, I was a computer scientist on a dare. And I gained a lifelong friend.

They say we become who we are by the time we are six. Although my mother died when I was young, her influence shaped my life. For the rest of my life, I sought incredible humans to follow—friends, teachers, supporters, coaches.

At Berkeley, I studied computer science and art. My art professor, the famous artist Jane Rosen, became a family member to me. I became her teaching assistant, and we focused our class on non-art majors. We taught that visual literacy can—and should—be part of the training not just for artists, but for scientists, doctors, and engineers. Visual literacy stems from the power of observation, the sensitivity of attention, allowing us to "make the invisible visible" by noticing, recognizing, and bringing it to our conscious mind.

A trained doctor will notice the hue of her patient's skin or thickness of hair, which might cue a diagnosis. A good scientist will notice a change in the pattern that will reveal a new theory. A good artist will recognize a fake by looking at the nose of a sculpture. My artistic training has been an advantage throughout my career. It has given me the ability to analyze across various disciplines, to synthesize and transfer knowledge across them.

Because I worked full time to pay my tuition, I ended up doing some interesting jobs. I worked for an assistive technology lab that taught me about people with a range of abilities and how technology can help give us extra powers but, more importantly, help us all truly harness our incredible potential regardless of our physical differences or even limitations. In the process, I learned not to overlook anyone just because they don't fit our stereotypical frame.

I also worked for a genetics lab at the Lawrence Berkeley National Laboratory. At the time, we were sequencing the human genome as part of a collaboration between Stanford and Berkeley. I watched scientists in front of a genetic alphabet soup trying to match DNA sequences in a process called genomic alignment. This observation led me to build a genomic browser that became critical to their work and landed us in "Nature" and other journals.

Over the years, Berkeley became the powerhouse in genetic editing, and I am proud to have been a part of the journey. I started my own company based on applying observation algorithms like those I used for genomic sequencing to stock market analysis. This "transfer learning" led me to later apply my knowledge in finance, banking, traditional software, telecom, media, health, and energy. Underneath it all was the foundation of science and art that helped me connect the dots.

By the time I was the CEO of the foundation behind Wikipedia (one of the largest websites in the world) and leading technology segments for Microsoft, this question of connected knowledge became top of mind. As humanity's knowledge far outpaces our capacity to contain it, how will we synthesize ever-growing depths of understanding and disciplines? What tools, what machines, do we need to build to go beyond the limitations of our physiology?

My ambitions have always been a bigger than I am. At the end of the day, we will all be forgotten. However, what we do and make can survive us, and that is what drives me. Technology is an incredible tool because it can make a disproportionate impact. It can amplify our human capabilities and enable us to supersede them. And for that reason, it can also be dangerous. How do we nudge the world toward a better outcome and a better ending? For that, I think we need more than blind ambition. We need expanded consciousness. However, this expansion cannot come from any one mind because the best ideas—like the best DNA—come from diverse origins.

From my days at the assistive technology lab, my drawing classes, and my early work experiences, I learned not to take anyone for granted. The person you least expect will teach you more than you have even imagined if you only open yourself up to listen. And the most important insights will come from those who did not travel the same path. By our very nature and nurture, we think differently. It is this diversity that safeguards us from being blindsided by single-mindedness and helps us build better products and, more importantly, better future.

And talking about products, Jony Ive, former Chief Design Officer of Apple, said,

"The most important ideas often come from the quietest voice."

Bringing out that quietest voice is how we "make the invisible visible." And what we learned through testing AI is that the quietest voice in a room is nearly always a minority voice—and often least confident and assuming.

How do we make space for this voice? How do we help people feel accepted and safe? How do we ensure they belong and are valued? How do we listen, even when what we hear can make us uncomfortable? When that happens, we can create magic, avert disasters, and amplify what we can do. And that is how I see future boardrooms.

Now that I serve on boards, I believe it is up to me and others in power to make a difference. I have a say in corporate governance, and I feel it is my duty to help bring this practice and balance to the companies I serve. I see people who are in the same situation I once was. They don't feel confident even when being recruited. When I ask candidates to apply for a role a little bit out of reach for them, they don't feel comfortable applying. But once those people are in, they bring with them a new range of abilities. They also bring others, and the diversifying effect becomes self-fulfilling.

Look beyond the obvious. Look for diversity in thought. If you have all engineers, bring in an artist, a biologist, an archeologist, an economist, someone who will question the groupthink. And once you do have that team—guided by mutual respect of differences and mutual trust in abilities—everything else flows. When we are all together, the diversity of our minds creates better outcomes and better products.

To those of you who are just starting, what can you do while the world is still catching up? Learn from jujitsu and turn your perceived weakness into your strength. A long time ago, in my early executive roles, a well-known, retired CEO give me this piece of advice.

"Lila, don't be afraid."

At the time, he was talking about a football-player-turn-sales-exec who was talking over me, dismissing me outright, and worse, talking behind my back.

"You have to go toe-to-toe. I know it is scary, but you must figure out how to get there. And once you do, they won't know what's coming,"

Don't try to be like others. Be you. This feeling of being different, or even being an "impostor," won't go away until we are all included around the table. But in this feeling lies your strength. In it lies your power. Harness it to chart your own path. To all of you I say: No fear.

Sincerely yours,

Lila

Lila Tretikov is a Corporate Vice President of Technology in the Office of the CTO at Microsoft Corporation, and a leading expert on Artificial Intelligence and business transformation. In her role at Microsoft, she applies a cross-disciplinary approach to creating solutions that address some of the world's most challenging problems and empower humanity through technology.

Prior to joining Microsoft in 2018, Lila served as Senior Vice President of Engie SA, a global organization based in France, with a mission to alter the Earth's ecology through energy transition to CO_2-negative systems, and was Chief Executive Officer of the Terrawatt Initiative, a non-profit organization launched by Engie.

She was previously Chief Executive Officer of The Wikimedia Foundation, the non-profit organization that supports Wikipedia.

Lila founded a company in the field of computational genomics while at college and has numerous patents and articles to her name in the field of technology-enabled business transformations. In addition to prior service on the board of a U.S. public company, she currently serves on the boards of a number of private companies.

YVETTE BRIGHT

Board of Directors: CSAA Insurance Group

"Michelle Obama once said when you finally make it to the table, you realize you're just as smart as everybody else there. I remember that very moment when I was getting this visibility just sitting at the table, being the only woman, and certainly the only person of color . . .I realized I could do this."

Dear Chairwomen of Tomorrow:

I was born and raised in New Orleans, Louisiana, in a middle-class family, the youngest of six children. My dad was the first-generation attending college, and my mom was a homemaker. As I neared high school graduation, I didn't know what I wanted to do, but my best subjects were math and science. At sixteen, I decided to attend an engineering school, like my older sister before me. It was an up-and-coming field for women, and I enjoyed solving problems. My first choice was Notre Dame University, but my father did not want me to leave home at such a

195

young age, so I enrolled at Tulane University and majored in computer science and engineering.

Between my sophomore and junior year, I pursued internships with IBM. That summer, I interned with IBM in Houston at age seventeen and met the woman who would become my lifelong mentor and friend. Looking back, that was the most influential summer for me as a young Black woman because my manager at IBM was also Black and from my home state of Louisiana. I had an example of a successful woman who looked like me so I could see what was possible. Additionally, she went above and beyond to give me exposure with clients and other leaders at IBM. I spent that summer working as an intern on the oil and gas team, enjoyed the challenging work, and learned how to navigate a large corporate environment. It just so happened another Black woman was also on the team, and to this day, both these women have been with me through every major life milestone, forty plus years later.

IBMers always joked IBM stood for "I've Been Moved." I spent the first eight years of my career in Houston, Dallas and then New Orleans. During that time, I worked with clients in different industries, including financial services and the public sector, which broadened my experience while leveraging my skillset of applying technology to solve business problems. During my final two years, I worked for IBM UK in London, England. That was another pivotal moment for me because being an expatriate in the early '90s was rare for a young Black woman in a technology field. I was leading a pilot program for the consulting arm of IBM, the goal of which was to deploy new hires who had just graduated from university to staff project engagements at a lower rate and drive incremental revenue. That gave me a good foundation in terms of managing a small profit-and-loss center.

At that point in England, there were not many people of color in corporate positions, and certainly no other Black women expatriates. It was challenging to adjust to a new culture on both the personal and professional levels. It was a huge test for me at that point, and I left with the confidence I could successfully navigate an environment in a leadership position among all-white male counterparts, in a foreign office. I have always subscribed to the philosophy of "keep your head down, do your job, and deliver. The rest will take care of itself." Eventually, that paid off, and two of the male executives took notice of my work and my ability to deliver outcomes, which gave me influence and a voice at the table. The experience also taught me how to build and nurture a great team to achieve common goals. I realized I enjoyed leading and developing young talent. My time in England helped me understand the importance of developing a broad skillset and taking charge of how I wanted my career to unfold. After returning to the States, I felt I had real success under my belt, along with broad experiences and a transferable skillset, so I decided the time was right to move on from IBM to new challenges.

Once I settled in Philadelphia, I took a part-time consulting position with Independence Blue Cross. They had just hired someone to head the sales and marketing organization and needed someone to help build technology solutions to enhance their prospecting and sales reporting. My skillset was a good match, so I took the role, and twenty-seven years later, I retired from IBC. During my time there, I held eleven different positions, which gave me a great opportunity to learn all aspects of the

197

business. More importantly, I could do whatever I wanted to do by applying myself and delivering results. My new boss recognized that, and in addition to being my direct manager, became my mentor and helped drive my career forward. He always ensured I had visibility with the CEO and the top executives from day one.

As a Black woman, sitting alongside my white, mostly male counterparts, I always felt like I had to be better. That mindset was how I approached this new career, and it served me well. I kept my head down and focused on building a great team and delivering outcomes. Even with those successes, it was important to have mentorship and, oddly enough, over my time in healthcare, three men mentored me and helped guide my career.

I remember clearly the moment I attained a seat at the executive table, being the only woman and the only person of color. I no longer doubted my ability, and it was my responsibility to use my influence, not just for other women or people of color, but for everyone under my leadership. When conversations inevitably turned to talk about meetings, outings, or events "the boys" attended together, I felt more and more confident to raise the concern and importance about workplace diversity and women in the executive ranks. To be honest, I found willing listeners among my male colleagues, and we worked to put programs and metrics in place to focus on diversity and inclusion.

It took me a while to realize my male colleagues just asked for what they wanted—the promotion, increased compensation, inclusion in an important strategic discussion—and women did not typically do that. In the last ten years of my career, I finally began to push those boundaries and distinctly remember the conversation where I told the then CEO my goal before retiring was to run a multi-billion-dollar profit-and-loss center and be a Chief Operating Officer. I knew I was capable of doing that job and doing it well. In the last three years of my career, that is exactly what I did.

Over thirty-seven years, all these experiences shaped my personal and professional growth and rounded out my technical and leadership skills. I felt prepared to begin my next journey, so I retired and set my sights on serving on boards, starting a nonprofit, and pursuing other avenues where I could influence organizations to focus on diversity, support women in executive roles and, more generally, help people of color achieve their career and life goals.

Now I am serving as a director on five boards, and I realize the experience of being in the board room as an executive was invaluable to understanding governance structures. I also had the opportunity to sit on boards of wholly owned subsidiaries at sizeable companies, as well as chair a human resources committee. That experience gave me a great foundation to serve on my first outside board. I joined a board in the life insurance industry, where it was easier for my experience and skillset to be of value.

Board recruitment and interviews were other eye openers. Although board recruiters get many placements, most placements are relationship based. If you have not cultivated those relationships, it can be harder to land that first board seat. As a result, I know so many accomplished women who have been on a board yet because they don't have the right relationships. All are experienced executives, brilliant, and no doubt would make significant contributions. Three years into my first outside board, I now have other board positions being presented to me on a regular basis. Some are being driven by the environment we are in with states passing legislation to require board diversity. I hope corporations will realize they have nothing to lose and everything to gain from having a diverse board.

Corporations have to be willing to take a chance on appointing directors who may not have deep industry knowledge but bring a skillset and other intangibles that will add value. The candidate may not have 100 percent of what the company wants. However, for this to take hold and for women and minorities to get some traction, governance committees will have to be more open-minded when conducting a search. The next challenge is to land a seat on a public company board. Generally, they go to the candidate who already has public company board experience. But don't give up! I just landed my first public company board. How? A colleague on another board referred me. Yes, relationships.

Future Chairwomen, know your value. Be confident about what you can bring to the table, and network, network, network. I see change happening, and I see the change I am helping make happen. I have no doubt the next generation of board leaders will be the vibrant and diverse group that mirrors the clients and customers enterprises serve.

I look forward to seeing you next to me at that table.

Yours Truly,

Yvette

Yvette Bright is a leader in the healthcare industry and brings a holistic perspective built on 35 years of experience in operations, marketing, IT, human resources and finance to inspire actions leading to winning results. Yvette has led organization-wide teams that helped the company grow top and bottom-line revenue, while serving over 30,000 employer groups with more than 8.5 million people in 27+ states and the District of Columbia.

Yvette recently retired from the role of Executive Vice President and Chief Operating Officer of Philadelphia-based Independence Blue Cross, where she was the first woman and business leader of color to have responsibility for the Commercial and Medicare P & Ls, with revenues exceeding $6 billion. She oversaw customer service, processing services, operations shared services, business process reengineering and business technology services (IT). Yvette has transformed Independence's operating model to increase targeted margins; improved end-to-end customer experience resulting in a retention increase over the long-standing annual average; and advanced innovative, new partnership agreements that led to substantial incremental revenue.

In past executive roles at Independence, Yvette led the company's eBusiness evolution; successfully transformed Independence's systems, migrating 2.2 million members to a new platform with ACA and market leading capabilities; and continually led efforts resulting in millions of dollars in increased revenues and reduced costs. Yvette spent the first ten years of her career with IBM in the US and Europe.

Yvette earned her Bachelor of Science degree at Tulane University School of Engineering and a MBA from St. Joseph's University. She currently serves on several Boards of Directors including National Life Group, Independence Health Group, Reveleer, CSAA Insurance Group, Myers Industries (MYE), and the Advisory Board for Clarify Health. Yvette is now President of Brighter Horizon Foundation, which she founded to assist first generation minority students reach the goal of attaining a college degree.

CAROL REALINI

Board of Directors: Angaza, CardCash, JourneyApps, Juntos Finanzas

"You are never alone."

Dear Chairwomen of Tomorrow:

Picture it: Silicon Valley. The mid-1970s. The dawn of the tech industry. A woman in her early twenties begins her career. Although I didn't feel it at the time, I was not alone.

My name is Carol Realini. At the onset of my career, I thought I'd just be an engineer. I soon realized I wanted to pursue leadership roles. Then, after ten years spent working in management, I shifted direction and left the corporate environment to take on senior management positions in start-ups. Best-laid plans and all that.

My journey to corporate governance grew out of wanting to become a CEO. In 1990, I self-funded my own company and ran it profitably as CEO.

In the 1990s, I was running myself into the ground, selling my company, and trying to raise capital to start a new one. Back then, there were no books or really any kind of information on how to raise money.

Until that point in my career, I had a lone-wolf mindset. Starting out, I didn't have a lot of support, nor did I ask for help. Then someone said to me:

"Carol, you need to ask for help. Your vision for your new company is impressive. To succeed, you will need help. Otherwise, you're going to fail."

That really kicked me into gear. Right away, I contacted fifty experienced entrepreneurs in my network, asking if they'd be willing to read my business plan. To my surprise, most people gave a lot of time and I received a lot of great advice. All these people gave me insight into how to improve my business plan and how to think about fundraising. Although it was difficult to raise Series-A capital as a woman, I was able to raise five million dollars on my own.

Sometimes, the best solution is to reach out and ask for help, explaining what you're trying to do and what you need. There will always be people willing to support you. This is truer today than it was back in 1995, when I learned the value of asking for help.

Since then, I've raised $200 million for my own companies and helped with millions for other companies. However, I wouldn't be talking about this today if I hadn't learned this lesson: although I'm able to do a lot, I can't do it all.

Just before my second company went public, my board told me they didn't think I would make a good public-facing CEO. There weren't many examples of women CEOs, and I think they made that decision partially because I am a woman. I was heartbroken. We eventually brought in a great person. It worked out well for the company and gave me the chance to shift direction again.

I spent a few years in the nonprofit sector and traveled the world. Then, I decided to launch another company. I ended up starting two. The first, Obopay, was a great company but too early for the market. The second, Omney, aided faster payments in the U.S. As an entrepreneur, I learned to master the challenges of an early-stage company. Along the way, I held a variety of board roles, including general member, chairwoman, and CEO.

In 2014, I decided to focus my board efforts on pre-public companies with good CEOs doing business in fields in which I had expertise. You've probably heard this, but once a woman gets her first board offer, she's about to get a lot of offers for other board seats.

I currently serve on four private company boards. They are all technologies companies that are profitable or moving toward profitability. Before I make the decision to join a board, I take the time to understand the company and the board itself.

Public and private boards operate quite differently. Boards of pre-public companies get into details about how the business is operating. On pre-public boards, you ask questions like:

- *"Do we have the right strategy?"*
- *"What are the big challenges for leadership in the company?"*
- *"Are we scaling fast enough?"*

- *"Do we have the team to take the company to the next level?"*
- *"Do we have the capital?"*
- *"Are our capital sources happy with our progress or are they frustrated?"*
- *"Are we managing our scarce resources wisely?"*

If you don't answer these questions correctly, the business can fail.

Having women on boards creates a whole different context for the corporation. Gender diversity brings something new to the board, just as ethnic diversity does. It provides a perspective you just don't get otherwise.

As you embark on your journey of leadership, remember, you are not alone. If you set out to accomplish great things, you will need help. So always have mentors, advisors, and supporters. You'll want expert advice, so look for people who have the experience you need.

Then it's up to you to make it a little easier for the women coming after you. The less alone they feel today, the less alone they will feel tomorrow. I have been fortunate to have had many experts advise me along the way. And I wish you the same—all you have to do is look, reach out, communicate in a compelling way what you are building, and ask for support. Not everyone has the time or inclination to help – that's OK. The ones that do help, can really contribute to success.

Yours truly,

Carol

Carol Realini is a serial entrepreneur, mobile payments and banking pioneer, a successful Silicon Valley executive and an expert in financial service innovation. She has worked with leading financial institutions as well as multinational banks. She is and has been a part of several Boards of Directors, was CEO and Chairman of Obopay and she was named 50 Top Women in Technology.

Carol is the author of *BankRUPT – Why Banking is Broken, How it can be Transformed*. Carol has a BA in Math from the Univ. of California, an MS in Comp. Science from San Jose State U., a graduate of the Stanford Univ Grad School of Business and the Exec. Program from Singularity Univ. She is a Board Member of PrepayNation.

KELLY FORD

Board of Directors: Bento for Business, ScaleMatters, Suuchi, Kinetiq

"When designing a high-functioning board, one cannot just look at one seat that needs to be filled, no matter how challenging it is to do. One needs to balance the desired board culture and diversity with the strategy of the business and the needs of the CEO."

Dear Chairwoman of Tomorrow:

My family's livelihood came from my dad's job with Polaroid. He spent thirty-four years there, and we valued the stability and security of his position. My dad's work ethic and "whatever it takes" mentality set an example for me. He brought an "earn-it" mindset that sticks with me and drives me, and my expectations of others, to this day.

I thought I would follow in my dad's footsteps with a big corporate career path. I interned at Polaroid, then after graduation consulted for a few big companies before going to work for Lotus around the time IBM acquired it.

But in my late twenties, I got the start-up itch.

My family couldn't understand why. How could I contemplate such risk when gainfully employed at big, stable, secure IBM? The answer was easy:

I wanted to build something.

I wanted to be part of something innovative, fast-paced, and high growth.

I have now spent twenty years working with small and mid-sized businesses and have never looked back.

Still, my big-company career and dad's experiences have shaped who I am. They gave me the critical skill sets for my former career—operating a start-up, growth, and mid-cap companies— and my current one—investing in high-growth technology companies. From them, I learned the value of strong culture and strategic alignment that makes a company, as well as its board, productive and successful.

My first exposure to corporate governance was as an operator inside a private VC-backed company. The board was composed of only investors. I attended every board meeting and worked with the CEO to prepare everything from quarterly updates to presentations around acquisitions and investment rounds. Outside of garnering board support for our plans, though, what mattered to me most was understanding board member sentiment on the business, how could they make us better, and how I could engage them productively both inside and outside of the boardroom.

Today, I'm an investor at a growth equity firm that puts a lot of stock into using the board of our portfolio companies as not just an effective governing body but as a strategic weapon. I did not have prior formal or academic board governance training per se. However, I was fortunate enough to join a group of investors with a time-tested board of director's playbook tailored to companies in the stages in which we invest ($10-30 million in revenue).

Our playbook, which is grounded in "governance plus" from more than thirty years of board experience, emphasizes board design that drives strategic alignment and accountability, has domain and operational relevance, and addresses the specific needs, and perhaps even gaps, of the CEO. When investing in a new company, we often consider the quality of the board as carefully as the management team. The management team that guides a young company to its first $15 million in revenue is often not the same as the management team that runs the company when it is generating $25 million to $50 million. The same goes for the board. It may need to change as the company grows and matures.

Today, it is my privilege to serve on six private company boards (four investor seats, two independent seats) for private companies at stages ranging from start-up ($1-5 million in revenue) to scale-up ($10 to 25 million) and beyond ($100 million+). I also serve on the board of a nonprofit.

In my initial years as an investor, the aspects of governance that were new for me pertained to the situations when a special committee needs to be created, typically driven by government mandates, litigation, shareholder proposals, CEO change, or other outside pressures. My first encounter with a special board situation was a crash course in an unfortunate case of board conflict. The company was in a board-approved, banker-led sale process and signed a term sheet for a cash transaction at fair valuation. Then a co-investor became involved in questionable dealings with the buyer, resulting in the original agreement being terminated in favor of a stock deal at a significantly lower value.

Everything went into flux. A special committee of disinterested board members was assembled. Legal letters were exchanged, which resulted in an outstanding board liability. These conflicts are not uncommon, but this was a particularly ugly situation I hope to never encounter again. We had to call into question the investor's ethics, as well as deal with the economic fallout. In hindsight, this was also a clear case of board misalignment—a lack of true connectedness.

I quickly learned from this experience and others that a board cannot be high functioning, never mind a strategic weapon, without leadership and a culture grounded in connectedness, communication, and accountability.

Connectedness means alignment on the three-year plan, strategies for hitting key milestones, shared vocabulary and definitions for metrics, quality of management team, capital formation, and other strategic and financial matters. Just showing up on a quarterly basis does not make for a connected, aligned board. That requires a cadence of one-way reporting and two-way / multi-way communication, including the delivery of bad news faster than good news.

A board member also has to be accountable, just like the CEO and her management team. CEOs designing (or redesigning) a board need to ask themselves - Is my board:

211

- comprised of folks who are actively referring customers, partners, and key talent;

- creating connections for me with peers in the market;

- helping deliver key (sometimes difficult) messages to employees;

- contemplating marketplace trends and evaluating and engaging on how best to harness them;

- preventing major personal or company mistakes;

- helping to navigate litigious or other stressful matters?

And when it comes to culture, I've found that you need the leadership of a chairperson or lead director, who may or may not be the CEO, to set the tone from the start. Getting culture right (or wrong) at the board level has a trickle-down effect, defining the relationship between the CEO and the Chairperson all the way down to the management team and the rest of the organization.

In all, when designing a high-functioning board, one cannot just look at that one seat that needs to be filled, no matter how challenging it is to do. One needs to balance the desired board culture and diversity with the strategy of the business and needs of the CEO.

Only one-third of the boards I have served on over the course of my career have had more than one female board director besides me. Yet I hear consistently from male CEOs that they'd love to have a woman join their board, and even expand their board to create room for one.

I do find women are more communicative, engaged, and prepared as board members than men—and I certainly strive to be. I have a hunch that women experience less board amnesia than men too, which creates more productive meetings and a greater respect for the management team and fellow board members 'time.

I'd describe my own style as a board member and investor as curious and constructively candid. I've walked in the management team's shoes, and I know how to drive accountability. I have found the best boards have fewer investors and more operators (independents) around the table. CEOs and management teams benefit from actionable insights from those who have seen the movie before. Also, co-investors can have different agendas, making it more difficult to drive alignment. Independent directors with executive operating backgrounds can serve as an effective bridge between the CEO and investors when alignment issues arise.

Although I most often hold investor board seats, I've found myself playing the bridge role on several occasions. For my first meeting on one board, I defused a situation where the CEO and board couldn't agree on the issue of board design and compensation. I led an open discussion, provided advice based on experience, and got the board members to compromise on their original views. My predecessor had not been able to achieve this outcome, leading to one board member thanking me for giving the situation the "woman's touch." I wasn't offended and didn't ask him to elaborate.

The validation of my style has been invitations by CEOs to serve as an independent director on their boards after my firm exits their respective companies. I believe this recognition is equally due to my contributions and to the favorable dynamic a woman brings to the boardroom.

I believe that greater gender diversity at the board level for private companies will come bottoms-up from local ecosystems and top-down from the investor community. Local ecosystems on the coasts are the strongest. However, many female executives who built their success in those markets are returning home to raise their families and start their next ventures. With more venture and growth capital backing them, the pool of qualified and diverse private company board candidates will likely increase.

Board design is a critical exercise, whether drafting one on a blank canvas or re-evaluating an existing board at different stages of a company's journey. One design might focus on ensuring representation across the company's key audiences: customers, employees, community, and shareholders. Another design might rally around a first-time founder / CEO, where having seasoned CEO, CFO, and/or CRO profiles can fill gaps in the CEO's experience. The fact that one or more investors typically occupy board seats means the opportunity for diversity and balance is more limited.

I hope we see more CEOs encouraging the women on their executive teams to pursue board work. There's also a growing population of investors saying they won't back a company unless at least one woman is represented on the leadership team. I haven't heard of similar requirements from limited partners (LPs) invested in venture, growth equity, and private equity funds. However, if the LPs put their feet down, that could have a powerful trickle-down effect too.

I hope my experiences can help you decide what type of board member you want to be and how to evaluate the qualities of the boards you consider joining. I'd encourage you to place your bets in a board with a strong culture and alignment with your value and specialties—your sector, stage, network, and so on. After that, make sure you will have the data and tools you need to drive accountability, which will set you up for your next board engagement. And don't be afraid to play the woman card if it helps you get the job done.

Yours truly,

Kelly

Kelly Ford is a tech industry executive turned growth equity investor with a specialty in building enterprise value for software companies from startup to $100M. As General Partner at Edison Partners, Kelly invests in growth-stage fintech and enterprise software companies and, as the pioneer of the firm's Edison Edge operating platform, advises portfolio companies on go-to-market strategy and operations. She currently serves on the board of directors for Bento for Business, ExecVision, Kinetiq, observIQ and Suuchi.

Prior to joining Edison, Kelly spent 20 years in high-growth emerging and established B2B and B2B2C companies, including IBM (NYSE: IBM) and LivePerson (NASDAQ: LPSN). She is a member of the Board of Trustees for TechUnited:NJ, advisory board for Michigan State University's Center for Venture Capital, Private Equity and Entrepreneurial Finance, and Rutgers University School of Business' Road to Silicon V/Alley. She has been featured in *Buyouts*, *Forbes*, *Crunchbase*, and on *Nasdaq TradeTalks* and *Cheddar*, and is a frequent speaker at local and national investor, tech and B2B industry events.

LAURA MATHER

Board of Directors: Modulus Data

"Listen to what people are looking for and deliver what they want, but never lose sight of your value, especially the one that lies beyond boundaries."

Dear Women Leaders of Tomorrow:

In my early career, I worked for such institutions as the National Security Agency and Encyclopedia Britannica. I then worked in cybersecurity at eBay before the field was called cybersecurity. Back then, I also handled cybersecurity for PayPal because it was part of eBay. At that time, about eighty percent of all cyber-attacks targeted eBay or PayPal. By the time I left, that number had decreased to 25 percent. I wondered where the hackers ' attention had gone, and which other companies may need protection. This prompted me to start my own cybersecurity company, Silver Tail Systems, through which I stepped into my first board role. In that situation, the only people who choose you are venture capitalists. I was CEO for a few years, then was succeeded by another CEO, which was a fantastic decision. I remained on the board and personally experienced the differences in managing at the board level as compared to managing as an executive, particularly when it came to board politics.

As an executive, I witnessed firsthand where the board influences and where it lacks power. It was my first lesson. As someone once said to me:

"The board has one job. Every day, board members wake up and decide whether or not the CEO should be fired."

It really put the board's role into perspective.

Let's be clear. Board members try to influence many other things, sometimes hilariously so. I've heard horror stories about dreadful boards. Fortunately, I haven't experienced any myself. I received a good board-management tutorial from my first VC, who told me board meetings themselves were actually superfluous. More important was to convene with each board member before an actual meeting to foresee what would happen and what everyone would say. With this process, things happen as expected and without drama during board meetings. You need about a week before a meeting to connect with all board members. The week after the board meeting, you're usually implementing the tasks the board members suggested you do. This leaves you about two weeks to run your company, which creates an interesting dynamic. Private company boards are curious in that way. I was on that board for about five years before the company got acquired. That was a good fit.

The second company I started, Talent Sonar, helped enterprises remove unconscious biases from their recruitment using data-backed approaches, such as removing names from resumés and performing structured interviews. That company did not succeed.

It was interesting to observe the differences between a successful company and an unsuccessful one, specifically in regard to their boardroom. At the same time, my first company, which succeeded, went through a year, if not longer, of angst. We weren't going to the moon the whole time. It was fascinating to observe board dynamics when things were going really well versus when they were not.

A few horror stories stick out. When a friend went to raise her second round of funding, she had two investors to choose from. She did a bit of due diligence but not much. After making her selection, she found out the investor she'd accepted money from was known for swooping in and replacing CEOs. Investors often feel like they need to add value, and this one was no different. This investor did what he always had and replaced her. It was a nightmare. She fought hard to stay but did not succeed.

In another example, an independent board member got upset about an offer from an outside group to acquire the company because he didn't think the offer was good enough. He tried to hold the company hostage and threatened to go to the acquirer to sabotage the acquisition. These types of situations all cause drama. When the board's expectations don't align with reality, it can lead to real problems. Another example is Theranos, where Elizabeth Holmes had celebrities on her board who didn't know the market well.

VCs have a huge interest in the operational parts of the board and in how much it is spending. Public and private boards are different in that way. On private boards, VCs expect you to "buy market share," and you lose a lot of money to become a monopoly. VCs can push for a lot of marketing spend when the business isn't there yet. I've heard of situations where people were pouring gas on the fire when there wasn't yet a spark. That situation can be tricky to manage. Hopefully, CEOs can push back with data.

The key to managing a board is through data. VCs want to add value, believe they're smarter than you and, in most cases, that they've seen more. One component of a board is identifying and optimizing people's strengths while placating those who lack that strength with a compromise so as not to antagonize them. It's very much a dance.

Two things caused my shift from working in cybersecurity to addressing unconscious biases. First, I had my own biases. While at eBay, I clearly remember having seen someone with a grey beard during an interview and thinking to myself:

"This person is not a culture fit."

When I look back on that now, I am horrified. eBay's company culture favored youth and promoted a fast-paced environment where one worked until 8:30 or 9 p.m. every night. The workplace accommodated mostly those without families. Still, I likely lost out on a talented individual because I wasn't willing to look past the person's appearance to find out if he could do the job.

Second, in 2015, Intel announced it was going to put $350 million toward a diversity program. Apple and Google followed suit with tens of millions each. I realized I'd been looking at diversity differently. To be honest, my first company was successful because our engineers were semi-diverse. Let's be clear. They were all white men. However, they had diverse training and educational backgrounds. Only one of them had a computer science degree. One was a linguist. Another hadn't finished high school, and another had a physics degree. Their diversity came from the fact they'd all been trained to think differently. Watching such a team accomplish amazing things made it clear to me I'd been missing out for a long time by having a cookie-cutter mold of whom I'd work with. It kick-started my studying of the landscape surrounding diversity. If even small amounts of background diversity showed such promise, organizations could expand on that and become much more successful.

My PhD is in computer science, so I'm driven by empirical evidence. I read the research in the field and found empirically proven ways to increase diversity. These included removing names from resumés or asking candidates the same questions over the course of structured interviews. I assumed organizations, upon looking at these proven methods and tools, would want to implement these approaches. They did not.

I think intergenerational diversity adds an important dimension which boards miss out on. It comes up in board interviews. When my seven financially skilled male board members ask me whether prospective board candidates are good at finance, my response is:

"You have seven people who excel at finance. Why do you need another one?"

I'm not skilled in finance. I'm skilled in cybersecurity and running companies. I'm great at understanding software service models and Silicon Valley culture. It's hilarious to me that boards seem to think it is a good idea to replicate what they already have. You don't bring a millennial onto a board because they have forty years of experience running a public company. That isn't the value they add. Their value is in understanding the way millennials think as it relates to customers and the way an organization interacts with society, which is paramount these days. I believe the more diversity we can embrace, including age diversity, the better. A certain perspective is lacking without it.

One of the boards I've interviewed for, which was composed of all white folks, was looking for diversity. I interviewed with a male VC, who suddenly felt threatened when I mentioned my investment was with one of the world's top investment firms. He started pushing back on everything I said. It was a fascinating moment. The fact I could know more than he did was threatening to him.

In studying bias, I found that, when someone feels uncomfortable, it's easy for them to dislike others. I challenge you to think of your best friend and decide for a day you hate them as a thought experiment. It's easy to find some things to dislike. We're all human. It's absurd to talk about diversity and yet become uncomfortable when people don't look like us. Let's be clear, 100 percent of the reason this comes into play is because the board power structure is being challenged. Boards are mostly pale, male and stale, and love their power. I don't blame them. I would too. As a white woman, I possess a lot of that power too. But I do think this is the final frontier. I think we will have a woman president before the board challenge is solved.

I know there's controversy over quotas. Personally, I have never had an issue with them. In business, we measure everything else. If Acme Corporation conducted a study that found moving its factory to Main Street would lower costs, they would do it. Evidence shows adding women to boards improves companies' bottom lines and shareholder performance, so why not measure it? It's a business measurement. Acme Corporation would always measure things because it's good for business. I believe the power structure is responsible for creating a taboo around quotas, which is irrational and silly. I think quotas are effective.

A few years ago, when I was looking for board positions for myself, a VC asked me:

"What happens if you're the token woman?"

I replied:

"Somebody has to be that first person. Maybe the role won't be great, and maybe it's a glass cliff situation where the board needs a scapegoat—that's awful and shouldn't happen—but I do believe imposing quotas and adding women improves board performance."

Board positions are usually filled by word of mouth, which is why most board members look the same and play golf. If boards truly value diversity, they can show they do by paying for it. Research shows exposure to one's biases reduces them. For example, when people with little exposure to Muslims watch a show featuring a Muslim family, their bias lessens. Let's use that data to show ways to reduce bias. Some women will struggle. However, gender and racial diversity on a board would be a beautiful thing.

When board members tell me I'm not "qualified" for a board role, and I see who they choose instead, I think to myself that the chosen board member doesn't possess the skills I was told I lacked. Intel conducted a study about women and promotions. The hypothesis was women didn't ask for promotions. In reality, the study showed women ask for five promotions for every promotion a man gets, and men don't usually ask for them. Men are typically offered promotions over a game of golf or drinks. It's obvious where boards get their talent. The method is easy and cheap. However, it doesn't add value. The biggest hurdle is those in power don't want to give it up.

I have a hard time believing current CEOs and board members will focus on environmental, social, and corporate governance issues. They will get fired if their stock price doesn't go up, so how can they focus on anything else? If corporations got to a point where they really cared about these issues, they would benefit from adding diversity to their boards. I don't believe we're there yet. It sounds cynical. However, it'll take time.

As far as female role models, I met with Heidi Roizen years ago. Heidi is a Silicon Valley executive, venture capitalist, and entrepreneur who is best-known for speaking out against the harassment of women in technology. I admire Heidi's "take-no-prisoners" attitude. I feel like she goes after what she wants. As women, we're boxed into a set of expectations that hurt us, in terms of our likeability. My advice is to not listen to what boards say they want, because again, my hope is that by the time women, people of color, LGBTQ+, and disabled people get to a place where they undeniably demonstrate their value, boards will notice. So don't try to stifle yourself to fit into this limited vanilla box.

Under-represented people will have to juggle knowing their worth and fitting into a set of expectations in order to get to the level where they can demonstrate their value.

Listen to what people are looking for and deliver what they want. And never lose sight of your value, especially the one that lies beyond boundaries. We are told the only way to climb the ladder is to fit in, and that needs to change.

Yours truly,

Laura

A pioneer of web security, Laura Mather worked for the National Security Agency, Encyclopedia Britannica, eBay and PayPal before she cofounded cybersecurity firm Silver Tail Systems in 2008. The company worked with global financial institutions to protect them from website security risks. Silver Tail Systems was acquired by cloud company EMC, which merged with Dell in 2016, for $250 million in 2012.

After Silver Tail Systems was sold, Laura embarked on her second startup, Talent Sonar. The HR platform is designed to eliminate bias from the hiring process by offering services like "blind" resume review options and interview scripts. Ultimately, the platform aims to help companies by boosting diversity and increase opportunities for women and people of color. Talent Sonar merged with hiring company TalVista in 2018.

TELLE WHITNEY

Board of Directors: Everactive, AI4ALL, CMD-IT, Power and Systems

"Being action-oriented made me successful in my job, but constructively serving on a board requires a different approach."

Dear Women Leaders of Tomorrow:

My name is Telle Whitney. I am currently a board member on three nonprofit boards and one industry advisory board.

My journey to board governance began, surprisingly, when computer science entered my life. I was born in Salt Lake City, Utah, and had no exposure to computer science or engineering while growing up. My father was a lawyer, my stepmother was a piano teacher, and my mother was a history teacher. I attended the University of Utah for my undergraduate degree and started out majoring in theatre. I then studied political science, and almost dropped out. I completed a "strong interest inventory test," which showed that computer programming would suit me well. This prompted me to enroll in a COBOL programming class.

226

I fell in love with computer science from that moment. A faculty member, Rich Riesenfeld, became interested in my work and introduced me to Ivan Sutherland, who had founded the Caltech Computer Science Department. Ivan's encouragement and Rich's recommendation led me to pursue my PhD at Caltech, where I worked with Carver Mead, considered by many to be the father of systemic VLSI design, which is widely used today to create chip designs. Carver has remained a good friend to this day.

Despite not having family members who were engineers or computer scientists, I did have people along the way rooting for me and pushing me forward. The most important advice these people provided was encouragement to keep going. Before "the" Rich Riesenfeld took interest in my work, no one had ever told me I could pursue a PhD. My father and stepmother supported me, and my mother always told me I could do anything. Even though she passed away when I was fifteen, that core belief allowed me to persevere during difficult times.

After graduating with a PhD in computer science from Caltech, I moved to Silicon Valley. At the time, it was literally Silicon Valley in that all the companies I worked with built silicon.

I wasn't around many women in California. Only about 13 percent of the student body at Caltech were women, and I was desperate to meet other women. I met Anita Borg upon arriving in California, and we developed a friendship and a successful partnership. Together we created the "Grace Hopper Celebration" event series. The series, which is named for one of the pioneers of computer programming. celebrated the contributions of women in technology. Five hundred people attended our first event in 1994, and the 2019 conference reached twenty-six thousand people, to become the world's largest gathering of women technologists. Since its inception, the conference has scaled globally. We now hold a Grace Hopper event in India and smaller events all over the world.

Anita started the Institute for Women and Technology. Unfortunately, she was diagnosed with brain cancer shortly after its creation. The organization was still early in its vision and was in serious financial trouble. So in 2002, I stepped in after she and the board requested that I do. When I stepped down, after fifteen years, the Anita Borg Institute (which was renamed AnitaB.org in her honor after her passing) now called) had become a $28 million nonprofit with sixty-five employees.

As CEO, I also was a member of the board. Through this dual-experience I gained a lot of knowledge about boards and effective board governance. When I joined AnitaB.org, the organization was young. Fortunately, a few key board members helped form the board and led the board governance. On their recommendation, for instance, we added a board member with a financial background, from whom I learned a lot about the financial aspect of running a board. Several AnitaB.org board members from the corporate sector left their corporate jobs and joined numerous public boards. Their stories and advice taught me a lot about effective board strategies that we incorporated into the AnitaB.org board. Their stories also highlighted the gender dynamics on corporate boards. Board governance became an increasingly important topic as the Anita Borg Institute grew and matured. We formed a compensation committee, an audit committee, and a nomination and governance committee, and we followed best practices regarding the structure and responsibilities of those committees.

228

When I left AnitaB.org, I evaluated what it would take to join a corporate board. As an experienced nonprofit CEO, my skill set didn't necessarily align with the skills desired by public boards. It is important to consider what skills you offer to corporate boards. A friend of mine who serves on several corporate boards coached me to consider what three words described me and to use those key descriptions in my profile. For example, semiconductor experience and nonprofit CEO are terms that, in essence, succinctly communicate your experience and skills. Additionally, you need to be able to quickly state what you offer. For example, one of my colleagues specializes in compensation committees. She chairs the compensation committees on a number of boards, so she's attractive to those seeking that skill set.

While still at the AnitaB.org, I joined the board of the Center for Minorities and People with Disabilities in IT (CMD-IT). CMD-IT hosts the Tapia Celebration of Diversity in Computing conference and is similar to AnitaB.org. It's a small organization with powerful leaders who seek to make an impact on under-represented minorities and people with disabilities in the computing field.

After I stepped down as CEO of AnitaB.org, I joined the AI4ALL board, which brings AI education to under-represented groups. The organization initially focused on high school kids and expanded to college age and beyond. Finally, I chair the board for Power and Systems, a nonprofit that deploys professional development for culture change in a fascinating and engaging way.

As I've learned more about my own skills, I have found that smaller companies, particularly start-ups, are more attractive to me, and I am talking to several start-up boards.

As I've had the opportunity to learn more about board work, one of the biggest surprises is the significant responsibilities inherent in board governance. The financial reporting for organizations is regulated, and it is important to have board members and staff with financial backgrounds. The compensation of the CEO and of high-valued employees is public and subject to governing laws, and needs to be documented.

I've witnessed people from operating roles who join a board and then struggle. As a board member, your job is not to do, but to advise and manage the governance of the organization. My particular expertise with my nonprofit board engagements is in advising CEOs because I've been in their shoes. What is important is to offer advice and listen to their issues, while realizing they are making the decisions. A board chair role includes additional responsibilities, ensuring that board meetings are effective and that all board member voices are heard. The board has fiscal responsibility for the organization and the chair needs to ensure all governance and financial oversight responsibilities are met.

Typically, a board's work is episodic. For the most part, board members show up at meetings, participate in any committees they join, review the material prepared by the CEO, and ensure they understand the business. Sometimes, however, the board needs to help solve significant problems or search for a new CEO. That's part of the responsibility.

Diversity of thought is extremely important on a board. It is certainly the catalyst behind pushing for more female representation on boards. It's important the chair (depending on the size of the board), the CEO, and the nominating committee reflect on the strategic plan with the organization's goals in mind.

They must consider which board makeup will help take the organization forward, while also inviting those who will challenge the status quo. At AnitaB.org, for example, we added students to the board. They had all the rights and responsibilities of other board members but served a two-year term. (Other board members served three years, and often served two terms.) These students became an important part of the conversation. They quickly learned to speak up and often brought forth great ideas, along with different perspectives.

More boards have embraced diversity. The women I know who serve on public boards often find their board work particularly challenging when they are the only woman on a board. These women have described how much a board dynamic changes when there are two women and how it shifts again when there are three. When three board members are women, they normalize female participation and become "just" three more board members. As an example of why the representation matters, a prominent male board chair often confuses the names of the board's two female members.

In my consulting work, which focuses on recruiting and advancing women into technology organizations, I see companies that reach the size of about one hundred people and, all of a sudden, decide they need more women. Adding women once a company has gained momentum is much harder than when it is starting out. This also applies to boards. Small company boards tend to be composed of investors only, which is classically male dominated, although this situation is changing.

It is important to understand how board searches work. My board positions to date, including the private companies boards I am considering, have materialized through people I know. Fortunately, many organizations provide training and expertise to help people who are considering boards understand the process. Many of these organizations also have board lists. The jury is still out about how effective these lists are, but some smart and capable people are trying different strategies. I encourage you to get involved with some of the lists. *TheBoardList* and *How Women Lead* are two organizations from whose trainings I have benefited.

I am sure you will find the right resources that will support you on your journey. I wish you all the best.

Sincerely yours,

Telle

Telle Whitney is a senior executive leader, an entrepreneur, a recognized expert on diversity and inclusion, and a true pioneer on the issue of women and technology. She has over 20 years of leadership experience and was named one of Fast Company's Most Influential Women in Technology. She is a frequent speaker on the topic of Women and Technology.

Telle co-founded the Grace Hopper Celebration of Women in Computing Conference with Anita Borg in 1994 and served as CEO of the Anita Borg Institute from 2002 to September 2017. She transformed the Institute into a recognized world leader for women and technology.

She has won numerous awards including the ACM distinguished service award, an honorary degree from CMU, and is an honorary member of IEEE. She serves on multiple boards and advisory councils. She is also the co-founder of the National Center for Women and Information Technology (NCWIT).

Telle holds a Ph.D. and M.S. in Computer Science from the California Institute of Technology and a BS in Computer Science from the University of Utah.

LISA HAMMITT

Board of Directors: Glassbox, Clear Channel Outdoor

"Boards with women board members cover topics that wouldn't usually be discussed if only one gender were represented."

Dear Women Leaders of Tomorrow:

My number-one hero is my mom. She was at the top of her class at Lowell High School in San Francisco. That is, in and of itself, quite a feat, especially when you look at the school's illustrious alumni. The school was academically challenging, and fostered in her a love for lifelong learning and a growth mindset. She was awarded an opportunity to go to Stanford. Instead, she married, as many women in the fifties did. She had four girls, then lost her husband at a young age.

What she stressed in all of us was that education is the great equalizer. You could come from any socio-economic background and, provided you loved to learn, were given an opportunity to fail fast and learn many things, you could do anything. It was neither a gender issue nor a socio-economic one. It was just really your ability to manifest that growth mindset in yourself. That was important to my mother because she stressed academic success in all her children.

She took it a step further, saying that you also had to give back, which she did. My grandmother, an Italian immigrant from a family of lawyers, did as well. She was a beautiful writer and wrote eloquent letters on behalf of women who had issues dealing with local administration laws or with getting a driver's license, for example. My mom grew up in that environment, so she emphasized giving back. When we were young, she told us:

"I want you to have a fair degree of responsibility, I want you to have a boatload of work, and I want you to have no time and little money. With that, you'll learn to give back."

Her mantra turned out to be true. As I look back at it now, that mindset kept me out of a lot of trouble.

I wasn't yet eighteen when I went off to college. I graduated from Berkeley. My mom had always said:

"Weave education into whatever you do."

When I entered the corporate world, there was never a question in my mind that I would follow what I was interested in. I would enjoy the intellectual stimulation and focus on that. Career wise, I was always chasing my areas of interest, which is how I ended up working in the field of artificial intelligence and bioinformatics.

I've always been a curious person, which motivated me to become a CEO when I was in my early thirties. I got exposed to the boardroom early on. I saw that the decisions were really made in the boardroom. My sisters followed similar tracks, although they didn't elect to go into corporate life. Two of my sisters are self-employed and work in real estate. Another sister has a modest profession. However, she is also a sommelier and gourmet cook and has used these skills to plan extensive events. She has passed on her passion to her daughters, who are thriving in the corporate world. My sisters followed what they were passionate about and have both been successful in their own right.

Being a CEO is daunting under any circumstances, as you find out when you start your own company as I did. I got an idea through graduate coursework and was funded by the first VC I approached. In my case, I had a sudden influx of capital and angel investors who came along from Oracle and PeopleSoft to round out my initial funding. I raised a lot more capital from other VCs. At that time, I realized that, as a CEO, raising funding was my challenge to own. The staffing up was different because I needed to assemble a group of people who had never worked together, to create a product that had never been built before.

As a CEO, I quickly learned two sobering lessons. First, 30 percent of my decisions were going to be wrong no matter what because I had imperfect data. This was equivalent to firing a missile and hoping to intercept a rocket. Second, while staffing up from zero to seventy-five people, I learned I could only control three fundamentals: setting the right culture and strategy, defining our seven KPIs (Key Performance Indicators), and hiring the best candidates.

Setting the right culture and strategy was paramount. I spent a lot of time thinking about the type of person I wanted to bring through our doors, the core values they needed to have, and how they'd fit into a concentric circle from which additional concentric circles would be built. We could include additional DNA. However, we couldn't stray from our core values, which involved a lot of discipline.

Because so many people came onboard and I couldn't make all the decisions myself, I had to clearly define our operational dashboard's seven KPIs so that everyone would know and espouse them as their own mission. I had to push decisions down and hire leaders who could think on their own.

You absolutely have to be excellent at hiring and spotting talent because wavering from your mission is too costly. I learned how little a CEO actually controls because he/she depends on teams to really carry projects forward.

Early on, the board members who shaped my board appreciated my unwavering commitment to my principles, which boosted my confidence. When I attended a board meeting, I'd set my intention and rules of engagement, after which we'd quickly get through the operational review. Because my board members were busy, sat on multiple boards, and didn't represent me but our shareholders, I needed to be clear about where we were in the red, what we were going to do about it, and use our board time to deal with exception reporting.

Joining an external board was a new experience to me. My hypothesis is that serving on public boards, in particular, dramatically increases the chances you'll be approached to become a member of other boards. Those boards are staffed by private equity firms and outside directors in the industry. Their members see the board as Swiss cheese in that they have many holes which they need to fill. They can pick a number of candidates. However, their selection is based on a key skill set needed to help the company go where it needs to and help ensure shareholder oversight.

The particular hole I fill is imparting digital transformation and technology know-how to boards. Traditional industries like media, gaming, financial services, consumer packaged goods or healthcare typically don't have that kind of data and AI in their DNA. I come in to advise on how companies can monetize data or use AI in their five-year growth strategy. I am operational in my focus because it's inherent to my role, as opposed to that of an investment banker. I serve on every committee. It's uncommon, because a lot of board members don't have an operational background. Having that background gives me a great advantage because I understand what the CEO goes through to build the business.

There are two other women on the board, but the function I provide is both targeted and specific because boards typically don't find someone who has run nine-figure businesses on data and AI. That is unusual. Few companies are at scale with their AI, and I'm often solicited to advise on their digital transformation. That's why, when activism comes in and someone asks if we'll be spinning off a business or placing key management with this skill set, I am likely to be brought into the conversations. In many cases, that's considered our catalyst for growth strategy.

And I do think board training is essential. I was invited to attend Harvard's program for board training, which I found quite useful for one main reason: it provides you with access to a phenomenal network of people. More importantly, Harvard professors stress case studies. For example, if Carl Icahn came into the equation, we'd study PepsiCo and the impact an activist investor had on the company. Other students, who actually sat on PepsiCo's board at that time, describe what the dynamic was like and what kinds of tough decisions were made. Students participate and provide insights on the situation. It becomes an evolution of what you think would happen if you encountered the same situation. I'd say this approach is a lot more valuable than just attending a session with Wilson Sonsini where they talk about D&O insurance and other things to consider when on a public board.

If someone asked me if they should attend the Harvard program, I would wholeheartedly endorse it because I think its case studies are helpful. At Harvard you get top-quality instruction. You are coached in-depth on how to handle your first board meeting, on what happens when the CEO comes in, and to remember the phrase "nose in, fingers out" when tempted to overstep your functions to handle work yourself. You do extensive role-playing. However, I threw some of the things that I was heavily coached on out the window when back in the real world.

When looking at me, people see an academic tech person with an AI background. They start to think about how to clearly reset all the things they should be thinking about and doing. I was called upon in the first hour of my very first board meeting.

The Harvard program's instruction on behavior during your first board meeting was skewed. It emphasized you should listen and take notes but not contribute. My experience was the opposite. I quickly had to think on my feet. It worked out well for me because I had familiarized myself with all the materials beforehand, so I was able to add additional color. It allowed me to speak out a lot more, and I've openly contributed with conviction ever since.

Had I had followed a more classical training, I don't know it would have represented my natural inclination for a competitive approach. I'm glad I proceeded as I did because I now have quite a good rapport with other board members. I have no problem pointing out that we failed to cover a specific topic and need to look at it. Board members will agree and engage in the conversation about the missed topic. As a woman, or as someone who hasn't come from a traditional industry, I don't feel like my opinion is discounted at all. In fact, I feel my opinion is "double-clicked" on.

Another interesting fact is that boards are made up of committees. I serve on two: audit and compensation. There's also the governance committee, where the board forms into classic work groups in addition to a voting group.

Having been trained at Harvard and having spoken to fellow women members with deep operational backgrounds, I was afraid I would identify so much with the Chairpersons and the CEO enough that I would want to run the business. That was not my job. My job was to advise and probe.

It came as a surprise when the sales team invited me to get more involved in the business than other board members with different backgrounds. The team was introducing a net new product with a net new revenue stream and a different flavor than the previously launched product. They wanted me to come in for a day so their product managers could give me a demo, ask me how to enhance it, pitch it, and advise them on their go-to market strategy. I was flattered and also surprised by the invitation.

A lot of times, you'd think there would be a clearer, brighter line between those doing the business and board members, who usually keep their distance and strictly advise. I'm delighted by this development because I've established a relationship with the sales team, regularly share steps with them, and advise them on which leads to pursue. I call people I know when they are involved in something of interest related to what the team has shown me. It's allowed me to become a valued board member and carve out special relationships.

Boards with women board members cover topics that wouldn't usually be discussed if only one gender were represented. What does diversity and inclusion really mean? Do we, as a committee, start introducing guidelines around it? Are there guardrails around it? Topics that weren't covered five years ago are starting to come up now. What I try to do, as a personal contribution, is encourage everyone on the board to play to the strongest hand. Women excel in certain science and technology sectors, for instance, in the new areas around data management and AI. Some women are Scrum masters, while others can rapidly prototype with a behavioral model when a new market needs to be tested. We can add value-added services like these to our stacks to create higher margin value. Women do really well in some of these areas. Quotas aside, I encourage the operational team as well the board to think about which core competencies are needed and how we can extend the net to women to fill the vacancy pipeline.

The U.S. gender diversity report card is not as strong as I'd like it to be. It has less to do with intent because I know that topic keeps coming up. As an AI and data person, it is really easy to want to apply sledgehammer techniques to solve the problem. It's much harder to remove bias on things we can't easily see. Going back to my mom, she wasn't born into a well-off family. Although she was gifted intellectually, she wasn't from a high socioeconomic background like most of her classmates. It is difficult to represent harder-to-reach populations because inherent biases exist, and systems are set up to maintain them. To improve our scorecard, we need to be much more creative when putting our boards together.

To help break down the barriers to diversity in board representation, I recommend figuring out how to represent underserved populations in our boardroom strategy. To get back to Harvard again, I remember learning about Sherry Riva, who now runs Compass Capital and helps women who've saved up and are on the threshold of buying a house. They need solutions where different vendors and tech companies can figure out how to manage their assets so that they're not living paycheck to paycheck. Sherry or other select representatives from that community or could impact the future of banking or asset management. It would be immensely valuable. I'm focused on this aspect of value growth.

Someone with nontraditional skill sets as opposed to someone with the right pedigree can be immensely valuable in the boardroom and help carry the company forward. By simply having that skill set, and a different point of view, such people can offer value-added services and competitive go-to market differentiation.

I am the executive sponsor for the return-to-work program at Visa, so I hire women who want to come back to work. On the one hand, you might have a woman who had graphics training, worked in marketing at Electronic Arts, and paused her career for eleven years. On the other, you might have a summa cum laude

Berkeley graduate. There's no comparison. My freshly-minted data science person has a line across her desk of sales reps whose accounts want to work with her. Women work returnees are an underserved population. HR can establish quotas on returnees, but if you don't have someone who owns the P&L hiring them, or discussing success cases, no one pulls strings on their behalf. It's completely analogous to bringing women on boards. Yes, it's great we have people touting how great it is and we have laws pushing for it. However, you still need somebody to pull strings on the other side to make it a success.

I'm a Gen Xer. My generation was reactionary to the baby boomers, who were focused on wealth creation. They don't have to carry thirty-pound rocks anymore and retire when they're sixty. They can continue working until they're in their seventies and contribute valuable knowledge to the rest of us. Gen Xers were always the independent latchkey kids who had working parents and were serious about excelling. It makes us well suited to mentor millennials, who came from helicopter parents and didn't have to make the difficult responsibility tradeoffs Gen Xers did.

The interplay I'm seeing is: Gen Xers and millennials work well together. You have people who are working and are almost born to be mentors. They reacted to the '60s where there was a lot of societal upheaval, so they hunkered down, did their schoolwork, and rejected the drug culture. And then you have millennials, who prolonged their childhood because they lived at home for a long time and are naturally going to attach to an adult figure inside the corporate world. For example, I mentor sixteen millennials right now. Many seek mentoring, and it works for them. The dynamic of a multigenerational workforce works really well.

I find the Gen Z generation interesting. My two sons are from that generation. They grew up almost exclusively relying on collaborative platforms to do work in a Scrum-focused way. They are accustomed to having knowledge and insight at the tip of their fingers. They're going to think about how to make the ten thousand digital workers already on my phone achieve maximum productivity so that I can get my idea furthered with all the data to back it up. They're going to approach their jobs differently.

We have a good balance right now in terms of intelligence multipliers with the intergenerational workforce. But when the Gen Z's come into the workforce, you will see gross transformation in the way we work. They believe their mission is to systematically dismantle every institution built eighty years ago. They're not unusual. Every eighty years, we go through a systematic dismantling of institutions. I liken them to the Dutch sixteenth century model because they will form their own ideas as the basis by which they determine their profession, using many tools to do that, and they will form nimble networks of trust predicated on shared values and shared currency. They will abjectly reject globalism because that was the outcome of World War II.

I just joined my dream board, if you can believe it. A Stanford incubator invited me to join any of their boards. I chose Quantum Thought, a female-founded board, and was asked to be the chairwoman. I chose it because the company is tapped in a way in which we will quickly spin up and spin out a lot of companies. The company will be taking advantage of the latest technology.

I really liked two main things about the founder and CEO, Rebecca Krauthamer. One was her pedigree. She is the granddaughter of the Cassini Project at NASA, so she has a wonderful background of mathematics and technology. Secondly, she is using AI for social signaling. AI is becoming more and more intuitive. Soon, user control will be extracted out of a user's emotions and senses solely at their control. Users will be able to use AI to monetize their own intentions. This will be new money that hasn't been exploited yet, and it's going to be user controlled, which is super important from an ethical point of view.

Rebecca is trying to influence Stanford's Computer Science Department to use the technology. If we amplify that, we will attract more women into the field of computer science and create a net new computer science discipline. We will reach a whole group of people you and I are working so hard to stimulate right now. It will be much more natural.

What I want to say to prospective board members is inspired by a James Joyce quote:

"Our battles will be fought and won behind the forehead."

Remember that. It is not going to be about the mechanics. It will be in fighting to get your seat at the table. That will happen behind the forehead and is solely based on your value contribution to that board. To serve really does mean to serve. Think about it that way. I wish you all the best.

Yours truly,

Lisa

Lisa Hammitt is a senior software executive with 34 years of industry experience. She is currently Chief Technology Officer and EVP at Davidson Technologies, a missile defense contractor headquartered in Huntsville, Alabama. She is also a board director at Clear Channel Outdoor and Glassbox and an advisor at Sumo Logic and Brighton Park Capital.

Prior to Davidson, Lisa served as global vice president, Data and Artificial Intelligence, at Visa; vice president of marketing for Community Cloud at Salesforce; vice president, Watson Cloud Services at IBM; and director of strategy and corporate development at HP. She earned B.A. degrees in economics and French from the University of California, Berkeley, completed graduate coursework in artificial intelligence at Stanford University, and received executive education at Harvard Business School.

ROBIN MACGILLIVRAY

Board of Directors: Simpson Manufacturing

*"Wisdom isn't just sharing what you know,
it's also asking a LOT of questions."*

Dear Future Women Leaders:

My name is Robin MacGillivray. As a girl, most of the adult women in my community were stay-at-home moms. Sure, I saw women working outside the home—my teachers, cashiers at the local grocery store, and the receptionist at our doctor's office. But in high school, my Girl Scout troop leader gave a talk about her career in the airline industry. That little moment was an "A-ha!" It opened my mind to a world of opportunity I had never dreamed of, and was my first inspiration to "think big" about my future.

My next "A-ha!" moment happened in college. Title IX had just been enacted, banning discrimination based on gender in U.S. educational institutions and opening new doors for women. It was another moment that helped me see the limitless opportunities before me and motivated me to proactively seize them.

When I began my career at AT&T in the late '70s, the company was the world's largest private employer and had just reached an agreement with the Equal Employment Opportunity Commission. This agreement settled a complaint that the advancement of women and minorities at the company had been unfairly limited and resulted in a tsunami of opportunity for these groups. It was another "light bulb moment" that inspired me to "Lean In," as we now say.

"Leaning In" empowered me to ride the waves of change in the telecommunications industry for over thirty years. I worked in many varied capacities from engineering, finance and sales to human resources and mergers and acquisitions. I grew from a frontline supervisor of eight technicians to the president of a multi-billion-dollar business unit.

While the government intervened and certainly enhanced my college and early professional experience, my success as a student and a business leader didn't happen because of my gender. I was recognized and promoted along the way because of my enthusiasm, my performance, and my results. That's a key takeaway!

Early on in my career, I absolutely appreciated the importance of our customers and our employees. But in my first executive role at AT&T, another "A-ha!" came when a boss challenged a decision I had made. He asked if my decision considered our customers, our employees, AND our owners. In that "light bulb moment," I realized our shareholders' voice, our owners' voice, was our board's voice, and it was a vital voice to be heeded. That was my introduction to the realm of corporate governance.

I had my first personal experience in a governance role when I was elected a regent at John F. Kennedy University (JFKU) in Pleasanthill, California, now an affiliate of the National University

System. A regent oversees the financial management of the university, its investments, and its property holdings and appoints the president of the university. They key learning for me was, unlike my role as an AT&T executive, governance is not management. Boards are responsible for oversight and planning while management takes care of the daily operations. Having been in management for two decades, this was an adjustment.

My next governance opportunity was with my local Girl Scout Board. I am a life-long Girl Scout and have always been a fan of the movement. After all, that high school troop leader set my early career aspirations in motion, so I feel forever indebted. While on that board, we created Camp CEO, a three day overnight camp where successful executive women act as mentors and role models for high school girls from under-resourced communities. As a side benefit, Camp CEO provided the opportunity for the businesswomen to network. Sleeping under the stars, hiking, campfires, sharing meals in the dining hall—it was a great way to form new and lasting relationships. Camp CEO continues to this day.

My corporate governance experience was provided by Simpson Manufacturing, Inc. I was selected to join the board because the company was about to embark on a round of acquisitions, and I had significant M&A experience at AT&T. I was recruited by a fellow regent who knew me through our work as regents at JFKU, another nod to networking.

I was fortunate that a renowned governance expert served with me on the Simpson Board. In fact, he chaired our nominating and governance committee. He served as a mentor for many years. He taught me that wisdom isn't just sharing what you know. It's also asking a LOT of questions.

In time, I was asked to chair the Simpson Board's nominating and governance committee and served in that capacity for almost ten years. Over those years, my committee oversaw the appointment of several new directors, new committee members and chairs, a new female CEO, and a first-ever outside, independent board chair. The Simpson Board has been widely recognized for having 50 percent female board and committee chair composition and recently was a finalist for an award celebrating achievement in diversity. I am passionate about advancing women to seats in the boardroom. Simpson Manufacturing is living proof it can and should be done.

To wrap up, I encourage you to be open to the "A-ha!" moments in your life, those sudden insights or discoveries that reveal new paths. When you step onto a new path, "Lean In!" but . . . don't rely on your gender to achieve success. It may open a door, like it did for me, but nothing beats energy and great results. If you find yourself on a board path—and I hope you do—recognize that governance is vastly different than management. The board speaks for a company's owners and is a vital voice. Once on a board, find a mentor, learn all you can, and ask lots of questions.

Yours truly,

Robin

Robin serves on the board of Simpson Manufacturing, Inc., the leading manufacturer of structural connectors in the US and Europe. Before her retirement she held numerous executive roles at AT&T. She headed the firm's Post Merger Integration team, leading hundreds of initiatives designed to integrate merged entities for optimal customer service, cultural alignment and financial performance. She was President of AT&T's Business Communications organization, responsible for small, medium, and large businesses across California and Nevada. And she served on the faculty of AT&T University, the company's leadership and executive development arm.

For nearly two decades, Robin served on the board of merger-formed Girl Scouts of Northern California, including as President of the inaugural board and chair of the 100th anniversary capital campaign. Robin graduated with her Bachelor's and Master's degrees from the University of Southern California. She also completed the Stanford Executive Program and the Harvard/MIT/Tufts Joint Program on Negotiations.

Monika Schulze

Vice Chairwoman, Board of Trustees: The European Foundation for Media Optimization

Supervisory Board: Atlantic Grupa, Sektellerei Schloss Wachenheim,

"It's important to form your own opinion and be clear about what you want to achieve in your personal as well as business life."

Dear Future Women Leaders:

My name is Monika Schulze and I studied business administration at Cologne and Hamburg University. My main focus was on marketing and human resources. After graduating, I looked at the companies I thought were the most attractive. My ambition was always to look at the big picture. I wanted to live and work abroad, see different countries, and have more of an international perspective.

My father was a high-level executive at P&G, so I lived in the U.S. as a young kid. He supported all three of his kids growing up and wanted us to have good careers. He believed it was important women progress, study, and be responsible for their own living. My mother, on the other hand, always worried career ambitions would get in the way of having a family.

In the end, I was influenced by both parents and decided to have both a leading role in a company and a family. Having role models in my life, be it my parents or mentors in companies, always helped me push things forward and develop a positive, can-do attitude.

I was fortunate enough to work at Unilever in Germany, The Netherlands, Sweden, and Hungary. I was responsible for brands and businesses in Asia, Japan, and the U.S., which gave me exposure to different ways of working and thinking. I also did two years of coaching and training board members and individuals to help them achieve their goals in a better way.

After almost twenty years in a global company environment, I decided to take a break and started my own company. One reason was I wanted to spend more time with my twins. Being a single, working mom on an international assignment was too time-consuming. At the same time, I had to decide what I wanted to focus upon next. It was important that I get out of the so-called "hamster wheel" and reflect on what I wanted to achieve in my business life as well as personal life.

That's advice I often give to other (female) managers: Sometimes there is a need to step back and reflect. Don't take things for granted. You always have a choice and can change parameters in your life, especially if you feel you are not doing well anymore.

I set up a consultancy company for strategic and brand development with a method called "strategy into action." I had learned a lot of things are well-understood in theory. However, doing something and getting started often didn't happen. I would help companies focus on a set of goals and win and see progress within a short time.

My business and consultancy developed well, and I had to decide to either hire people or go back to the corporate world. The advantages of having support teams like legal, finance, and so on won over my intention to build up my own company. I realized I was too influenced by the ways of working in a bigger company, so I decided to go back.

When I was asked to have an interview with an insurance CEO, my first reaction was to decline. Luckily, I had a persistent headhunter talk me into at least taking the interview.

That is another key piece of advice: always listen to your gut feeling and remember your first impression (which is sometimes better that post-rationalizing with facts) and then make a decision.

In the case of the insurance CEO, the interview went well, and I decided to join Zurich, even though the industry was completely new to me. The CEO, however, wanted somebody to challenge and set up a new way of working on a strategic level. I like challenges and doing things in a different way. If somebody would have told me about the hurdles and resistance I would face, I am not sure if I would have said yes.

That's another key lesson from me: You have to dare, and you have to think outside of the box, believe in your skills, stay confident, and always learn new things. In the end, I convinced my colleagues with facts and data about, for example, customers and their expectations, which was part of the expertise I brought to the table.

One of my mentors prepared me early enough to think about a board membership and, in the end, helped me get my first assignment. He still gives me tips on what to focus upon and has helped me realize the difference of being an executive board member and an advisory board member. Apart from his sponsorship, the company was looking for a female member, preferably somebody with food and drink expertise and digital skills. I fit their profile perfectly. So, the tip I would give is: build a strong profile and a strong network.

Before I joined the board, I felt it was important to strengthen my skills by getting some training. I signed up for board academy training with different modules, for example legal, compliance, and strategy, with a test and certificate at the end. That gave me the feeling of being prepared and gave me a deeper understanding of what a board seat means and what is expected of me.

In the meantime, my second board seat at a start-up in New York ended after a year when the company was sold. Another opportunity came up through my network I had established when I had my own company. I am now also a board member at a food company in Croatia. It feels good to be back in the business I originally came from and to have the additional financial services expertise.

The advice I can give about board memberships: be clear about your expertise and what you can bring to the table. You have to be conscious about what drives, motivates, and fascinates you. If you love the details and digging into things, a board seat may not be right for you. You need to give the executive board the confidence to drive the business, intervene if things go wrong, and be clear about the vision, strategy, and direction in general.

People pretend there's a formal process in finding board members. In the end, my experience says it's about people knowing people. There are also headhunting companies that objectively analyze the structure of a board and what kind of people, personalities, and skills are needed for different kinds of boards. In my mind, that is a very good approach as this might help support diversity on boards in terms of skills, experience, and ways of thinking.

In a more traditional structure of advisory boards, diversity is still relatively low. That will hopefully change, and the board will drive valuable insights that help executives understand the importance of diversity and inclusion to drive business success.

Likewise, it is essential to give younger people and women the confidence to develop either into executive roles or board members and have a view about what they want to achieve.

Meanwhile, I encourage three daughters to be clear about what they want, be conscious about their decisions, and set up a vision about what they want to be and a plan for how they're going to get there. I think it's good to have a direction and be exposed to as many experiences as possible. Even if it doesn't go well in all cases, learn, adapt, and keep a positive attitude.

Life is, after all, a grand journey. I wish you all the best on yours.

Sincerely,

Monika

Monika Schulze is the Head of Customer & Innovation Management at Zurich in Germany and member of the Executive Committee with focus on building strong businesses in the context of massive industry transformation and digital disruption. Before joining Zurich Insurance, Monika run her own business as a strategic business consultant. In the last two positions at Unilever she served as Vice President Brand Development Europe and as Business Director Foods with P&L responsibility in Hungary. She has a Master of Business Administration degree from the University of Hamburg.

Monika is Member of the Board at Schloss Wachenheim in Germany, at Atlantic Grupa in Croatia and until end of 2019 she served as Board Observer at CoverWallet in the US. Moreover, she is a member of the Board at G.E.M (German Society for Research on Brands).

Monika was listed by Hubspot as one of the marketing experts to follow in 2021 and by Martech as one of the "Top Twelve Tech Women CMOs to Follow on Twitter 2018". She was nominated by Ad Age as a "Woman to Watch Europe 2017" and in the same year recognized by Forbes as one of the World's Most Influential CMOs.

KIM VOGEL

Board of Directors: Trico Bancshares, Orimar, Inc.

Board of Trustees: Saint Mary's College of California

""Don't feel you have to do it all by yourself. It takes a village to build a successful family, company and board. Seek out the best and brightest people to work with."

Dear Chairwomen of Tomorrow:

My name is Kim Vogel, and some may call me a technology entrepreneur. As a child, I would never have guessed technology would become my life-long career.

I am a first-generation college graduate. I learned about college for the first time during my freshman year of high school. Intrigued, I went home and told my mom I wanted a bachelor's degree.

My mom responded:

"Honey, I'm glad you want to get married and make sure some man does not remain a bachelor."

In that moment, I realized the obstacle in front of me. My family didn't even know what a bachelor's degree was. My mom is one of the most amazing women you could ever meet—incredibly hard working, passionate, and giving. However, she never graduated from high school and knew almost no one with any kind of higher education. As a result, I navigated my career path without guidance, often falling into each new step.

Now, some thirty years later, I aim to use my life experience to provide others with an easier path. I make it my personal mission to mentor career-minded girls. This is why I am writing today, in order to teach driven young girls, the chairwomen of tomorrow, the three most important lessons I learned in navigating my own career.

First, never underestimate the power of education. Second, find your niche. Third, stay true to your roots, and remember where you started. Above all, have faith in your journey.

The first crucial lesson I learned in my career journey is to never underestimate the power of education. Of course, education gives students the academic knowledge required to succeed in a particular career. However, what the professors don't tell you is education provides much more than that. It gives you a network and exposure to a world beyond one's own. It is an unparalleled opportunity to grow, not just as a student but as a person and businesswoman.

I completed my undergraduate studies at St. Mary's College of California. Growing up, I did not have a "dream school." I barely knew what college was. When it came time to decide where to attend college, I did not know where to start.

St. Mary's was local, and I discovered it while performing at basketball games as a member of my high school's drill team. It seemed as good a choice as any. Little did I know how pivotal this decision would be in aligning me on my particular path . . . but we'll get to that later.

Once I began my studies, I found I was best at math and accounting. I took the safest route in the book and became an accountant, heading to KPMG after graduation.

At KPMG, I worked alongside a woman pursuing her master's degree at night school. She sparked my interest in going back to school for my MBA. I looked into night classes at a local university. However, with the intense hours that accompany a career in public accounting, I never took the plunge.

A few years into my time at KPMG, the economy crashed. KPMG laid off my entire level, and despite having taken the "safe route," I found myself unemployed.

Lost and discouraged, I found the silver lining. Suddenly, I had time on my hands. My mind kept returning to the prospect of an MBA. Now, with more exposure to the academic world, I thought of the "dream schools" I had not even known about when applying for my undergraduate studies.

One school always stood above the rest to me, so I applied to Harvard Business School. It was a long shot. Honestly, I didn't expect to get in. I just wanted to ensure that at least I tried to reach for the stars. And then one day, I saw a letter from Harvard hidden among the junk mail and bills.

Opening it to find a "yes" was one of the most joyous moments in my life. I knew this was a game-changer. With no hesitation, I accepted, put my house up for rent, quit my job, and moved across the country, completely upending my life to become a full-time student. My time at Harvard was by far the two most impactful years of my life.

I received far more than a top-tier education. I gained international exposure, a network of some of the smartest and most interesting people I've ever met, and fantastic professors, many of whom are legends in the business world. I took it all in, feeling like I had won the lottery or slipped through the cracks thanks to some clerical mistake at the admissions office. Yet, eventually, I shook the feeling that I didn't belong. I acknowledged that I earned my spot and developed confidence in myself that I never had before.

Young women need to find that moment for themselves—it is in that moment that you truly believe that you can try anything. For me, that moment was thanks to my educational journey.

The second lesson I learned on my career journey is to find your niche. While you may think you know what your perfect job is, in reality, the job you enjoy the most may surprise you. At Harvard Business School, perhaps the most sought-after job was that of a Wall Street investment banker. While attending, it was hard not to get caught up in the competitive, fierce, and glamorized portrayal of life in banking. After graduation, I headed to an investment bank where I gained invaluable business experience and, perhaps most importantly, learned to navigate the crazy hours and become an even harder worker.

Still, business school dream job and all, I couldn't shake the feeling I was not passionate about what I was doing. Soul searching, I thought back to Harvard where I had the privilege of studying under a professor renowned for board governance. Interested, I began studying different boards and soon set the goal that, one day, I would serve on a public board of directors myself. However, serving as a director to a corporate board is no easy feat. Always realistic, I told myself it was a goal for retirement, after my career was already well-established.

My career progressed and I became the chief financial officer of several companies. Each of these companies had a board of directors and, as CFO, I found myself working closely with them on a regular basis. I enjoyed the different dynamics of the board members, each contributing something different to our company. Most of our boards were venture capital backed, with the venture capital funds giving the company a lot of money and a lot of grief.

One board member I worked with was particularly impactful. He was a Fortune 500 executive at an acquisitive financial services provider. His firm ultimately bought two of the three companies I helped build.

One of my most interesting boards was that of mFoundry, the mobile-banking-software company that took us ten years to build. Besides our fair share of venture capitalists on the board, we had several large corporate investors, including MasterCard, Intel, PayPal, and Bank of America. This provided a completely different insight into corporate governance.

What began as a sparked interest in a business school class quickly evolved into figuring out my areas of expertise. Without realizing it, I was already well on my way to solidifying the skills needed to be a successful board member. My MBA, technology background, and finance/audit skills and, later, my time serving as a C-suite executive of various companies all came together to provide many of the skill sets boards look for. Unintentionally, I had found my niche. Now it was just a matter of getting on my first board.

That leads to my last piece of advice—trust in your journey. Life is not about a perfect plan. No one gets everything they want, and in difficult times, it is important not to give up, but instead, have faith you will end up where you are meant to be. While it is helpful to set goals, life will inevitably throw curveballs your way. My key to success is to stay open minded, focusing on opening new doors, and creating as many opportunities for yourself as possible. From there, just trust your journey. Your life will take the path it is meant to take.

Years into my career, I found myself living near my undergraduate university, St. Mary's College. I was a new mom attempting to stay at home with my baby daughter. I applaud women who stay at home because it is the hardest job I have ever had, much harder than my work as accountant, investment banker, or CFO. Once again, I was at a crossroads in my life and found myself plotting my next move.

Right back to where it all began, I sought an informational interview to understand what the requirements were to be a university professor. I left the informational interview with a textbook in my hand and an adjunct professor position. Within a few weeks, I started teaching my first graduate course at the business school. Working with the business school led to my involvement with the school's advisory board and exposed me to a different type of board, a large nonprofit board. Eventually, my advisory board work gave me my first board position as a member of St. Mary's Board of Trustees.

Every board meeting left me mesmerized, excited, and encouraged. Board members had different personalities and backgrounds. Every member tackled the problems we faced differently, and I tried to learn from each member's approach. Most importantly, many years, different universities, jobs, and home states later, I was able to give back to the place that started it all, to the school that put its faith in a girl who barely understood what a bachelor's degree was. Sitting in one of those meetings, it crossed my mind that my path was different. I was probably one of the few St. Mary's undergraduates who used a liberal arts background to progress to Harvard Business School and become a financial executive, and was now back where she began, focused on giving back.

At one meeting, a former CEO spoke to the St. Mary's board. As I watched him work the boardroom, I was stunned at how his confidence and energy took over the room. With the goal of expanding my board work past the nonprofit space and wanting to get to know him better, I asked if he would meet with me before an upcoming board meeting. I asked him what was needed to do public board work and his answer was simple—do exactly what you are doing right now, tell people like me and everyone you can find that you want to do public board work.

264

He introduced me to a partner at an executive search firm, and it turned out the firm was looking to fill a female board position at a public community bank. Of course, I was interested. However, I had to be patient. The process took about two years. Every few months, I got a phone call asking if I was still interested. I was. Finally, I had an interview.

I put everything I had into it. I spent hours preparing. It paid off—I had my first public board position. The structure of my first board meeting was similar to the other board meetings I had attended. However, one moment stood above all of the rest. Before I joined, the board was composed of twelve people, eleven men and one woman. The company's headquarters is in Chico, California, a rural, conservative county. And yet this one female board member had been on the board for ten years. An African American woman among white men from old-school industries, she hadn't had an easy path.

During that first meeting, she stood up and spoke of passing her baton. She was inspiring. Observing the respect she had garnered with this group, I realized she had paved the way for me to be there, and that one day, I would pave the way for someone else. All at once, I had found my path, reached my highest career goal, and realized my greater purpose—using my experiences to provide others with guidance on their career paths.

Now my daughter and I are in the midst of the college acceptance period. It is a tough time, filled with stress and life-altering decisions. The advice I give her is you do not have to decide everything, just make sure you open the doors.

I talk to many women who are unhappy at their current jobs and ask me if they should start looking for other jobs. I give them the same advice I give my daughter—you do not have to decide. The journey gives you the answer. Get as much knowledge as possible and then listen to your gut. Like my daughter, the future ahead of you is extraordinarily full of promise and potential. While the ground has been set by the pioneering women board leaders before you, there are new doors to open and new precedents to be set.

I am confident in the future of our female leaders and their contributions to the business world. Good luck!

Yours truly,

Kim

Kim Vogel is a serial technology entrepreneur and dynamic executive with more than 25 years of experience helping companies finance, grow and monetize their business. She is focused on innovative, high-growth businesses with products and services that are transformational in nature and deliver above-average returns for investors.

Kim has successfully completed more than a half a dozen mergers as both buyer and seller, and has served as President and Chief Financial Officer for several high growth Bay Area companies. Earlier in her career, she worked in Investment Banking and is a Certified Public Accountant. Kim earned an MBA from the Harvard

Business School and is a former professor at St. Mary's College of California.

ANDRIJANA CVETKOVIKJ

Chairwoman: Ambassador's Council

Board of Directors: Del Sole Corporation

Advisory Board: Okinawa Institute of Science and
Technology Foundation
(former) Cartier-Japan

"Dream with passion, act with strong willpower, be kind."

Dear Chairwomen of Tomorrow:

I was born in Skopje, Macedonia's capital and Mother Teresa's birthplace. You might guess that Mother Teresa has been one of my role models, and I know her a bit differently than many others do. Although I never met her, I know where she was born, her family background, and the environment that nourished her to become who she was. I consider her not as a saint, which she undoubtedly deserves to be called, but as a real person, someone who walked the same streets I did, grew up in the same warm homeland as myself, and perhaps as a young girl shared similar dreams and aspirations: to see the world, to serve humanity with humility, to overcome obstacles no matter how big they seem to appear. I was always impressed by her willpower—despite being a physically fragile woman, she made a remarkable mark on our history, our humanity.

When I think of my childhood and what has shaped my understanding of adult human interaction, I remember that I'd accompany my father, who owned a publishing company, to many of his meetings. It was usual for me to do so, so I did not think anything of it. I watched how he skillfully negotiated terms and publication deals with partners, how carefully he crafted his words when talking with competitors, and how excited he was when a new business prospect would arise on the horizon. I was his silent partner and confidante as he shared more and more of what was truly happening behind each interaction. He opened the world of business, negotiation and compromise, decision-making and the weight of making one i.e. the world of an entrepreneur who is the master of his/her destiny and the one who has to accept the responsibility of failure or success.

FIND WHAT MAKES YOUR HEART MOVE

Despite my father's expectations to take over his business I decided to be the master of my own destiny and pursue the dream that I had to be a storyteller I studied film directing at the National Academy for Theatre and Film Art of Bulgaria, one of the most prominent and most challenging schools which only accepted four to six students out of about four hundred applicants every year. My class only had two women, including me. One came from an already well-established family in the film industry. I was the only foreign woman in the class.

Film directing, compared to business, management, law, or any industry, is one of the least gender-diverse industries with few female directors. There was much opposition in my family to my pursuing directing because the career was "not meant for women." I had a great passion for cinema, a tendency toward stubbornness and an appetite for risk taking, all of which were decisive for what followed -- years of hard work, away from home, and often against the odds I could complete what I had started. Against all hardships I never questioned my decision and the path I have chosen, since I loved every second of it!

It's imperative to be always guided by one's passion or what makes your heart move. Be governed by logic and sound thinking as well, but when you make the big decisions of your life, listen to your heart. My favorite author and scholar Joseph Campbell would say, "Follow your Bliss," which means follow the path where your gifts and blessings are. If you are good at singing and enjoy music, be a singer or musician. If you are good at communication and enjoy talking to people, find a profession where that is 90 percent of your job. Make your talents work for you, and you will enjoy effortless success.

TRY IT, MASTER IT, FORGET IT, EXPERIMENT WITH IT

Another lesson from my past is always to challenge something new in your area—master, forget, and experiment with the new. Don't be afraid of opposition or being ahead of your time. During my postgraduate studies, I decided to do my masters on the subject of digital cinema. It was 2003. At that time, I was pioneering this discipline as digital technologies were not "a thing." I had a lot of trouble convincing my professors to approve a master's dissertation on that subject because it was not considered relevant, since back then, digital technology only applied to television, not cinema.

I succeeded in convincing my professors that digital technology was the future and completed my master's degree. However, I decided to go deeper into the subject and applied to one of the best universities in Japan (Nihon University) to research the subject even further. That is what brought me to Tokyo. I arrived in Tokyo only to discover that none of my professors spoke any English. I had to learn Japanese to reach my goal of conducting the research I came to do and eventually entering and completing the doctoral degree program.

If I were to succeed here in Japan and enter the PhD program, I had to put myself on an ultra-high-speed Japanese-language-learning path. I often studied fourteen hours a day, almost without any break. In retrospect, the tremendous effort I put into acquiring the Japanese language skills, which is certainly among the most difficult languages in the world, was so rewarding. That language training allowed me to pursue and complete the doctorate studies in the subject in which I was interested. Additionally, my Japanese language skills later helped me land job opportunities that enabled me to merge fully into Japanese society. As I have mastered this difficult language, I was no longer limited in any way to fully immerse myself within the Japanese society. I used this skill to try out new things-such as joining a haiku club and creating my own poems in Japanese which were published in a book, or writing scripts for Japanese period films, one of which (Purple and Gold) was even produced by the legendary Shochiku Studio in Kyoto.

I worked at Japan's national television network as a writer and director, and was often invited as a guest at TV shows to comments about current events and culture. I was later hired as a head of an artificial intelligence team at an AI company in Tokyo. I headed a department that developed smart and emotional robots. I felt so comfortable living in Japan that it allowed me to feel confident to get engaged in many endeavors, such as teaching at universities, becoming a director for the TED Talks in Kyoto, and co-establishing several start-ups, some of which were acquired by bigger companies.

WHAT YOU DO TODAY IS A REHEARSAL FOR WHO YOU WILL BE TOMORROW

When I was nominated to become Macedonia's first ambassador to Japan in 2013, I was working as a Visiting Associate Professor at the prestigious Kyoto University and had to return to Macedonia for the first time since I was seventeen. I was hired by the Ministry of Foreign Affairs of Macedonia and worked closely with the minister on Foreign Affairs on a new digital diplomacy initiative while preparing for my ambassadorship.

Everyone I knew was shocked to hear that I will abandon my academic career and embark on an unknown journey of diplomacy, which is a very delicate profession. The only person that wasn't shocked was me. I felt as if my entire life and career so far from living in several countries, mastering several languages, being a public speaker, an entrepreneur, a director, a Project Manager and many other things has prepared me to do this job with great competence.

Serving as the first Macedonian Ambassador to Japan for four years (2014-2018) gave me the opportunity to meet many different people with whom I previously could not have met, known, or seen. This experience showed me the big picture of Japanese society and allowed me to engage closely with people from various fields and at all levels, from top political leadership and decision makers to the public and private sectors to universities and nonprofit organizations.

WOMEN, BE AMBITIOUS

During my ambassadorship, I came to consider boards in a new light. Of course, I'd previously been aware of boards. I'd known many board members at my father's company. However, I had not thought I would be interested in being on a board. During my ambassadorship, I spoke at several international women's conferences. One international conference in particular has helped women for the past twenty-eight years. I presented there, along with many amazing guest speakers from different countries—politicians, business executives, athletes, and men and women in decision-making positions that support female empowerment.

The panel where I was a speaker was themed *Women, Be ambitious*. I realized that most of the guests were young females. They were eager to hear our stories, observe our example, and learn where the glass ceiling is, the limit of their career aspirations. Many of them were already employed and were on good career tracks, so I heard them ask:

"Can we go even further and dream bigger?"

Among the panelists were many female board members and male champions, male CEOs advancing the female board agenda. During one of the panels, a member of the audience asked me for the secret of joining a corporate board. I could not answer that question since I had never been a board member, apart from being an advisor to several advisory boards of governmental agencies and committees.

273

At that time (in 2016 and 2017), females held less than 10 percent of board positions in Japan, and the numbers are not much better today, even though we are seeing great progress in the diversity agenda as a social discourse. Prime Minister Shinzo Abe was dedicated to fostering female diversity and encouraging companies in Japan to appoint female board members. I urged Prime Minister Abe to dispatch a female ambassador in my country as the number of female ambassadors in Japan is extremely low. I was delighted when a female ambassador was appointed. While I was contemplating my own personal career aspirations after the ambassadorship, I realized that the lack of gender diversity on Japanese boards was a real problem, and that women could contribute toward better corporate governance and bring new energy into Japanese corporations by participating as board directors.

At age thirty-three, I was the youngest ambassador out of a total of 169 ambassadors in Tokyo. I was also the Head of Mission of one of the most active, dynamic, and successful embassies in Tokyo, judging by the number of cooperation agreements forged among companies, universities, and institutions, as well as the grants secured, the high-level political visits concluded, the awards of excellence granted, and the amount of publicity we received for our work.

This gave me confidence to think that if I could do this extremely sensitive and delicate job with integrity and make positive changes in my field, maybe I could move the needle forward for women in Japan by becoming a role model as a board member. I also thought it would be an excellent opportunity for me, personally, to view how companies work and operate from the inside. Besides having a PhD in digital technologies and cinema, I

274

have an Executive MBA from Temple University Fox School of Business, which additionally qualifies me to be a responsible member of a board and to contribute toward corporate governance based on my knowledge and experience. I made my ambition clear and known to the circle of my business associates and acquaintances, and not long after my openness that I would be willing and happy to accept a role on a corporate board, several offers were presented to me, and I accepted some of them.

GOALS, QUOTAS & POLITICAL WILL

I am often asked what it would take to achieve gender balance and diversity in society and my simple answer is -political will, goals, and quotas. Of course, the longer answer would encompass many other factors, but I draw this conclusion from observing the diversity shift in my own country using these tools. Historically, in Macedonia, women did not play a significant role in the political discourse. However, after our proclamation of independence from former Yugoslavia in 1991, women fought to pass a law that would guarantee that in any general election, 30% of the candidates for a parliamentary seat must be women. Of course, the number is not limited to 30%, but it is a guaranteed low threshold and guidance for gender diversity in our legislative house.

In our system, when someone is appointed as an ambassador, they need to present a plan showing what they are going to do for four years, and they have to defend it in front of the parliamentary foreign affairs committee. When they complete the position, they are required to write a report.

The international committee members are often rigorous and critical. Political dynamics are always present. Opposition parties tend to criticize the proposed candidates for ambassador by the other side and vice versa.

When I presented my final ambassadorial report last year, all five women on the committee gave me great comments, praise, and support, even though they were from different political parties. That meant so much to me since the comments came from the heart of women with high professional standards. In their comments I recognized support from fellow women who worked so hard to get where they were in their careers, and they recognized right away how much effort I had put in the four years of my ambassadorial term. One of them is now the Minister of Health, playing a crucial role for the country as we tackle COVID.

THE RISING SUN OF DIVERSITY

I think Japan is making significant changes to improve gender parity, even though we might argue these changes are too slow and insufficient. Still, the Japanese Government, as well as many corporations and multinationals, have publicly promoted the diversity plan. The Japanese government organizes a women's empowerment conference every year and invites many heads of states, ministers, and important female figures from the international, bilateral, and multilateral arenas to talk. When Japan was the host of G7 or G20 meetings, they insisted on having the female empowerment and diversity issue on the agenda, which is commendable. The Cabinet of the Government of Japan has pledged a quota of 35% of the seats in the Parliament to be reserved for women by 2025.

I can see the changes already taking place when looking at board member representation in Japan. The percentage of women included is still meager compared to other countries, However, the numbers are growing each year. Some foreign investment firms, such as Goldman Sachs, are showing the lead in this area and have pledged to vote against listing top companies in the stock exchange if they do not have at least one woman on their board.

I joined the charge to mount that soft pressure. As of July 2020, 63 percent of the four hundred biggest companies in Japan had at least one female board member, which is an increase. (In 2018, they were at 54 percent). However, in the United States and Europe, 90 percent of the top companies have at least one female director, so there is still a lot to do.

The board I joined has 30 percent women board members. The founder and Chairwoman of the company is a woman, who is also the first Japanese female executive to list her company on the stock market. The company's CEO is the long-time former president and CEO of KFC Japan. He was one of KFC's first employees when KFC opened here back in the 1970s. Both the Chairwoman and CEO are both highly respected veterans in the food industry, and it's an honor to support them and learn from them.

Several women's organizations here in Japan are active, with many female executives and board directors. There is a 30 percent Club Japanese chapter, with many corporate leaders, both male and female. Part of their agenda is not only women supporting women but also the concept of "HE FOR SHE," which cherishes the male champions for female empowerment. We have to be real that the business and political worlds in Japan and in many other countries are male-dominated, so the gender-equality agenda won't happen overnight. Increasingly, businesspeople are committed to taking these small steps and finding ways to both emphasize diversity as a value in our society and also securing board members to represent the diversity reflected in their customer base. Diversity and inclusion are not only moral virtues, and part of the sustainable leadership approach for global. They bring significant economic benefit for the companies investing into this long-term vision for the future. Diversity and inclusion are also not only good for the economy and the future of sustainable life-work balance, but the diversity itself is defining our democracies in the globalized world we all live in.

THE PICTURE OF THE JAPANESE BOARD ROOM

The traditional Board meetings in Japan are generally formal, almost scripted and mechanical. Very different from the West. You should not break the harmony in Japanese society, so most of the issues concerning the company are rarely challenged at the board meeting itself. Instead, lots of information is exchanged before and after the meeting, so people have time to smooth out differences and get the necessary explanation and information before they vote on a certain issue. These discussions can often be long, and members, especially outside directors, are encouraged to talk freely and offer their views.

The Japanese corporate governance code was recently drafted and extended, so corporate governance is becoming more important for Japanese companies. More and more Japanese corporations have at least one foreign national on their board.

While most corporations still use only the Japanese language, some board meetings are held in English. Multinational, international, and global corporations understand the need to have not only gender but also racial diversity on their boards as they aim to become accountable, transparent, and inclusive players in the market. I believe that corporations will recognize the rich pallet of diversity and will gradually open their doors to people from various groups on the diversity spectrum.

BECOMING *BOARD-READY*

I also believe that serving on a board is a tremendous opportunity, but it's also a big responsibility. I'd encourage those interested in joining a board to learn as much as they can about the company, the economy, and the industry they are pursuing. Take your time when the opportunity arises. It will be crucial for you and your career, so learn and prepare now.

Once you join, you will be flooded with numbers and information. I am trying to learn every day and stay on top of everything. I completed an executive MBA to become a more capable board member. I believe in lifelong learning. We should never stop pursuing knowledge and never decide that there is a limit to what we can learn. As a board member, I feel a significant responsibility toward the shareholders and stakeholders, as well as a responsibility to uphold sustainability on the macro-level. And to that end, I am a big supporter of the United Nations Sustainable Development Goals (SDGs). I was a speaker at the Sendai UN Conference (Sendai Framework for Disaster Risk Reduction 2015), and a speaker at the World Economic Forum (2016) where I could present more of my views about the future in relation to the SDGs that are an agenda that I identify with. Many companies pledged their alliance with the UN and the public sector to implement some of these goals, which are not meant to exist only on paper. We must incorporate these step-by-step on a corporate level because corporations are the fabric of society.

I am excited for what lies ahead for you, the next generation of leaders, and the impact you will have on how we move forward and thrive together. Don't forget that even "a journey of a thousand miles starts with a single step", and you have already made that step by reading this book and this letter. See you at the Summit!

Sincerely yours,

Andrijana

Andrijana Cvetkovikj was the first and the youngest ambassador of Macedonia in Japan from 2014-2018. She is a founder & CEO of BrioNexus KK- firm focused on innovation in the workplace and re-defining human interaction in the digital world, and a Chairwoman of Ambassador's Council, a Think Tank based in Tokyo.

Andrijana has a Doctorate from Nihon University, Honorary Doctorate from the European University, and an Executive MBA from the Fox School of Business, Temple University. She currently sits on the Board of Del Sole Corporation, the first company led by a woman (Merle Aiko Okawara) to be listed on the Japanese stock exchange. Andrijana also sits on the Advisory Board of the Okinawa Institute of Science and Technology Foundation and is a former Advisory Board member of Cartier-Japan, JATA (Japan Association of Tour Operators) and several other organizations. Andrijana was the Head of the Public and Digital Diplomacy Unit at the Ministry of Foreign Affairs of Macedonia, and a Project Manager for A.I. company in Tokyo, focused on linguistic computing. Andrijana is a committed advocate on diversity, inclusion, and the promotion of the UN's SDGs (Sustainable Development Goals), with demonstrated active leadership in this area. She advocated for these issues as a speaker at the World Economic Forum 2016, the UN's Conference for Climate Change in Tohoku, and by organizing the "Ambassador's Roundtable Meeting with the first female Governor of Tokyo-Yuriko Koike, where she delivered the "*Resolution for gender inclusion* and empowering women through sports and culture", endorsed by all-female ambassadors in Tokyo. Andrijana served as a Chief Jury Member of Miss International twice (2015, 2016) and initiated the Women's Entrepreneurship Initiative.

Andrijana is also a filmmaker and an artist. She directed the TEDxKyoto events (2012, 2013) that have been streamed on the Japanese national television. She worked on numerous international film productions, has won prestigious awards, and is a Member of the Directors Guild of Japan.

IRIS CHAN

Board of Directors: East West BankCorp

Board of Governors: San Francisco Symphony

"You don't want to be asked to join a board for the sole sake of fulfilling a government policy. However, if you really have something to contribute and it is your only opportunity, why not seize it?"

Dear Chairwomen of Tomorrow:

My name is Iris Chan. I grew up in Hong Kong and moved to Taiwan to attend high school and college, following my father's move there. I was the youngest girl in a household of five children. I attended an all-girls high school, so I didn't experience any gender discrimination. This experience built up my self-confidence, even though socially, I wasn't exposed much to the male gender. In college, I studied finance and business. I grew up in a secure environment, in a loving family that allowed me to pursue my interests and build up my self-confidence. I was a happy child.

My brother and I, the two youngest, were raised as could-do-no-wrong in the family. Having been born after World War II, my brother and I felt a little rebellious because the world was rebuilding itself. We grew up in a different environment than my three other siblings had known at their age. My parents instilled in me the belief I could overcome any challenge if I put just my mind toward it, even though, in those days, girls were supposed to be coddled and weren't expected to study business. I chose to major in finance, and after I graduated, I accepted a job at Citibank.

After a year, I left to pursue my master's degree. After graduation, I got married and moved within the U.S., first to the South then to the Midwest. My experience in these regions was vastly different than on the West Coast, where Asian women were fairly well assimilated and represented. Back then, fifty-six Asian women lived in Durham, North Carolina, where my husband was studying. All fifty-six of us became close friends. However, we felt like outsiders in the workplace and in the community.

We moved to Nebraska after my husband transferred from Duke University to Creighton University to pursue his medical degree. In those days, people couldn't relate to Chinese women or understand what China meant to America. Chinese people definitely felt like foreigners. I worked at a small savings and loans bank where I was the only Asian and non-white employee.

They'd often tease me by saying:

"Good morning, merry sunshine! How does the garden grow?"

People never took me seriously. These biases made me feel discriminated against for being foreign and forced me to think about how to overcome prejudices. Chinese women weren't given the opportunity to further their careers. The three years I spent in South Carolina and Nebraska were the most important ones of my career. I felt treated differently, and learned about different parts of the U.S. I understood how foreigners in the U.S. are forced to blend in and make a career or life on their own. I understand how Southern and Midwestern Americans thought in those days.

The biggest lesson I learned was that people are naturally biased and don't instinctively treat you as one of their own. You're not considered for every opportunity, no matter how capable you are. The biggest question I learned to ask was:

"What are you going to do about it?"

I could choose to be a good citizen, not make waves, accept what I was given, and move on. Alternatively, I could fight the situation while going nowhere. The third path was to try to blend in with my differences because others were different too. By learning from each other, and through reciprocity, we could develop common ground and find mutual acceptance. That's the foundation of inclusivity.

As I evolved in my career, I became the Chief Executive for Commercial Banking at Wells Fargo. As a global business, commercial banking experience provides a good understanding and insight for corporate governance. When delivering speeches in San Francisco, Salt Lake City, and Houston, I'd adapt my wording to each location. Corporate governance exists to provide the oversight necessary to ensure not only a successful business operation but, more importantly, it serves the market and community with a good conscience.

284

As a board member, your first priority is to align your company and workforce with your market and customers while keeping their distinct characteristics (e.g., identities, genders, race), expectations, and needs in mind. Once there's alignment, you have to design your strategy, analyze risk levels, and employ a diverse workforce to achieve the objectives. In the end, governance revolves around mitigating risks in every area of the company: strategy, customers, markets, employees, regulatory environments, social media, and the like.

The lessons I'd learned from having lived in different areas of the U.S. could be applied to corporate behaviors. In the Midwest, for example, people don't have dinner on weekends. They have "supper" instead. Understanding living habits, cultural behaviors, and reactions to initiatives is extremely important because a company cannot market or sell a product that's offensive and does not take its customers into account. Pepsi-Cola's "Live for Now" commercial, for example, backfired because it lacked sensitivity toward the plight of African Americans suffering from police brutality and arbitrary arrests. Acknowledging social and cultural issues is as important as examining regulatory issues.

Imagine a board strictly composed of white males. Would they really understand women's needs and responses toward a product? Although society is changing, I think women still rule the household: They make purchasing decisions for the kids and home, take care of scheduling, cleaning chores, meals, and caregiving. Women are still the primary decision makers in many areas. That's why the board structure has to evolve.

I always say the board culture, or how governance is being managed, is important because one gender or ethnic group might not understand what is happening around them. If a company is half women and half men, does one group really understand the other 50 percent of employees? What are their preferences? What makes them tick? What motivates them to give more to the company? What issues do they face when selling products to customers?

I got my first board seat when someone tapped me for the role. When I worked at Wells Fargo, an informal corporate rule stipulated that those in my role weren't allowed to serve on the board because it could lead to conflicts of interest. Many people asked me to join the board, but I wasn't allowed to. Only after leaving Wells Fargo was I able to join a board. As an executive and member of the management committee, I had attended all Wells Fargo's board meetings. That experience helped me better understand board interactions and structure. I learned how to conduct follow ups, how to deal with challenges, and how to liaise with C-suite executives to ensure their interests, priorities, and governance goals aligned.

I was involved with many private boards over the course of my career before joining a public board. The boards were for both business entities and a few nonprofits. I learned a lot because every board is different. Nonetheless, their goals are the same: maintaining good governance and making sure the company is acting as a good corporate citizen while not incurring too much risk to its reputation. Even if a company is not financially at risk, potential risks to its reputation could ruin the entire business. People need to pay more attention to reputation risk.

These days, the political landscape has become slightly toxic. With age, we settle into our ways and in the way with which we manage affairs. Nevertheless, we all need to practice our listening skills. The opinions of younger generations should not be ignored but considered and reflected upon. Listening doesn't mean doing what someone says but finding common ground to move everyone forward.

Boards are trending toward being more diverse, both in terms of gender parity and in terms of age. Most boards consider women closely and look for younger board members. The board structure is still in a transitional phase because those who chair the board feel the most comfortable promoting the board culture. Until women are significantly represented on boards, not much will change, Fortunately, that transformation is underway.

You don't want to be asked to join a board for the sole sake of fulfilling a government policy. However, if you have something to contribute and it is your only opportunity, why not seize it? Once you're a board member, you can make sure you're better than what you're labeled as. Life is unfair. How are you going to convert the unfair into the more equitable?

To advance diversity, we need to showcase the companies which reflect diversity, exhibit thriving performance, and lead in their industry. The primary goal of their boards isn't more diversity per se. However, a diverse board can help drive performance goals. We need to address it that way to make sure people understand. Because the market is so diverse, there is no such thing as serving just one group anymore.

Women who want to join a corporate board must pursue leadership roles. Everyone defines leadership differently. However, it involves the will to lead, recognizing that there is no one there to tell you what to do. As a board member, you hold a leadership role. You're part of a group tasked with helping the company grow. That's important. You have to ask yourself:

Why is being a leader important to me?

Do I have a wealth of experience?

Do I want to help enhance the company's performance in every way to actualize its potential?

Serving on a board is a tremendous responsibility, both in terms of fulfilling the responsibilities for the organization itself and in terms of being part of a meaningful challenge. I am inspired with where we are today, while I also know there is so much more to change. With you engaged, everything is possible.

Sincerely yours,

Iris

Iris S. Chan is currently the CEO of Ameriway, which she founded in 1989. Ameriway focuses on technology innovation investments and cross-border trades between North America and Asia. She was the former Executive Vice President and Group Head of Wells Fargo's National Commercial Banking Group, and a member of the Wells Fargo Management Committee. Prior to her retirement from Wells Fargo in 2009 after over 20 years of service, Iris oversaw more than 90 commercial banking and loan production offices throughout the United States. Earlier in her career, Iris held various management and international banking positions with Bank of America and Citicorp.

Iris is involved in many community and professional organizations. Currently, she is on the board of governors of the San Francisco Symphony. She served on the Board of Directors of Wells Fargo HSBC Trade Bank, N.A. from 2003 to 2009. Previously, she was a member of the business advisory board of University of Southern California Marshall School of Business and Carnegie Mellon GSIA.

Iris has received various awards and recognition for her work. In 2007 and 2008, she was named one of the "25 Most Powerful Women in Banking" by American Banker magazine.

Sarah Hofstetter

Board of Directors: Campbell's Soup

"The power to determine that perspective is yours."

Dear Women Board Leaders of Tomorrow:

I grew up in a sea of sameness. I was in an all-girls class where we dressed alike, ate at the same places, and rarely left our enclave. As an observant Jew, I attended a school where equal investment is paid to Jewish studies and core curriculum, meaning my school day was twice as long as the public-school kids.

I lived and continue to live through the ideals and rules of the Old Testament, which includes eating exclusively kosher food and completely shutting off all outside stimuli, including phones, cars, electricity, for twenty-five hours each week from Friday night through Saturday night. I also pray before and after I eat food, and even after I go to the bathroom, thanking g-d for the ability to do so.

Every single choice I make—what I eat, what I say, whom I speak with—is considered and, in many ways, conforms, to a way of living. Every choice is a reminder there is a greater being and a greater purpose well beyond what I'm doing.

290

Parents and teachers told me from a young age we are all built in g-d's image. In my young mind, that literally meant there was a mold for us, and we were supposed to conform to it. So when you're raised with the mold mindset, being different is a bad thing.

My first exposure to being different from my mold came around the age of nineteen—after fifteen years of private Jewish education and a full year of college living in Israel—when I started at a public college. But other than a few discussions and collaborations at the school paper, I largely stayed with my enclave, even in college.

Even after college, I ended up working for a firm owned by an observant Jew, which meant I never had to engage in discourse around kosher food or explain why I was leaving early for the Sabbath. I stayed within my bubble, possibly unconsciously.

Then I took a risk and decided to leave the bubble. At the age of twenty-nine, as a mother of two preschoolers, I had reached the ceiling of my limits staying within the bubble. My professional curiosity was bursting. I wanted to learn more and grow more, so I started my own consulting firm, helping start-ups build their brands, including a fledging advertising agency called 360i. While consulting, I started its social media practice, and it grew so quickly I decided to resign my clients and join 360i full time.

Being different—being an outsider in the agency world—was awful. I couldn't eat with my coworkers because I couldn't eat at the non-kosher restaurants. When everyone went out for happy hour on Fridays, I went home early for Sabbath. There was a noticeable difference between me and everyone else. Agency life requires lots of bonding, happy hours, shared experiences . . . things that were challenging for me.

It didn't matter if there was a huge client deadline. If the sun was setting, I was, as my colleagues would say "turning into a pumpkin" like Cinderella at midnight. It drove me crazy and probably drove my coworkers crazier. How could I make up that deficit?

Well, I worked more hours, just not the ones around Friday night and Saturday. All my colleagues knew exactly when Sabbath ended because of the onslaught of emails coming from me Saturday night, making up for lost time. I'd always aim to beat a deadline by a long shot, to avoid any risk of having to miss having to make changes on the Sabbath. If I had to travel, I went through convoluted planning to ensure I never had to travel on the Sabbath. This extra planning was further exacerbated by raising two little kids, each of whom had doctors, after-school programs, sports, and the occasional trip to the emergency room. (They know me on a first-name basis there.)

There's also the issue of being a female CEO, and a mom at that. When I was CEO of 360i, of the best thirty agencies listed by Ad Age in the U.S., only two are led by CEOs who are moms.

The other difference was my lack of agency experience. What, you say? You're running an ad agency and you've never worked at another ad agency? Yep, that's right. I don't have the agency pedigree of coming up through the ranks, nor do I have the contacts from hopping around from agency to agency.

We all need to look at whether our differences are really liabilities, or if they can be turned into assets. In my case, I've taken the approach my vulnerabilities are my biggest assets, and this has been a key to my success. Half full versus half empty.

Let's start with the religious element. First, the Sabbath. When I was raised in the mold, Sabbath was all about what I COULDN'T do. It was about not watching TV, not going places. But now, living outside the mold in an always-on, diversified, multi-sensory world, Sabbath is my recess from everything. Without a doubt, the ONLY reason I haven't burnt out is because of Sabbath.

How many of us never unplug? How many of us are glued to our phones, outside of the occasional workout or yoga class? For twenty-five hours every single week, I am completely absorbed by my family, my friends, and my thoughts. I play board games with my family. We talk about all kinds of topics. We eat like kings. We take naps, yes naps. It allows me to recalibrate, regain my center of gravity, and remind me why I'm working. It changes my perspective. My "liability" of checking out for twenty-five hours is actually the top asset that has kept me going. In fact, Katy Perry is now promoting the virtues of unplugging.

Second, eating. Over the past twenty years, I've worked with clients who are often exposed to amazing food experiences. I can assure you it's challenging to find a kosher establishment outside major metropolitan areas that are client friendly. So client entertainment is a challenge for me. Unless you turn it into an experience.

A few years ago, I received a last-minute invitation to a dinner with the CMO of Enterprise Car Rental in New York City at one of the hottest non-kosher restaurants in the world. There wasn't enough time to pack a kosher meal, so I joined the dinner and just didn't eat. The CMO couldn't understand why I wasn't eating, and I explained that I ate exclusively kosher. He felt awful that I couldn't eat and insisted the next time I came to visit him in St. Louis, he'd take me to a great kosher meal. I didn't have the heart to tell him there was not a single good kosher restaurant in the city, let alone a great one.

A few months later, I was visiting him in St. Louis, and he insisted on taking me to this great kosher meal. We drove for forty-five minutes and, upon arriving at this restaurant, we see that the special of the day is Jumbo Shrimp, which is not kosher under any circumstances. His Midwestern hospitality compels him to continue our journey, driving another forty-five minutes until we arrive at a dilapidated structure, which indeed happened to be kosher . . . just not great.

I acknowledged to him that this is indeed kosher, but far from top notch. He is so excited he was able to find a place for me to eat, and got even more excited about the authenticity of it, that it was contagious. We had a great adventure together and created more memories than a foodie experience. My liability became an asset and a memory sticker to boot. And so instead of being the outcast, I was different. And different is memorable.

And that was a good thing, once I got comfortable with it. I have adventures and stories from all over the world, eating kosher meals in the most unlikely of places, from the Swiss valleys with Nestlé to kosher sushi at Dentsu in Tokyo and in Cannes celebrating my first advertising award with a bottle of kosher rose. Growing up as an outsider, I had no choice but to see beyond any comfort zone.

I wasn't just an outsider because of my religion. I also was an industry outsider in most of my jobs, whether that was an ad agency or technology leader. Because I'm more aware of what that's like, I'm more attuned to making sure I don't fall into that "insiders-only" trap. That's a huge asset in and of itself. Because I grew up in such a different mold, I am more attuned to ensuring our talent does not look like "the mold." Do we inadvertently hire people who are just like us? Could this be a source of our industry-wide diversity challenges?

The skills and experience I bring to the boardroom are different than those of my fellow board members. To get variety and diversity of thought, backgrounds and experiences, boards conduct skill matrices to ensure the multitude of hard skills needed are represented in a balanced way in the boardroom. A board strictly composed of CFOs would not be desirable because everyone would be focused on one thing and not the others.

The diversity I bring includes a lot more than gender and age. I am a marketer by nature so have expertise in marketing, advertising, and sales. I've also operated digitally led businesses for many years, which brings a different experience in an increasingly digital world. Working with many packaged goods companies has taught me to understand the food and packaged goods competitive landscape. I know the market well, despite not having the typical resumé of a board member.

My liabilities as an outsider also gave me something special: the freedom to be unencumbered by legacy. As you think about your next steps toward getting to the boardroom, there are plenty of hard skills to learn. However, mindset plays an important role too. Consider the following:

1. **Examine assumptions:** Had I been a good soldier and followed convention or anything resembling a career path in any of the jobs I had, I wouldn't have made it this far. What's guided me is the deep desire to do something different by making a difference. I've never wanted to be ordinary, and anyone who has dined with me while I eat vacuum-packed kosher meals in a fancy non-kosher restaurant can tell you ordinary is not one of my issues.

The root of being different stems from a question that has burned inside me since I was a kid: "WHY CAN'T I?" Why can't a woman be an observant Jew, raise a family, contribute to the community, and be successful in the workforce?

I suppose the fire in my belly to challenge convention dates back to my grandparents. Ironically, I don't think they meant to inspire me to challenge convention. Rather, they just did what it took to preserve their lives and their faith. The way they did so, however, was anything but conventional.

My maternal grandfather got out of Poland as a teenager right before World War II. This orphaned, penniless child taught himself English, went to college, earned a master's from Columbia and a doctorate from NYU, was ordained a rabbi, started his own synagogue, taught in two universities, and wrote more than a dozen books in multiple languages.

My father's parents are both Holocaust survivors, having been through Auschwitz. Once liberated by the Russians, these sick teenage skeletons retained their faith and were incredibly resourceful. My grandfather used his typesetting skills to forge documents that helped dozens of others get out. He eventually traded cigarettes, packs of salami, and broke out of an Italian prison to make his way to America. Once here, since he was unable to get a job that didn't require him to work seven days a week and they were Sabbath observant, he started his own insurance brokerage. The business is flourishing today. My grandparents could have given up on their faith. Instead, they achieved a special kind of destiny—their way.

I was lucky to be raised surrounded by role models of fighters and scrappy, curious, passionate leaders, qualities I try to embrace myself.

2.   **Different is memorable:** The stories of my journey across the St. Louis plains to find kosher food is an experience I will

remember for many years, much more than the latest celebrity chef's delicious meal. Sometimes you may remember the food, and not the person you were with. It takes no special skills to take a client to a fancy dinner, to network over cocktails at an industry boondoggle, or to play a round of golf with colleagues. (OK, maybe an outgoing personality and ability to swing a golf club is helpful.) But these types of activities are so standard in the corporate world that they're a tired cliché. What makes you different, and how you can share that with the people around you—from colleagues to clients—in a memorable and meaningful way? Sometimes, people don't know what they don't know.

3. **Balance some chutzpah with respect**: "Chutzpah" is a Hebrew word, and the English translation means "audacity." Now, as with much of this speech, audacity can be good or bad. More often than not, it's perceived to be bad. The voice I strive to balance is the good kind of audacity—a chutzpah that is delivered with respect and with the most generous interpretation. For example, don't apologize for the things that make you "different." That's a sign you're viewing them as vulnerabilities or liabilities. Don't be afraid to speak up, respectfully. As an "outsider" in a sea of same, your perspective is invaluable. From marketing to politics, there are plenty of examples where poor decisions were made because people were working in an echo chamber.

Those who are "different" may be comfortable being uncomfortable. They may be used to sticking out in some way. On the flip side, it can make people uncomfortable to embrace someone or something different when they're accustomed to being surrounded by the same. This gives you an edge in which you're already used to being out of your comfort zone and can be a champion for others who don't look like you, love like you, pray like you, or whatever it is that makes you an individual.

I challenge you to think through your perceived vulnerabilities, and you can turn them into assets. Is your glass half full or empty? Is today worse than yesterday or better than tomorrow? The power to determine that perspective is yours.

Yours truly,

Sarah

Sarah is currently the President of Profitero, a leading eCommerce software provider helping thousands of brands improve their eCommerce ROI. But this is far from Sarah's first run at helping brands navigate change, as she has a 20+ year proven track record of driving tremendous growth in multiple disruptive environments. She is the former Chairwoman and CEO of digital marketing agency, 360i, which under her leadership grew from 30 to 1,000 people and was recognized by Ad Age as a top 10 national advertising agency every year that she was CEO and President.

Sarah is also a member of the board of directors for Campbell Soup Company. She has been recognized by Ad Age's "40 Under 40," and Adweek 50, and has been inducted into the AAF Hall of Achievement and Word of Mouth Marketing Hall of Fame. Sarah also has taken the stage at Cannes Lions Creativity Festival and Fortune Most Powerful Women Next Gen Summit, among others.

PATTI LEE-HOFFMAN

Board of Governors: San Francisco Symphony

"As Kamala Harris's mother famously preached to her daughter, 'You may be the first to do many things, but make sure you're not the last.' This letter is an important part of the work we must do to insure the latter."

Dear Future Chairwomen:

Like my mother, grandmother, and great grandmother, I was born in San Francisco's Chinatown. The advantage of starting out life in the ghetto is that it gave me lots of runway to collect firsts—the first girl to become student body president and a member of the school board, the first girl to wear pants to school and take shop classes (part of my election platform), and the first girl to join the boy's track team. When it became clear I did not have the means to go to college, my community crowd-funded the considerable gap between scholarships and four years of college expenses, earning me another first—the first in my family to go directly to college.

I was also in the first group of women hired by an international assurance firm. I was fired after one month because I had inconveniently found fraud, thereby upsetting the client. Fortunately, I convinced my employer to transfer me to a larger office rather than terminate me. At the larger office, partners fought over me to staff me on their one-man projects in order to be alone with me. While I was able to fend off the advances, the devil's bargain I made was, in exchange, I was able to accelerate my learning and bypass layers of management that through which my male counterparts had to apprentice through.

But being a young Asian woman, whose work was dominated by a few dominating men worked at cross purposes to ensuring I would not be the last woman hired. I knew I had to start Triage Consulting Group. It's the kind of company that is a great place to work because everyone is respected. It's been on the list of great places to work in America for eighteen consecutive years. Women are hired in equal numbers or more as men. Honest, anonymous feedback from employees is required.

Thus, some of my first board roles were in my own companies or companies in which I had equity.

Do women help women?

When I start companies, I have the opportunity to pick whomever I want to join my board. Without exception, everyone I invite demurs they are too busy, and yet all agree to help. A few even agree to join. It is enormously helpful to have the advice to jumpstart a company while avoiding costly mistakes.

In rounding out my own boards, I seek successful women who have different experiences than I do. They may have deep

301

contacts in a region or area in which we haven't fully explored. Or they may have deep knowledge in risk areas, such as cybersecurity.

When I turn down an invitation to join a board, I always suggest other, more talented women than I—especially women who have not served on boards and may have the time to do so.

I serve on two boards thanks to other women. I sit on the San Francisco Symphony Board because I was endorsed by members of the Women Corporate Directors (a sorority of women board members) who also serve on that board. We take our nominations and endorsements seriously because we are putting our reputations on the line, and we are confident the recommendation is a good one.

All board members are asked, at some point or another, to suggest candidates. I keep a dynamic list of potential candidates I'd want to see serving on my boards and names of the women I'd want to be replaced by the time I retire.

What do women board members offer that men do not?

Like my male counterparts on the board, I was initially attractive as a potential board member because, as a CEO, I have a lot of experience starting up, growing, and selling businesses. Being a CPA is also helpful.

At a time when multiple generations are represented in the workforce, I've noticed the men I serve with are not as concerned as women with culture or sustainability, and those issues are more important to younger generations. Companies with great cultures outperform the S&P 500. Research shows solid a company culture creates a healthy company. I think the attention I place on these issues of culture and sustainability brings value to the boards I serve on and are obviously necessary to good corporate governance.

During the Great Recession, companies—especially consulting firms—shrank headcount and went on starvation diets. During this time, Triage had its best years. The following story illustrates why Triage's culture makes it so successful.

I was summoned to a termination meeting with a CFO of a hospital. To convince her to retain us, I reminded her the year's revenue growth was made possible by our strategic pricing initiatives. When that did not elicit a warm reaction, I reminded her we'd conducted hospital-wide training free of charge. She was still unmoved when I mentioned we had absorbed all the legal fees in a recent lawsuit that yielded a handsome settlement.

Out of desperation, I asked:

"Do you know we improve your patients 'clinical outcomes?"

She laughed, rightly so, because we are financial consultants. She was familiar with the study showing improved clinical outcomes for patients supported by friends and family. But she was not familiar with the fact our team hosted children's birthday parties at the hospital's Ronald McDonald House. She was finally engaged.

I told her we recycled the unused items in sterile surgical kits and sent them to local clinics and disaster zones around the world. The hospital that was saving its own patients 'lives was also saving lives around the world. For good measure, I told her our staff regularly donates blood to the hospital. She ordered us to resume work the following Monday. Culture makes employees happy and businesses successful. It's a self-fulfilling prophecy.

Key Takeaways

1. Like the adage, "To be interesting, be interested," attractive board members attract interest with deep and wide experience and networks. Boards deal with difficult issues that are not day-to-day occurrences. It's important to have hands-on wisdom dealing with complicated financial, legal, personnel, and risk issues.

2. Don't wait to be asked. Find the situation where you can add value and go for it.

3. Ask a woman for help.

Truly yours,

Patti

Patricia Lee-Hoffmann co-founded Triage Consulting Group (now Cloudmed) and Flutter Eyewear. She has a successful track record of building companies: that produce critically necessary and beautiful products that customers enjoy purchasing again and again; with happy employees; and that benefit the communities in which they operate.

LIANE HORNSEY

Board of Directors: BUILD

"I have learned that success in the world of work is not about status. It's about influence, and influence is best underpinned by kindness."

Dear Chairwoman of Tomorrow,

When I think of my teenage self, I am shocked by how narrow my priorities were. "Boyfriends, boyfriends, boyfriends." No ambition, no hopes or dreams. Being raised by my dad, who was a postal worker at night and a driving instructor by day, a career was never on my list. My life was like looking at a watch face. I could see my past, present, and future in one place at the same time and in a specific order.

Envisioning potential is hard when you have restricted role models. No one from my extended family had been to college. I was pregnant at fifteen and teetering at the edge of an abyss.

I wish I could say differently, but sometimes success is about chance. When I was sixteen, I had to decide between going to work or staying in school. Fate took a hand, and my boyfriend at that critical time was determined to go to university. It was that simple: I suddenly had a role model. I categorically wouldn't have gone to college otherwise. I saw a future opening up. Education cracked open that watch face of inevitability.

At college I became politically aware for the first time. I realized social injustice is endemic and so many others far worse off than me would fall directly into the abyss I avoided. So, I trained to be a teacher, and, like Don Quixote, I went charging into an East London special priority school area thinking I could change the world, one pupil at a time. It became the most exhausting, challenging, yet rewarding three years of my now rather long career. (Side note: I recommend everyone to have a Teach First (UK) or Teach For America experience if they can.)

Teaching (ironically) taught me the fundamentals of success in the world of work. I learned to question power and status while embracing influence and developing relationships. My pupils worked hardest when they believed I was on their side. There's no substitute for kindness, literally none.

My first job as a board member was in the UK at Lastminute.com. I worked directly for the founder, Martha Lane Fox. She had a poster behind her desk that read, "Bollocks to Poverty." That's how I knew it was the place for me. It was an online travel start-up based in Buckingham Palace Road (next door to the Queen of England), which it gave me pause for thought, but I did it anyway. Does that make me a hypocrite? This is one of the most difficult moral dilemmas for anyone with left-leaning principles in business. "Champagne socialist" is an epithet that has unnerved me for years. But I decided long ago it's better to have just principles side by side with some righteous actions than none at all.

When I joined Google in 2006, my "wonder woman" boss Shona Brown taught me so much. Shona is, in my opinion, one of the key architects of Google's business success, and even today I think in terms of "what would Shona do." Her influence in terms of using data to make decisions and being scrupulously fair-minded remain guiding lights for me.

My recommendation to my own adult children is not to map out a career or jump into a corporate or societal straitjacket. In fact, it's all about finding a passion for whatever you do. Not many of us can be Barak Obama, Nelson Mandela or even Elon Musk. That doesn't matter, Commitment and passion are in your head.

When I was happy as the first woman VP in HR at Google, I got close to joining the UK's leading rat-catching company. That's not a mistype. I almost left Google to join a pest-control company. Leaving Google in 2009 was pretty much unheard of, and I didn't do it in the end. However, the reason I got so close was the infectious enthusiasm of the founder. Lesson learned: you can be a glass-half-full regardless of what bar you are standing in. Enthusiasm is self-generated, and it will never let you down I have relied on it through every career high and low.

Shakespeare wrote about the seven ages of men and women. A shift has definitely happened to me. I don't know whether it's nature or nurture, but as a leader, I reflect on my own behavior and value relationships more today than ever before. Today, I am delighted that twelve of my previous direct reports are now CPOs with their own seat at the board table. Several of them are women.

In my current job I could not be happier with my relationships. Palo Alto Networks is a great place to work. It's a company that has goodness at its core. My boss today, Nikesh Arora, is the smartest, most loyal, most thoughtful person I have ever met (never mind worked for), and the leadership team is driven to do the right thing. It's a joy to work in a compassionate, employee-centered culture. A further lesson: dig deep to determine the culture before you join any company. Does what you see and hear resonate with your personal values?

More than anything, I recommend kindness at work and, of course, in our personal lives. I know firsthand that work can be a long haul. Don't sweat it. It's work. I feel Zen when I see people who understand that life, not work, takes precedent. That's the priority. I also feel saddened when people dismiss the work part of life. Work is meaningful. It's complex for sure. However, that's no reason to give up trying to solve the puzzle. Self-esteem can become tied up in your title, the laptop you carry, or the company you work for . . . be aware. :)

Yours truly,

Liane

Liane Hornsey joined Palo Alto Networks as Chief People Officer in September 2018. She previously served as chief people officer at Uber Technologies, Inc. where she helped transform the culture during a period of significant turbulence. Prior to that, she served as chief administrative officer and operating partner at SoftBank Group International. In this role she traveled the globe helping portfolio companies scale and achieve unsurpassed human capital success.

For almost ten years before joining SoftBank, Liane led People Operations for Google's Global Business and became Google's first female vice president in human resources. She has held senior leadership roles at lastminute.com Group, Virgin Media and BMG Music. Liane is widely recognized as one of the world's pre-eminent practitioners in people operations as well as organization and leadership development. She serves on the board of BUILD, a nonprofit organization that provides real-world entrepreneurial experience to empower youth from under-resourced communities to excel in education, lead in their communities and succeed professionally.

LIZ TINKHAM

Board of Directors: Headspin, Athena Alliance, Washington STEM, Particle

"Find the time to establish your external brand in your thirties and forties as it will pay dividends for opportunities in your fifties and sixties."

Dear Future Chairwoman:

My career started with a coin flip and a phone call that were prescient signals to a fantastic run at Accenture.

As an aerospace engineering graduate from Ohio State, I envisioned my career would be designing jet propulsion systems for rockets. But a coin flip and phone call changed that trajectory.

In the middle of my senior year interviewing season, an older friend, whom I much admired, told me about this fantastic company he worked for, Arthur Andersen (AA), and encouraged me to interview. Because the two of us were similar in energy and interests, I interviewed with AA's consulting division and really enjoyed the interview. They flew me to Chicago two weeks later and made me an offer.

At that point, I had several offers from aerospace companies and really liked a jet engine company called Garrett Turbine Engines. I couldn't decide between Arthur Andersen and Garrett, so I flipped a coin—best two out of three—with Arthur Andersen's Management Information Consulting Division winning the toss. I graduated from Ohio State on a Friday, started with Arthur Andersen on Monday, and never looked back.

Arthur Andersen went onto to become Andersen Consulting and then the public company Accenture. I retired thirty-three years later after an incredible global career riding the technology boom and being able to participate in an IPO. The aerospace industry went through a recession in the '80s, and Garrett was bought by another company. While the phone call and coin toss did play a role, it was my gut that made the right decision, and that instinct played a part in my professional success.

The best thing that can happen in your career is to be pushed upward before you feel ready but with a good team around you to help. You are capable of more than you think. I was fortunate because that was always the case with me. I was ahead career-wise for my tenure because no one else senior to me could do the job. When I started, there were five thousand employees. When I left, there were 425,000. Accenture grew exponentially every year.

I was thrown into many different situations that went well most of the time, but not all the time. I was forced to step up, learn, and grow. In 1997 I became a partner (now managing director) and began taking on new leadership roles with clients. Then within Accenture, I began defining some of the changes the company would make or growth strategies it would implement.

311

Every five to ten years, I took part in sessions to envision what Accenture would look like in five years. I sat on some of those committees as well as on CEO-related ones. I held various management positions throughout my career, with increasing amounts of responsibility and authority.

I was lucky to have many women mentors early on in my career, which was almost unheard of, given the small number of women who worked at Arthur Andersen / Andersen Consulting in the '80s and '90s. My primary mentor, one of my first managers in the late '80s, became the company's Chief Human Resources Officer (CHRO). I'd tell her about a potential job change, which might be a big step up, located in another city, or require different skill sets.

She'd shake her head and ask:

"What are you afraid of?"

Of course, there was nothing to be afraid of. She was always right. Yet, I'd go back to her every time, and she'd say the same thing. She was a terrific mentor and sponsored me. She left a few years before I retired. However, she remains my best mentor. To this day, I call her when I have a career- or board-related question.

I also had many male mentors and sponsors within my industry group. One of the things I did was use my peers as mentors. I was part of a perfect class of people who'd started around the same time and had basically come of age in our Communications, Media, and Technology Industry Group. Our code phrase was "Permission to vent?" when we needed help with our client, advice on getting promoted, or needed to truly talk. These men and women are my lifelong friends. We continue to support one another in and out of the company.

The thought of being on a board of directors occurred to me late in my career, which is unfortunate. To get a board position, a person should do a lot of prep work before retiring, such as building an external personal brand and laying groundwork with your professional network. Because I worked hard to the finish, I did not invest the time needed for me to be prepared. At the time, my colleagues and I joked about retiring from Accenture: If finishing your career at Accenture were a football game, you'd go over the goal line with the football and just lay on the ground. Exhausted and unable to do much else.

But my retirement is not panning out that way. I realized I was still young, had a lot of energy, and could make it over the goal line standing, so I needed to think about doing something else. A friend from San Francisco told me I'd be great in board governance and a local group helped women gain access to boards, so I attended a few of their meetings. I'd been advising senior executives for most of my career and had participated in board meetings before, so board governance seemed a natural transition. It was a part-time role, which suited me. It relied on wisdom, which I hoped to have gained during my career, so I started looking into it. I was asked to take part in a board governance onboarding program for women in public companies which was a great learning experience for how to become part of a public board. I also joined The Athena Alliance, which helps women get on private and public boards.

Currently I am the Chair of the Board for Washington STEM, a large Washington State nonprofit, and that role has provided me with an exciting learning experience. Selecting a CEO, bringing on new board members, dealing with racial justice and equity in our school systems—these are all rich topics that I love. Moreover,

STEM (Science, Technology, Engineering and Math) is a passion of mine after all those years of math and science in school. The board is comprised of C-suite leaders and educators throughout Washington. It's helped me to broaden my network and grow as a board member. To my readers, do not overlook joining a nonprofit board early in your career to gain experience and meet people. Just make sure it aligns with your passion as you will be expected to contribute both time and money to the cause.

I am also on the board of a private company. When I joined, I was the first independent board director, as well as the first woman on that board. I enjoy this board a lot as the company is small and growing, so the issues are similar to what I handled with my clients at Accenture, although on a smaller scale. The Athena Alliance helped me get the interview with this board. I am also about to join two more start-up boards and look forward to knowing more about smaller, private company board governance when I start.

Since my retirement, gender diversity on boards has become a popular topic of conversation. I don't have the stats. However, I believe that most U.S. public companies in the Top 200 have women on their boards. Private companies typically have fewer. Many privately held boards are composed of a mix of VCs and the founder. They have to wait until an independent spot opens up. Could companies do better? Yes. However, I believe there needs to be significant focus on the diversity not just of women but also of people of color (POC).

One of the biggest issues with candidate selection has been board members tend to seek out the same type of candidate as themselves. I understand why they want a CEO or a CFO, particularly on public boards. However, there are too few women and POCs in that pool.

Boards should open their candidate selection aperture to include other functions, like CIOs, CMOs, CHROs, and heads of large P/L divisions or departments within companies. Doing so will significantly expand the qualified selection pool of both women and POCs and, more importantly, will improve the quality and diversity of thought on the board.

As I reflect on my career, I could have done a better job in building an external profile and establishing thought leadership earlier in my career. My generation did not do much of this, and we are catching up. I advise Generation Z and Millennials, regardless of whether you ever intend to serve on boards, to think about your external brand and what you can become known for. Take opportunities to network and speak externally.

This can be more difficult for women as many have children. When I was working, I would say:

"I have work and three children; that's all I can do. That's it."

However, I probably could have squeezed in one more thing. It does not need to be a big thing, just something to push your external brand along. A bit of early branding in your thirties and forties will help open opportunities for you in your fifties and sixties.

My second piece of advice is to strive to become a CEO rather than a board member. A friend of mine who runs a venture capital firm kids me, saying she appreciates my trying to get more women on boards. However, she says there simply aren't enough women CEOs, particularly in smaller companies. There are opportunities galore for women to be CEOs long before they are ready for a part-time board role.

I like what many board groups like BoardSeatMeet are doing to help women advance to the boardroom. I especially think the opportunity groups like that provide for networking with current board members is beneficial because most current board members are men. I've worked with men all my life, and their insight is different than women.

I think the BoardSeatMeet platform will help men as well. Most of the men I know are keen on helping others, so I think the platform will provide a good way for them to share insight and advice.

My best wishes for your rock-star career!

Yours truly,

Liz

Liz Tinkham is a dynamic leader and respected advisor to C-level executives on issues of technology, digital transformation, and leadership. She currently advises companies on the challenges and opportunities inherent in the shift to digital technologies. She serves on the Board of Directors of Particle.io (Particle - Welcome to real IoT), a San Francisco-based, full stack Internet of Things company, of Headspin.io (Digital Experience AI Platform - HeadSpin), a cloud-based mobile test automation platform company, and The Athena Alliance (Home - Athena Alliance), a digital platform for community, learning and access to CXO and Board opportunities for top women in business. She is senior Digital and Technology Advisor to Gryphon Investors, a private equity firm specializing in mid-cap investments, and formerly served as an advisor to the CEO at Delphix, Levyx and EQITII. She also advises the state of Washington on educational and equity issues through her position as the Chair of the Board of Washington STEM.

Liz most recently served as a Senior Managing Director at Accenture where she was a member of the Firm's Global Leadership Council and the Global Lead for Microsoft. As a long-time member of Accenture's Global Leadership Council (top .02% leaders), Liz helped craft and lead the implementation of several initiatives that have contributed to Accenture's significant growth. For example, Liz framed a discussion around the retention of senior women for changes in succession planning that increased women in Global Leadership Council positions by 75%.

Liz teaches a management consulting class at the University of Washington's Foster School of Business. She also teaches a graduate seminar class on Nonprofit Board Management. Additionally, Liz served as an advisor to Ohio State's College of Engineering Dean David Williams on the future of Engineering education.

In December 2020, Liz launched her own podcast, "Third Act" (Athena Radio - The Athena Alliance), where she talks to guests who have found meaning and passion after their big career is finished. Liz hopes to inspire men and women age 50+ who have more to give in their retirement years.

Liz enjoys hiking, SoulCycle, travel and spending time with her husband and three children. As a proud graduate of The Ohio State University, where she received a B.S. in Aerospace Engineering, Liz is an avid Buckeye fan.

MARGO WEISZ

Chairwoman: Texas Energy Research Institute (TEPRI)

"A worthy inheritance: passion and perspective."

Dear Chairwoman of Tomorrow:

I had an epiphany. The year was 1993, and I was sitting in a class on Race and Social Policy at the LBJ School of Public Affairs at the University of Texas, Austin. Epiphanies are not to be taken lightly. They are climactic moments of clarity. I like the word "epiphany." When you say it aloud, it is punctuated with a summit. The word represents the moment we mentally and spiritually connect to the divine.

My epiphany took life in a remarkable direction. As an idealistic graduate student, I was struck with the not-uncommon notion that we can create our world. My passion was (and remains) the great democratic ideal that all people have a voice in our society. The integrity of our humanity lays in dismantling gender and racial barriers and entrenched poverty. Opportunity and justice for all people lay at the heart of the American ideal.

319

I came to graduate school from California just after the race riots of 1992. The riots were sparked after the acquittal of four police officers in the beating of Rodney King. Poverty, prejudice, and frustration bore witness. But the seed fueling my conviction was planted earlier on.

My father was a mythological figure. He died of cancer when I was three. The power of his presence was felt through the stories told around the dinner table. So, as one story goes, my parents were having a small party and a couple was running late for the meal. One of the guests was frustrated and said, "Where are those N#!!s ?" My father stood up and asked the guest to leave. Heroes live large in the mind of a child.

So it was in this vein of fire that I found myself in Professor Wong's class vehemently debating urban poverty and race in America. And in this class, I came across a story about a bank that opened up in the South Side of Chicago. My undergraduate degree had been in English literature. However, I fell in love with this bank.

Southshore Bank was started by an uncommon group of bankers. Fueled by the civil rights movement, the founders had an idea for a bank whose mission would be to rebuild a devastated neighborhood. This bank resonated with me. I loved the psychology behind it. Rather than approach the community as a place of deficit, this bank viewed the community as a place with untapped potential. And then, I had my epiphany.

Poverty is about money. It is about how money flows in and out of people's pockets and their communities. To solve the problems of poverty, I had to learn about money. Finance. Capital. Assets. I realized I couldn't sit at a decision-making table with any credibility if I didn't understand financial implications. And I certainly couldn't lead the way. I was going to have to do numbers.

Twenty-five years ago, upon graduation from my Master's program, I helped launch and then lead PeopleFund, a community development financial institution (CDFI) providing financing and serving the economic needs of low-wealth communities. Under my fifteen-year leadership, PeopleFund grew to a nationally recognized and award-winning CDFI and thought leader on economic opportunity, housing, and social entrepreneurship.

While the mythology of my father's fervent ideals may have guided my passion for equity and justice, my mother's deeply practical nature influenced my leadership. Despite being a single parent with three young children, my mom was a paragon of balance. She navigated life's unexpected direction with steadiness, curiosity, and humor. My youthful travails were met with a heavy dose of perspective as my mother would have me look at the big sky full of stars and realize how small and fleeting my personal challenges truly were. My mother is the anti-victim.

The word "perspective" guides my decisions. See the whole chessboard. Explore all relevant points of view. Understand implications from a financial, operational, political, risk, ethical, and human perspective. And then, allow this vantage point to ground me—not letting emotions, ego, fumbles, or seductive ideas get the better of me.

I began serving on nonprofit boards around the same time I began managing my own board as the CEO of a nonprofit organization. Experience on both sides of the table helped me understand my role, leverage my expertise and networks, and serve in a way that supported and respected the staffs. My twenty-five-year participation on boards has yielded a panoply of experiences on local, state, and national boards and on both founding and longstanding boards. I have also had the privilege of serving in every board role, including secretary, treasurer, and chairwoman.

Working with a group of people who share my values and commitment to justice, environmental stewardship, equity, and opportunity has been a deeply satisfying experience. I love the sense of purpose and camaraderie in building a vehicle for progress. Conceptualizing, governing, and building a nonprofit organization in any role, pulls together my passions for entrepreneurship and social mission.

Despite the tremendous joy board participation has brought to my life, I have mixed feelings about nonprofit boards. Most boards I have been on have been functional and productive. However, there are inherent challenges in their structure that distinguish them from corporate boards, primarily the qualifying characteristics for board membership and compensation.

Nonprofits often depend on contributions as they serve a market rarely ripe for generating sustainable profit while pursuing the organization's mission. Therefore, qualification for board membership is often measured by the size of a candidate's pocketbook, or the candidate's network of potential donors. Sometimes a board member will have nominal subject-matter expertise or nonprofit operational experience, yet their role provides them high levels of decision-making power. While differing perspectives can be extremely valuable, there is a power dynamic not always in line with expertise. This dynamic can be held in check by an accountable board governance structure.

However, the issue of "compensation" has a strange impact on governance.

Nonprofit board members are not paid for their time. For many board participants, sitting on a nonprofit board of directors is their "feel-good" volunteer work. But governance and accountability can occasionally require difficult conversations or require substantive time. For some board members, the volunteer nature of the position can provide an easy excuse for cutting corners that would never be cut in a paid role. And again, the power ceded to nonprofit board members can be out of sync with their willingness to responsibly wield it.

Despite these structural challenges, many nonprofit board members rise to their calling. And many nonprofit boards adhere to healthy governance practices that directly address these common tensions. The antidote is clarity of roles, meaningful accountability, a diversified revenue structure, appropriate board expertise, and, most importantly, an empowered and competent CEO.

Today I have a strategic consulting firm called City Lights Group, where I focus on the nexus of entrepreneurship and social mission. I have helped conceptualize the creation of, and sat on the boards of many nonprofits, such as AustinUP, which serves the older adult community, and Texas Energy Poverty Research Institute (TEPRI) to inspire sustainable and lasting energy solutions for low-income communities. My heart still lies in addressing the needs of underserved communities, and I work on a variety of issues, from workforce development to lending and impact investing.

Throughout my career, I have learned to be confident in my perspective, while listening to the differing ones around me. I have learned when to lead out in front, when to pass the torch, and when a solution will require more backend engineering over time. I try not to sweat the small stuff but not ignore red flags. I inherited my most potent tools—a good sense of humor and camaraderie—from my mother. And I always try to be curious, be kind, and do what I say I am going to do. For me, this recipe has been tried and true. Perhaps it will be for you.

Sincerely yours,

Margo

Margo is the founding Partner at City Lights Group, a strategic consulting firm established in 2011. Margo's work focuses on the nexus of entrepreneurship and social mission. She works with private and public sector clients to create strategic roadmaps, devise revenue and capital models, and conceptualize and build new impact programs.

Margo has a distinct interest in energy solutions for low-income people and communities that address today's climate challenge. The result was the creation of a statewide nonprofit, Texas Energy Poverty Research Institute (TEPRI), which launched in 2017. TEPRI has grown quickly to play a primary role in engaging energy stakeholders across the state and country, and piloting an array of projects to test solutions that address both cleaner sources and cost burdens of energy. Margo currently serves as the Chair of the TEPRI Board of Directors.

Margo has served as Chairwoman for the Austin Mayor's Small Business Task Force, and as a member of the Mayor's Task Force to Address Institutional Racism in Finance and Banking. She has also served as an adjunct professor at the LBJ School of Public Affairs and the McCombs School of Business at the University of Texas at Austin, where she has taught graduate level courses on designing effective community initiatives and impact investing.

A champion of innovative ideas, Margo has authored numerous editorials and reports, including the chapter Small Business and Entrepreneurship for *"The NEXT American Opportunity: Good Policies for a Great America."* She has provided leadership on national and local boards, including the National CDFI Coalition and the Texas Association of Community Development Corporations.

Margo has received extensive recognition for her work, including the Exceptional Executive Leadership Award (Austin Community Foundation); "Profiles in Power" winner (*Austin Business Journal*); Social Entrepreneur of the Year (Ernst & Young); and "Austinite of the Year" (Austin Under 40).

COURTNEY BEALE

Board of Directors: Pencils of Promise

"Female representation in the boardroom still needs progress in almost every country around the world."

Dear Chairwoman of Tomorrow:

Serving on a nonprofit board is an incredible way to use your skills to make a difference. My motivation to serve on boards comes from the role of service in my upbringing, how I view leadership, and most importantly, my desire to support issues about which I care. Having served on two boards at different stages of my career, I'd like to share some tips to help other women achieve their board goals.

I grew up in St. Louis, and I think I have a Midwestern outlook on life. It's one of modesty, friendliness, and a strong work ethic— which I know has been instrumental to me thus far in my career. My father was in the military. My mother stopped working when I was little and became active in our community. She was the senior warden of our church, on the PTA, and our Girl Scout leader for thirteen years. I very much grew up with a sense of:

"Those to whom much is given, much is expected in helping others."

That really formed my perspective about deciding to become a diplomat and to serve in other ways, such as on nonprofit boards.

I was in college when 9/11 happened, and it struck me I didn't need to go into the military to make a difference. I could instead serve my country by becoming a diplomat, which would also let me pursue my love of international relations, explore new places, and learn new languages. I wanted to help build a stronger foreign policy for the United States and, hopefully, a more peaceful and prosperous world.

With this in mind, I graduated from the School of Foreign Service at Georgetown University. I interned with the State Department while I was in college. I took the Foreign Service exam while I was in school, so in a way, diplomacy is the only career I've really ever known. I've been in this field for seventeen years, and despite challenges, it's been rewarding. I really love this way of serving my country. As a diplomat, I represent our country as I meet new people, form relationships, and learn about new parts of the world. It's a way I can continue my family's tradition of service, and is a fulfilling career.

Serving on boards allows you to see leadership in action and gain leadership experience. When I entered the Foreign Service, I saw firsthand the importance of having a strong ambassador so the team functions well together. I understood the importance of setting out clear rules and regulations and holding people accountable to them without micromanaging or getting in the way. Leadership made a big difference whether I was serving my country in India or working as a special assistant for the Secretary of State.

I believe my diplomatic experience has helped me understand the role the board can play. The board needs people with defined roles and whose own personal vision and values meld well with the organization, to both support and serve as a check and balance. I've also learned a lot about leadership through other board members, as well as the leadership of the nonprofit organizations on whose boards I have served.

I first had the opportunity to serve on a board when my husband started a nonprofit organization at the beginning of our careers. The organization worked on an issue we both cared a lot about, so I joined the board and served as the secretary. That's how I first learned about being on a board. I learned about how you get an organization off the ground and how the board can support the organization's growth and governance.

The board was small and hands-on for the first few years. Once the organization and the board expanded, I learned about the types of people you need on a board. I saw how you need to recruit board members with different skill sets, such as finance, development, and communications. I also enjoyed having a view into the nonprofit sector through the board. There is a risk when you're working in government that you see everything through a government lens. It's really important to understand what's going on in the private sector and what's going on in the nonprofit sector. A government needs to be partnering and working with all sorts of different entities. So I really valued the view into how a nonprofit organization works.

I stayed on the board for almost ten years and stepped down when my kids were young. Once they were out of diapers and I had a little more time, I was ready to join another board. I set it as my New Year's resolution for 2019.

I talked to friends about my resolution to join the board of a nonprofit working in international education, and a friend told me she knew of a great organization. She connected me to the CEO of the organization and the chairperson of the board to see if there would be a good fit. As luck would have It, they were a large organization with almost fifteen years of experience looking for board members who could bring an international perspective. After four interviews about my experience and motivation, they asked me to join the board. I started out on the impact committee and recently joined the executive committee.

My first tip for anyone who wants to serve on a board is to figure out what kind of an organizations is going to motivate you and how you can add value to the board. Board service can be a big-time commitment, so it is important to choose an issue where you feel passionately about making a difference. Look for something that will make you get back on your computer and do something to try to help this organization even when you're tired, the kids are in bed, and you really want to watch Netflix. Serving on a board connected to something important to you and where you feel like you're making a difference is crucial to keeping you going with that organization.

You also need to be prepared to explain your value-added to a board when you interview. You need to know what skills you'll bring, and what the board is expecting in terms of time or financial contributions. Some organizations have an explicit "give and get" requirement while others are more informal, so I recommend being transparent about expectations and what you can give during the interview process. When I started interviewing, I didn't know whether I was supposed to ask or wait to be told. I've learned you need to be up front about board expectations.

In my case, as someone working for the government, my value-added was less the financial contributions I could make and more about how my international perspectives could support their work. However, from my past board experience I also know that making a significant financial contribution is also important.

As you pursue your journey to the boardroom, try to find a mentor who has been on a board. One who's willing to walk you through the process and make it more comfortable. Even though I had lots of experience and confidence in my own career and had served on a board before, I felt like a little girl in a big-league, non-government-organization (NGO) world when I joined the second board. It was a different environment, and I did not know how it worked, so I asked around for advice. You need someone who's going to hold your hand, teach you how it works, and give you that confidence. Fortunately, lot of leaders are ready to do that for you. All you need to do is find them and ask.

This may be my Midwestern upbringing, but early in my career, I felt embarrassed or I had to learn how to ask for things. I thought if I worked hard and was good at what I did, people would think of me and bring opportunities my way. That's not how the professional world works. You have to know what you want and tell the right people in the right way. I had to learn to phrase it in a way that was comfortable for me.

For example, I want to serve on a board because I want to help this kind of organization in this way. You have to get the word out there, whether that's adding on your LinkedIn profile you're interested in serving on boards or connecting with people who are on boards and/or in leadership positions on boards.

Learning these skills is important because female representation on boards—and in other professional areas—is an issue that still needs progress in almost every country around the world. Some countries and sectors have made more progress than others. Most of the areas of the world where I've worked are under-represented in just about every professional endeavor, including on boards. Thankfully, this is a huge topic in the United States and one most professionals recognize now. But in Latin America, where I live now, female participation in boards is lower than it is in the U.S., and the conversation is a little more nascent. There isn't the same recognition that a lack of diversity on a board is a problem.

I heard a great story from a successful businesswoman. After achieving amazing business goals, she wanted to join the board of one of the biggest banks in the country where she lived. Her grandfather had been on the bank's board, but it did not have a single woman on it. As a favor, she asked a senator to put in a good word put in for her. Admittedly, she said she probably only got the position because they knew her grandfather. Even as an amazingly talented businesswoman, it took asking for favors and capitalizing on family connections for someone like her to become the first female on this board.

When she got there, she felt nervous about speaking up. It was awkward because she was the only woman. Finally, a year or two later, another woman joined the board, and they backed each other up, which made it much more comfortable. This story is so indicative of the fact that even if we're incredibly distinguished, talented achievers, we can still be nervous and need some connections to get on a board on which we're perfectly qualified to serve. This is likely true for many women in America too.

Based on my experience with boards, I think progress is coming. It has taken longer than we wanted, but it's coming because of pushes from the staff at the organizations who are now calling out the lack of diversity on their own boards. I hear teams saying: "If we're going to work there, we want the board to represent us too." So now I feel a responsibility to help diversify the board on which I sit, which I realized is not as easy as I first thought. I've been shocked at how hard it is to find the people I know are out there. I'm just not connected to them.

We all need to be a part of increasing female representation on boards in order to bring about progress around the world. So I encourage women who want to serve on boards to think about their motivations and value-add, speak up about their interest, and work on finding the right fit. I'm so excited for your journey.

Sincerely yours,

Courtney

Courtney Beale is a U.S. diplomat currently serving as the Consul General and Principal Officer at the U.S. Consulate General in Merida, Mexico. Prior to Merida, she was the Senior Director of the Global Engagement Office and Special Assistant to the President at the National Security Council. Courtney has served in diplomatic assignments in Havana, Cuba; Monterrey, Mexico; Islamabad, Pakistan; Bogota, Colombia; and New Delhi, India. In Washington, she was a member of the advance team for Secretaries of State Rice and Clinton and a Special Assistant to Secretary of State Clinton. Courtney graduated with a Master's in Public Policy from Princeton University and a Bachelor of Science in Foreign Service from Georgetown University. She is a term member in the Council of Foreign Relations and is fluent in Spanish, Hindi, and Urdu. She enjoys spending time outdoors with her husband and two rambunctious sons.

SAORI OSU

Board of Directors: Komehyo

"I'd recommend women be ambitious and relentless in reaching their goals. If you devote yourself to something passionately and persistently, you will achieve results."

Dear Future Women Leaders of Tomorrow:

I grew up in Japan, and my parents really encouraged independence. I sensed my mother, who didn't have a job outside of our home, regretted not having a career and did not want me to experience the same regrets. She encouraged me to attend university and dive into industry, which is what I did.

I didn't have any mentors at the beginning of my career, but I did have a role model. A woman who went to university with me started her own company in 2005 after graduating. She wrote a book on how to start a business as a woman, which was my inspiration to launch my own company later on. She has also served as an external independent director at several major Japanese companies

Following university, I worked for Hitachi in various departments: sales, advertising, marketing, and PR. I worked hard and fortunately had the opportunity to learn from top executives while in my twenties. Hearing about their experiences and working alongside them helped me advance professionally and gave me insight into corporate governance during the early stages of my career.

In my twenties, I devoted myself entirely to my job at Hitachi. I began in a low-ranking position and through various internal negotiations, in a very short period of time, I was able to obtain the position in marketing, including public relations, which had been one of my long-standing aspirations. Two years after I joined Hitachi, I got a new position in the advertising department, and this role was a good experience for me. I interacted closely with many of our headquarters-based employees, as well as board members - most of whom were good, middle-aged, male leaders.

If you want to achieve something, use strategic approaches and aggressively pursue your goal. My job at Hitachi was incredibly difficult. However, I learned a lot which helped me start my own company. In addition to my hectic work at Hitachi, I also focused on building my business network outside of the company to prepare for the future. Through that network, a mentor who was a marketing consultant supported me in building my company.

I created Global Stage Inc - a marketing and business consulting firm - which soon evolved into one of the most unique companies in its field. Later, in 2013, I founded the Working Mothers Association of Japan, a business school and a community for working women and mothers. We also have a program for children of working mothers and run occasional workshops (such as Design Thinking and STEM workshops) to help these young students become the next generation of leaders.

One lecturer who gave a talk to the membership was a board member of a large tax accounting company. She had been asked to recommend a candidate to join Komehyo's board. She recommended me. Soon I was introduced to the company and interviewed with one of the board members in charge of administration. I then met with the Komehyo's President to talk about the company's goals, operational geographies, and prospects for its future. When Komehyo held its annual shareholder's meeting, I was voted in and subsequently joined the board of directors. It is interesting because I first heard about corporate governance while at university but never explored it further until I joined Komehyo's board.

Several corporate governance training courses are offered in Japan, but I've only taken one. It lasted about three hours and covered basic corporate governance fundamentals. When I worked at Hitachi, there was a considerable amount of training available to board members. Mid-sized companies do not have many opportunities for trainings like this. However—and interestingly enough—I'd never considered myself a natural leader. To that end, I trained myself by attending seminars, workshops, and by gaining experience.

Before joining the Komehyo Board, I had gained experience running a global marketing company. In addition to promoting female leadership development, which was their original request to me, Komehyo also welcomed my advice and business experience across international borders. I think the other board members paid attention to my opinions and experiences that provided a perspective that they did not have. As a woman leader and board member, I am focused on goals and strategies, not on the fact I'm a woman.

Komehyo is a mid-sized company dealing in second-hand luxury brand goods. With more than 70 years of history, it's organized in some areas and in others it is still in development. I've supported many companies in their expansion abroad and found they share similar shortcomings, one in particular being unable to harness the power of technology. Komehyo, which embraces challenge as its corporate mission, just began developing AI-powered technology-based authentication solutions for luxury goods by scanning products to determine whether they are authentic or fake.

The directors of Komehyo are working in accordance with the Corporate Governance Code established by the Tokyo Stock Exchange. The Corporate Governance Code is a set of principles and guidelines that listed companies should refer to as guidelines in their corporate governance. Once a year, before the shareholder's meeting, its board members complete a questionnaire, and their answers are summarized. Board members then decide what should be done for the following year. Only one of these questions pertains to gender diversity.

In a rapidly changing and technologically advanced world, we needed the wisdom and opinions of people from various different backgrounds to help us develop further. What needed to be on the agenda included Komehyo's investment in this technology and how we should transform our business model to take advantage of new technologies and also expand globally. I try to support the board, but feel it needs more tech-savvy directors. Our core business and trends change so quickly. Even though our branded luxury bag company is still number one in its market and category, it is a competitive market, and if other players entered this field, it would be a problem for us.

When I first joined Komehyo's board, I sensed from the male board members' facial expressions and body language that they were unsure how to deal with their first female executive since the company was founded – i.e. me. All of the executives were male and had decades of industry experience. Their discomfort likely derived from their lack of knowledge of how to deal with female board members. Another woman joined at the same time I did, and we are still the only two women on the board. It must have been a big decision to accept female board members. After a few months, the atmosphere improved as opinions were exchanged openly and frankly.

Board meetings should be structured according to diversity and gender in general. In addition to the need for more gender diversity on Japanese boards, there is a large need for more diversity. I also felt that we needed executives who understood the highly technical aspects of business and the global environment for our future development.

I found the biggest challenge to gender parity on Japanese boards is the dearth of potential women candidates for those roles because female managers currently represent less than 10 percent of the Japanese workforce. The demand for women board members in Japan has seen an upward trend. For instance, a recruitment firm recommended me to a Japanese restaurant chain company's board, which was looking for executives to fill a few board seats. The company, which employs many part-time female employees, invited me to join the board. They wanted me to manage these part-timers, motivate them to work more, and foster a dynamic work environment. The company had a long history and a good reputation, yet the board of directors was made up entirely of men with a lot of industry experience or specific skills such as law or accounting. By that time, I had decided to move to the U.S. to the San Francisco Bay Area, and so I did not pursue a role on this company's board. In June 2020, I resigned from Komehyo's board of directors at the shareholders' meeting. I am now the president of Global Stage Inc. and Global Stage USA Inc., as well as the Working Mothers Association of Japan.

Japanese corporations are looking to increase their number of female leaders. In order to qualify more women for board governance roles, both the Japanese government and corporations should focus on fostering leadership in young and middle aged female employees. Even though women make up almost 50 percent of the Japanese workforce, Japan is still struggling to increase the number of women in board governance.

On the other hand, some women do not aspire to become leaders in Japan because they don't see the benefits and don't identify with the role. They are discouraged by the burdensome aspect of working longer hours and taking on more responsibility. As a result, they don't want to work harder and don't have ambitious goals. In Japan right now, women lack a go-getter spirit, due in part to the education they have had and the family environment in which only men work. I am encouraged by the signs that this too is shifting.

If you are a woman who wants to get married or have children, you have limited time to develop your career in your twenties. During this decade, just try to work and study hard. Everything should be challenging, especially for women. These experiences will support you in the future as you reach your thirties, forties, and fifties. Having a family and working at the same time is a good way to continue growing in your career. I'd encourage women to be ambitious and relentless in reaching their goals. If you devote yourself to something passionately and persistently, you will achieve outcomes beyond what you imagined. I know, because I did.

Sincerely Yours,
Saori Osu

Saori Osu has created new value and opportunities for society by launching new businesses and projects in dynamic and rapidly changing markets. She has numerous achievements in the education, food, human resources, consumer goods, and IT industries. Saori is the founder and CEO of a global marketing company that supports Japanese companies to expand their business aboard, and a non-profit organization that fosters the success of women and youth in Japan.

Saori severed as a board member at a TSE-listed company for five years since 2016. In 2020, based on her business experience in various areas such as Japan, greater Asia and North America, she launched InterEd, a global STEAM education program for middle and high school students around the world, and pursues the goal of creating global STEAM education opportunities for a cumulative total of 100 million students in 10 years. Her passion stems from the idea that all students can become changemakers who create new values based on their own interests and contribute to a better society.

ROBIN TOFT

Chairwoman: We Can Rise

Board of Directors: Synapse, T2 Biosystems

"There are many bold moves along your career journey. You have to be confident in communicating your accomplishments and your achievements in order to ask for the next opportunity."

Dear Chairwoman:

I grew up in the Detroit suburbs. My dad worked in the factories, and neither of my parents went to college. I'm fortunate to have survived and thrived. My dad was one of my greatest inspirations. He told me I could do and be anything, and I believed it and just ran with that. I remember lying on the grass as a kid looking into the sky and thinking that anything and everything is possible.

I like to share the "3-minute story of me" in four chapters. I studied pre-med in college and aced all my classes. Everyone said I should be a doctor. Somehow, I knew that I was going to be in business and not medicine, even though I loved science. I ended up with a medical technology degree and walked into a lab, put on a white coat and thought, "*What have I done?*" It took me about 10 years to get out of the lab. I used to teach a medical technology course at a local university. However, from the day I put on the lab coat, I kept raising my hand to talk about business instead of science. Looking at the microscope was just not my thing.

I got my chance while working for SmithKline Beecham. They didn't have a sales role for me because they thought I was a scientist. So, I walked across the street to the competitor, LabCorp, and told them I needed to be in sales. This was a pivotal moment because I asked for the sales job when I had absolutely no sales background or understanding. From the moment I started, I became their top performer out of 400 people. All I did was follow the formula, constantly asking myself: *what's in it for the customer?* If I could identify at least three good reasons for them to make a change, I could make it happen. As a result, I created 10 years of through-the-roof sales performance in multiple settings. Using the "3 reasons rule," I was always the top performer everywhere I worked. My employers grew to expect it, and I worked hard and delivered.

I was then recruited by a biotech startup in the San Francisco Bay Area. That was a pivotal moment because I worked with an HIV and AIDS research team for about 10 years. At the time, the global view was that a pandemic was raging. In fact, in 2020, 26 million people have been affected by HIV, and it's still over 30% prevalent in many African countries. I introduced the first HIV viral-load test to the market, and my start-up developed a better way to monitor and treat people using a combination therapy. We quickly built sales from zero to $30 million, and then I decided to resign my executive role and ride off into the sunset.

At the time, I was married to a wildlife photographer and everyone would ask, "Do you go everywhere with him?" So...I decided I *would* take a year and go everywhere with him. Eventually I realized that being the CEO of his company, running his photography and travel business, wasn't rewarding to me personally. I needed to return to the industry I loved so much.

Upon re-entry, I was recruited as VP of Virology at Roche. The SVP who hired me became a great mentor, and I still revere him today. About a year later, he resigned. he brought me into his office and said: "I've decided you're my successor, and I want you to have my job. In fact, I've already told everyone that you're our new SVP." Shortly thereafter, I became a Senior Vice President of Commercial Operations for Roche. Life became busy and stressful. I commuted to Europe every two weeks. On one return trip I got sick on the plane and ended up in the ER. After a litany of tests, it turned out that I had colon cancer with an obstruction. It was a near-death ER experience. I knew I had cancer for one day, within 24 hours I was in surgery, which was followed by chemotherapy.

I was 45 years young.

I knew that life had to change. The job caused too much stress, and my health was being seriously compromised. I ended up quitting my job. However, it wasn't long before I was back working and founded a life-science executive-search firm for empower leaders that would change the way cancer is treated in my lifetime. It was a cosmic experience. I had minimal experience with executive search except as a buyer. However, I felt I knew enough that, with a clean slate approach, I could make the company successful.

I built a completely different search firm, unlike anything that existed in the industry. I built it like biotech where I put a giant mission in the middle, hired amazing people and paid them exceptionally well. The rest is history., We went from start-up and zero revenue to over $10 million. It was a blast to be a founder and a builder of my own company. I never knew I wanted to be a CEO, as I had always been comfortable in the second-in-command seat. But I had drive and ambition to try new things. I wanted to go out, build the brand and write a book for executive women to accelerate their careers.

As we continued to scale, I hired a CEO and a CFO, and took the position of the forward-facing executive of this company. My whole mission for the next decade was to advance women in their roles.

I wrote a book called "We Can" based on the Women's Executive Career Advancement Network that I had created. We created a community that is bringing together women in San Francisco and San Diego who need to know each other. It's called the We Can Rise Community. The book was named on the Top 100 CEO books of all time by BookAuthority, even though I'd never written a book before.

I followed this up with an accompanying companion We Can Journal to serve as a woman's practical guide on how to personally navigate her career path. In the book, I recommend women first create value, ask for the chance to win the next growth opportunity as they advance their careers. If you've created value, your company should not hold you back. If it does, you may decide to go look somewhere else, which is exactly what I did when I walked across the street to that other company to get the sales role that I mentioned earlier. You have to make many bold moves along your career journey. I recommend you be confident in your accomplishments and your achievements and learn to promote yourself.

I originally tried to sell my company when we had reached about six-and-a-half-million in revenue, and the valuation did not reflect our true value. That's when I decided to hire the next CEO and CFO for the Toft Group. I would go out and build the We Can brand to accelerate women in their careers. As a result, we achieved $10 million in revenue two years later.

In 2019, I decided to sell my company because I wanted to follow my passion further and advance and develop women full time. I sold my company to ZRG Partners, and they have provided a good home for my people. I stayed on at ZRG to help build the company while I launched *We Can Rise, Inc.,* my new startup to accelerate women's careers worldwide. In parallel, I continue to lead the Women on Board practice and also its Global Life Sciences franchise.

In 2019, the year that I sold the company, California had introduced Senate Bill 826. As I had been such a champion of women and diversity since founding Toft Group, I had fourteen women - out of a team of twenty - working for me as I built *We Can Rise.* I told them their job was to go out and meet all aspiring executive women in the industry. That would differentiate us. I bet on two things when building my search firm: fast and female. Ten years later, that made a big difference, because I knew all these executive women when the board legislation passed to advance women to the boardroom. I have been focused exclusively on advancing women to the board level for the past two years. We did more board search work in 2020 than we had done in the previous 10 years combined. I'm currently launching a new book for women seeking board roles, which will provide my insights into how women can rise to board level as quickly as possible.

It's been a tremendous ride. I am enthusiastic about where things are now with respect to women leadership in the boardroom. I've worked in life sciences, healthcare, and high tech, which in California are booming fields, in spite of the global pandemic.

Women in the boardroom creates a competitive advantage to companies and simply makes sense for four reasons:

1) Enhanced profitability.

2) Increased innovation.

3) Better product design for today's diverse customer base.

4) Better talent

I educate everyone that I speak with all the time about these four competitive advantages.

Healthcare and life sciences talent was already in demand before COVID-19. With the pandemic, the demand for talent has only grown, and the industry is extraordinarily short on talent. There are simply not enough qualified people to fill all the slots. In my opinion, the best way to attract and retain people you want is to achieve diversity at the top of an organization. This makes the company more attractive to diverse candidates who will want to work there.

I was speaking with someone we recently placed in the CEO role. The company wanted to diversify its board further with two women. And he said afterwards that I would not believe the change in the reception of his employee base. It had been remarkable. The employees are thankful that women are represented at the top of the company. I should note that most companies are proud to have 52% women employed at entry level, the bottom of the pyramid. However, companies typically have only 20% at the officer level, and only 5% of companies have a woman CEO. I believe it should be 52% all the way up.

I've realized that, when the new board legislation on diversity was announced in California, the most competitive employers started racing to make the top of their companies more diverse, even though were not required to do so. These companies realize now that diversity is an undeniable competitive advantage and data has demonstrated this fact. The healthcare and life sciences industry is progressive, and most companies now believe that advancing gender parity across the board is logical, reasonable, and appropriate. The history of board search pre-legislation is that 70% of searches did not even go to an executive search firm. Historically, most board placements were achieved through the board or CEO's network. If you think about it, the network in this setting is usually 95% male, and their networks do not include many women. So, when the board-diversity became law in California, these boards realized they didn't know any qualified women, which is why now the vast majority of board searches are being handled by executive search firms.

Additionally, the historical pattern of board membership is that, to be considered qualified, you typically needed to be a CEO or CFO. Today, in advance of board restructuring, most companies are doing a formal board assessment and realizing they need to add some more functional roles around the boardroom table since companies have changed dramatically over the past 10 to 20 years. Many healthcare companies today rely on big data and consumerization of healthcare information. Progressive companies are using this opportunity to fill their board seats with additional functional expertise. For instance, the role in highest demand in our industry requires someone with M&A and finance background who can also serve on the audit committee. More importantly, we are seeing companies seeking regulatory and clinical expertise, strong commercialization experience, product-consumerization expertise and/or an understanding of big data. We are not dropping the bar. We are changing the bar.

Meanwhile, networking with companies you aspire to serve is more important than ever. I advise women to build their own network and identify 5-10 companies for which they have a high level of personal interest and where they could add value. Then meet the chairman of the board, the CEO, and the head of the Governance Committee, to insert yourself into their network. You have to create that network yourself. Most women don't realize this and prefer to wait for the phone to ring. Keep in mind that all boards would prefer not to hire an executive search firm given the expense. Inserting yourself in a board's network is the fastest, cheapest, and easiest way for them to find you. If you are already in their network, you're the first person they will call.

It's important to realize that you cannot be elevated to a private or public enterprise boardroom if you've never spent time and/or been instrumental in any sort of boardroom. Within your own company, you should ask for projects that would put you in front of the board for formal presentations. I advocate that effective executives should meet with their direct manager and design a plan for themselves for the year. Share your goals and aspirations for personal growth and ultimate board service during these meetings. And the individual you work for should know definitively that, on a quarterly basis, you're going to tell them how your career plan is going. Please note that in their eyes, your entire job is to create value for your employer. If you think anything other than that, you're not thinking properly about the workplace. Your job is to create value and, once you do so, you have earned the right to ask for opportunities. Having that clear conversation on a quarterly basis will differentiate you, and you will likely see opportunities come your way. Always be crystal-clear about your aspirations and share the fact that they include board service.

I personally encourage the next generation of female board leaders to explore every way to build your network and gain governance experience, which definitely could include joining the boards of non-profits. In fact, that's how I made my way into the boardroom. I continue to serve on many non-profits today. You need to gain boardroom experience, and that is a good path. Typically, when you begin non-profit work, do something you're super passionate about. They're going to want you to volunteer your time, energy, talents, and money if you can. I recommend that, as you go through your career, do the work expected from a board member. Roll up your sleeves and get involved. I recently joined a board of the CLSA (California Life Sciences Association). This working board has 40+ members who are all CEOs of companies. They clearly stated that they don't want people to represent CLSA who aren't willing to do the work. I have already been instrumental in their racial and social justice committee and have personally supported these projects with my own finances. Now they've asked me to be on both the compensation and the governance committees.

I recommend you target non-profits with a formal committee structure and an impressive group around the table. For example, another of my boards, LEAD San Diego, has many industry leaders from different sectors, including government, hospitality, and military. I am the only life sciences representative on the board, and the only life science person they know. They introduce me to every life-sciences opportunity they find, since I'm the person they know. The cross-functional connections are important, and the board experience is invaluable.

Most of my board are seeking to have the most diverse board possible. Of course, I'm happy to help since advancing women is my passion.

I'm certain that we're all here to use our gifts and talents, and that we all have a purpose. Whether your aspiration is at the corporate board level, community governance or anything in between, we have entered a new era of female empowerment and democratizing leadership.

Together, We Can and We Will all RISE. Hoping you are resilient, inspired, self-confident, and energized about your career. It's your time!

Sincerely yours,

Robin

Robin Toft is the founder and CEO of Toft Group a ZRG Company, where she combines a deep inside knowledge of the life science industry with a passion for building game-changing management teams. A champion of diverse executive teams, Robin has built a reputation for recruiting women and minorities into top roles and helping the life science industry overcome unconscious bias in hiring. Having successfully sold Toft Group to ZRG Partners, Robin co-founded We Can Rise in 2020, a B-corporation aimed at helping aspiring female executives to confidently reach their potential while achieving balance and collaborating to build healthier companies that change the world. Prior to founding Toft Group in 2010, Robin served 20+ years as a biotech executive.

Robin's first book entitled *WE CAN, The Executive Woman's Guide to Career Advancement, is* recognized within the list of 100 Best CEO Books of All Time by BookAuthority and won Gold for Best E-book in the International Business Awards. In the American Business Awards for 2020, Robin won Gold in the three major individual categories of Lifetime Achievement, Maverick of the Year and Woman of the Year. She also won Gold for Most Innovative Woman of the Year in the Women in Business Awards for 2020. Robin currently serves on the boards of T2 Biosystems, Syapse, California Life Science Association (CLSA), The Clearity Foundation, and LEAD San Diego. Robin holds a B.S. in Medical Technology from Michigan State.

GAYLE CROWELL

Board of Directors: Envestnet Inc, Pliant Therapeutics, Hercules Capital

"I never aspired to be a CEO and certainly didn't aspire to be a board member. But when something came my way, mentally I would say to myself, what's the worst that could happen? I can go back to what I did before. Even if I fail, I will have had this experience."

Dear Chairwomen of Tomorrow:

My path to being a board director was certainly not a traditional one. I hope that by reading my story, you will be inspired to create your own path.

I started my career as a first-grade teacher. I became enamored with the idea of technology in the classroom. While teaching children how to read, I had this idea that if they could write their own stories and then read them to others, they could become much better readers. Obviously, young children can't write well enough with a pencil to craft narratives, but they certainly love telling stories, and I knew I could teach them how to use a simple word processor. I purchased an Apple computer and a large-font word processor to use in my classroom. My students wrote and illustrated their stories, which we then bound into mini books and published in the classroom. By the end of the school year, we had created an entire library of stories written by the students, which they would read to each other and to their families. As a result, my students scored high in reading.

Excited by this success, I knew we could expand the program if we could get enough computers and software for the school. I went to the school board, which acknowledged the program's phenomenal results but did not have the budget to purchase computers, software, or any of the items necessary for the program's success. Undeterred, I decided to look to my local community for financial support.

Since I was teaching in Nevada, I went to local casinos, corporations, and a few high-net-worth individuals to raise the money needed to purchase the computers for the school. I also believed in the power of partnership and approached several software companies to get the necessary software donated. Soon we were able to purchase the necessary hardware and technology with the funds I had raised. As a result, I was able to implement the program throughout our entire school.

Other teachers in the district were excited by my program and vision. I began conducting a few workshops teaching other educators how the program could be implemented in their classrooms. The Nevada State Department of Education then approached me, asking if I would be willing to educate teachers in other school districts around the state. Eventually, I began spending my weekends with two of my other teaching colleagues traveling to other school districts teaching educators how to use technology to reimagine reading and writing curriculum in their schools.

After some positive local publicity, I was approached by the CEO of a local computer hardware company. He was inspired by the success of my program and by my vision and drive to bring technology into the classroom. The CEO, the president, and I had a number of conversations about me joining their company. I resisted as I saw myself as a teacher first, with a passion for technology second. The CEO persisted, noting that he was more interested in passionate and innovative thinkers than he was with having employees with specific skill sets. Eventually I knew I was ready to trust in my passion and myself, and I joined the company.

At first, I had no job title or job description and worked on the CEO's special projects. Over time, these two smart co-founders taught me everything about building a company, and it was truly a once-in-a-lifetime experience. I was exposed to many parts of the business and worked on multiple cross-departmental challenges. I even had the opportunity to go down on the factory floor to build a computer, which gave me a hands-on experience of the inner workings of a computer. I was open to learning and challenging myself, and these entrepreneurs believed in my abilities to succeed at anything I put my mind to.

After about two years at the company, the CEO decided to part ways with the VP of Sales. Confident in my previous successes, the CEO asked me if I would run the sales organization. Since I had not yet had a true sales role within the company, I questioned the CEO's choice. He reminded me that selling isn't limited to a transaction but more about bringing solutions to customers and building customer relationships. Through our conversation, I understood I had been selling all along. They gave me the job but not the title and not the pay. After a few quarters, I demonstrated I was capable of leading a top-performing sales team and, upon this recognition, I was given the VP title and the appropriate pay. My success at managing a large team led me to consider what other opportunities there might be in a different company.

Before I joined this technology company, I knew I had a passion for technology. Having the opportunity to grow and explore this passion, I knew that, if I wanted to be really successful in the technology world, I needed to be in Silicon Valley. Soon after, I relocated there and worked for some large companies specializing in both software and hardware, including Oracle. Building on that success and continuing to learn new technologies and skills, I eventually moved to several venture-backed software companies and, over time, worked my way up to become a CEO.

The start-up world was quite different than working at a well-funded corporation with tons of resources. You learn quickly how to be scrappy, and many of my earlier experiences at my first technology company served me well at this stage of my career. As a CEO, you are essentially the chief sales officer. You are ultimately responsible for customer success. As all CEOs know, without a growing base of satisfied customers, your company has nothing.

The CEO is the face of the company and must do a great job telling the company and/or product story in a compelling way. In the same way I loved teaching educators about the promise of technology, I enjoyed coaching and developing highly motivated teams to work with customers in the same way. The more my teams loved the challenge of building successful, high-growth businesses, the more excited I was to work with them.

In January 2000, I sold my company, *Rightpoint*, a real-time personalization software company. As a result of our success, the company generated a fifty-times return for our investors. Around the same time, my dad became ill. My parents were struggling and asked if I could help them.

Though I was interviewing with multiple companies for my next CEO role, I knew it would be hard to take on a new CEO role while managing my father's care. During this time, I received an offer from a large private equity firm, Warburg Pincus. The opportunity with Warburg allowed me to work at a world-class firm, and gave me the flexibility to manage my parents' care. As was the case with my first technology company, I had no real job title, and there was no precedent for my role. Ultimately, I became what would be their go-to-market, sales, or marketing expert.

I worked across a portfolio of forty to fifty software and technology companies at a time. I advised many amazing CEOs and helped guide them on go-to-market strategies. At the time, I thought I would do this work for a year or two and go back to being a CEO. But I loved the fact I was able to work across a variety of companies and observe best practices, not only from my own experiences but from a wide variety of successful companies.

Given that Warburg Pincus is a successful private equity firm with a broad portfolio of high-achieving, high-growth companies, my tenure there allowed me to acquire even more skills in building and scaling businesses. Working in the private equity world was a rewarding experience, and it gave me a great perspective on understanding what drives investors and shareholders. While I had successfully raised capital as a CEO, I found it was different sitting on the other side of the table. Ultimately, it was my ability to see through the eyes of a successful operator and investor that created the platform for my success during this stage of my career.

Thinking back on my first board role, I can still remember when the private equity partner first asked me to sit on the board of one of his portfolio companies. It came up during a conversation about my interest in taking a CEO role. Given the nature of private equity, partners often find themselves traveling around the country meeting with prospective executives and portfolio companies, but never staying long enough to create meaningful, long-term relationships. His suggestion that we work together on a board really resonated with me because it opened a variety of opportunities for both of us. When you create opportunities to spend time or collaborate on a project with someone or a firm, naturally that will generate more projects and opportunities to work together.

I believe it is one of the reasons women initially had such a hard time breaking into board service. Board members tend to recommend people in their network and early on, most board members had male-dominated networks. Utilizing that personal network is one of the key drivers that resulted in men recommending other men so often for board roles. Because of this factor, women need to create these types of opportunities and leverage their networks in different ways.

358

The advice I frequently share with women is to get your name out there and have real measurable results and success associated with your name. Whether it's in independent value creation or working at a successful company where you have made a significant contribution, it is important to continuously share and amplify your brand and successes. Once your name gets out there, more people will want to talk with you and spend time with you and getting on a board becomes a bit easier. For most people, getting the first board seat requires a well-thought-out strategy and plan. After that, it is a matter of making the right decisions to continuously execute against that plan.

I have been fortunate to be able to build and drive success at companies that had great financial exits for all stakeholders. My first board seat gave me the visibility I needed to be recruited for subsequent board seats.

Upon becoming a board member, I realized that yet again, I would have a lot of new skills to develop and cultivate. When I think back to the early part of my technology career, I was first and foremost a successful operator. As a board member, I had to change hats and transition away from being a hands-on operator. Different than previous roles in my career, board members are there to essentially provide strategy and oversight. By being removed from the day-to-day operations of a company, board members can guide the company with a particular focus on investors and shareholders. Understanding the balance of risk versus reward is critical as board members provide valuable guidance to management as they build a company. This change in perspective allowed me to step back and see the big picture, which guided my transition from being an operator to being a successful board member.

Since those early board seats were often male-dominated, as a woman, I had to quickly learn and adapt to a new environment. As an executive and a board member, I have always been confident in my own knowledge, expertise and value. My communication style is direct. However, I have always been aware of the dynamics in a room and that intuition has served me well, especially in the early days of my board service. An imbalanced gender dynamic was pretty much the norm up until the last six or seven years. Earlier in my career when I was a CEO, however, there simply were not a lot of women CEOs. The prevailing recruiting criteria at that time was that you had to be a CEO to serve on a board, which meant I was often the only woman in the boardroom. Thankfully, this has changed over time and companies have begun to broaden their thinking about the many executives and entrepreneurial roles that can add value around the board table. As more women joined boards, I began to appreciate the change in board dynamics. I could see where women had a collaborative style that was different than some of my earliest board experiences. Ultimately, that diversity of experience and thought made for the strongest boards.

Though board composition and diversity are shifting, women still need to present themselves in a knowledgeable and direct manner. It is not enough for women to have a seat at the table. They need to show up informed and prepared to discuss a wide range of topics. I have a natural intellectual curiosity for business and technology and have always been eager to learn about a particular company and/or sector. This willingness to learn about new fields or developments has served me well. My colleagues and network know I have a broad set of interests and skills not limited to one role or sector. This reputation has allowed me to be recommended for a role in a field in which I may not have previous experience, as I have the drive and ambition to master any topic and field.

I think being a teacher may have primed me to be this way. People who are not familiar with my background still ask me occasionally if I was ever a teacher. I try to make everything simple and understandable. I bookend things and wrap up information in a digestible way. You become so totally invested in a company when you sit on a board, and there's a great deal of pride around that. You want to add tremendous value and make a significant contribution.

I remember in college that I was nervous about public speaking. Someone told me that, if I didn't want to be nervous about public speaking, I needed to know my topic inside and out. You should know so much about your topic that you could just talk about it forever. This advice is also true when it comes to being prepared in business. If you want to speak credibly on a topic, you must go into the meeting thoroughly prepared. I am much more relaxed knowing as much as I can about a particular field or topic. Being able to confidently present and defend your points of view demonstrates your strong commitment to the company and helps ensure you add value to any topic of discussion. Solid preparation will always give you that edge.

Most people, regardless of gender, go through their corporate lives without understanding what a board actually does. In a company, a tremendous amount of management work goes on before a board meeting. People are somewhat in awe of board members, but they may not actually know what happens behind closed doors. Those involved know they must present to the board members, who are incredibly important, but overall, the presenters may not really understand how a board adds value.

This is a way in which society indirectly limits the pool of candidates for board seats. If we taught employees earlier in their careers how board members add value and shared with them the kinds of work the board does and how the members represent the shareholders - perhaps more individuals would be better prepared to consider whether a board role is for them. We need to educate potential board candidates early on how to network and create their own branding and value proposition. The way the system works now, we wait until candidates get to a certain executive level when they raise their hand to be considered for a potential board seat. As I stated previously, if we did a better job of helping individuals prepare for board service from a younger age, interested candidates would be able to present themselves as ready for board service all along, rather than as an afterthought of a successful career.

Similarly, we need to move faster. There is simply no reason boardroom composition shouldn't be aligned with the population demographic—period. If the workforce reflects the diversity of the population, then boards should be lined up accordingly. Some may say there are not enough talented or experienced women to join boards. I have never believed that. Instead, we need better mechanisms to expose talent and diversity to our boardrooms.

This will require each of us to think outside of the box and not simply rely on the same old networks. A first step is to develop a greater and more diverse pipeline of women executives who are C-suite or CEO ready. Additionally, we need to collectively promote the accomplishments of women who have already had a fair amount of success to our existing networks. There are some incredibly talented women who might not normally surface as a board member candidate, unless they've done something extraordinary as entrepreneurs.

Many younger women have the potential to add so much business value. However, they might not surface to the board level for another ten years. Limiting these pipelines is costly for organizations that could utilize these women's innovative thinking and perspectives. By working to expose the second and third layers of talented women in organizations, we would make much more progress toward a gender-equal boardroom in a shorter period of time. We cannot afford to wait another decade to have equal representation at the highest levels of our corporations. More importantly, this issue is not solely a gender issue. Boards add the most value when they are truly diverse across all spectrums—gender, race, age, ethnicity and culture. The diversity of thought and experiences create high-value board experiences.

Having said this, I have been impressed with the many women's organizations springing up over the past five years and are working hard to get more women on boards. They have created comprehensive educational programs to teach and coach qualified candidates every step of the way to their first board assignment. I highly recommend women work with one of these organizations early in their career. The work you do will help you create your own personal brand and develop a strong value proposition that will also help you in your current career trajectory. These organizations also help board candidates understand the difference between looking for a career role as compared to a board role and how to position their value accordingly.

Finally, Covid-19 has shown us the importance of having women at the table to have meaningful conversations about school, childcare, and employees 'future productivity and stressors. Women are reminding us employees are burnt out. They're now teachers and mothers and workers still chartered with forty hours of work a week with educational responsibilities at home as well. Having made career choices based on the needs of my family, I understand all too well the burdens women carry in the workforce. I don't know if the collective male perspective can be as empathetic in those conversations. We are seeing the mental and emotional toll this new life has taken on women in the workforce, and it is important to have a board that recognizes this shift.

The pandemic has compressed the digitization and transformation of companies by accomplishing in a few months what would have taken years to achieve otherwise. Many companies had to pivot and almost immediately implement what they had in their five-year roadmaps. This compression alone has rapidly accelerated opportunities. Vast corporate changes have been executed in a short period of time, adding great economic value for shareholders and incredible value for the businesses themselves. There are a lot of ways to look at this, but a holistic view is important. It requires a diverse mix of viewpoints that are not just gender-segmented but racially segmented as well.

In looking back over my board service, I have been fortunate to have served on over two dozen boards. My extensive board experience runs from technology to financial services to supply chain companies. Though my board work has spanned across many industries, I have always been attracted to successful companies that were often the market leaders in their sector.

A few years ago, I decided that, since I was fortunate enough to have enough board experience to be in demand, I wanted my next board to serve humanity in a more direct way. I looked at several sectors and decided I wanted to join a biotech board since most biotechs are involved in incredibly important and lifesaving medical work. I became laser-focused, ignoring other technology board opportunities that came my way. This focus provided me with the opportunity to have many conversations with CEOs whose companies were developing treatments to significantly change the lives of individuals affected by particular diseases. Ultimately, I was offered a director role for an exciting biotech that is developing breakthrough therapeutics for halting the progression and reversing fibrotic diseases. My previous experiences as a public board member have proven to be useful to this growing biotech, and I am fortunate to contribute to their success.

I want to continue to make a difference by being a part of companies that are going to change the world for the better. Another example of this strategy is when I originally got involved in financial services. I wanted to be part of a company in a position to use data to meaningfully impact people's personal financial lives. One of my public boards, Envestnet, is doing just that by creating a financial wellness platform. Just as much as your own physical health is important, your financial wellness affects everything in your life, your children's lives, and your families 'lives. As such, my later boards have been about changing the world and impacting individuals for the better. Just as I knew back then technology would make my students better readers, I know there are so many companies and sectors utilizing technology to greatly improve our personal lives.

In this time of the coronavirus, reimagining work and rethinking how businesses operate has been at the top of my mind. It is clear the coronavirus pandemic will have short- and long-term effects on people and businesses. It is my hope I can continue to work with talented women so they will be poised to lead businesses and employees as this next generation of business models evolves.

My advice to younger women is to embrace whatever comes your way and be willing to take risks. This was, by far, the biggest differentiator in my career. I never aspired to be a CEO and, early in my career, I never imagined being a board member. When a new challenge came my way, I always considered the worst thing that could happen. Yes, I could fail. However, I never let that stop me because I knew that if I needed to, I could go back to what I had been doing before. In fact, I believed that, even if I failed, the experience I gained would help me be successful in my next role.

As women, we are led to believe we are not risk-takers. Society has taught us we are to think of our collective circumstances before we can take on a new role or challenge. I encourage women not to think that way. Instead, take a risk. Had I not trusted in that first risk to leave teaching behind and join a technology company, I would not have had the diverse and successful career opportunities I have enjoyed. Trust in yourself. You are smart and talented and capable of learning along the way. You will figure it out. Take the risk!

I wish you all the best on your journey. I have no doubt it will be more exciting than you could have ever imagined.

Yours truly,

Gayle

Gayle is a highly experienced Board Director, CEO, C-suite executive, strategic business advisor, executive coach and speaker with extensive experience in both venture capital and private equity-backed technology companies. She spent the last decade as a Sr. Strategic Business Advisor across the portfolio of one of the leading global private equity firms, Warburg Pincus working closely with high growth technology, financial services, logistics and healthcare companies.

Gayle currently serves as an independent corporate Board member of three public boards: Envestnet (ENV), Hercules Capital (HTGC), Pliant Therapeutics (PRX) as well as two private corporate boards: Resman and GTreasury. She has extensive Director experience as a public and private Board member, having served as a Chairman, Lead Director or Independent Director for over twenty-five public and private corporations driving value creation at the highest level for customers, employees and shareholders alike. She is currently the Chairman of the Compensation Committee for HTGC and the Compliance and Info Security Committee for ENV. She serves on the Audit committee at PLRX, the Compensation Committee at ENV and the Nominating and Governance committee at both ENV and PLRX.

On the nonprofit side, she also serves as a Fellow of the prestigious Desert Research Foundation, a world leader in environmental research. In addition, she served as Chairman and on the National Board of Directors for Watermark, a non-profit women's executive organization. As a passionate environmentalist, she is the co-founder of www.conservingnow.com, a large community of earth-friendly individuals who care deeply about children and the future of our planet.

She is a member of the National Association of Corporate Board members (NACD), Women Corporate Directors (WCD), Boardlist, Athena Alliance, Women in the Boardroom, Women Who Lead, Digital Directors Network, 2020 Women on Boards and Watermark.

ENDNOTES

1. 2020 Women on Boards, "Women Now Hold Record 22.6% of Russell 3000 Board Seats in the US," News Release, (September 16, 2020).

2. "Women on Corporate Boards: Quick Take," Catalyst, March 13, 2020, https://www.catalyst.org/research/women-on-corporate-boards/

3. "2020 Global Board Diversity Tracker," Egon Zehnder, accessed March 1, 2021, https://www.egonzehnder.com/global-board-diversity-tracker

4. Ross Kerby, "Women's share of U.S. corporate board seats rises, but not top roles: study," Reuters, February 3, 2020, https://www.reuters.com/article/us-usadirectors-women/womens-share-of-u-s-corporate-board-seats-rises-but-not-top-roles-study-idUSKBN1ZX1K3

ABOUT THE AUTHOR

Rika Nakazawa is a senior leader, entrepreneur, investor, board director, and frequent public speaker on technology-powered business transformation and diversity in leadership. She is the Co-founder of BoardSeatMeet Inc. a social impact venture that is diversifying both the board room and C-suite by empowering minority executives to build and leverage social capital with an intelligent orchestration platform.

Trilingual in Japanese, German and English, Rika grew up in Japan and moved to the U.S. initially to attend Princeton University. Rika has since worked internationally for over two decades in senior executive roles in strategy, business development, account management, and marketing with Fortune 500 companies—NVIDIA, Sony, Aricent (now Capgemini), Accenture, American Express—and technology ventures. She is a technology industry veteran and has served on multiple venture boards in next-generation computing and artificial intelligence ecosystems.

Throughout her career, Rika has been an avid advocate for advancing women's leadership in governance, technology, and business across industry verticals and global dimensions. While at American Express, Rika launched the West Coast chapter for AMEX's Women's Business Resource Group, and today she is the Executive Sponsor for the Women's Impact Network at Conduent. She is also passionate about deepening the intersection of analog and digital experiences through transformational innovation and the pursuit of purpose-driven collaboration.

While Rika has authored screenplays registered with the Writer's Guild of America, *Dear Chairwoman*, is her first book. She plans to follow up with *Dear Chair.X*, in late 2021, featuring letters from racially diverse and LGBTQ board leaders.

Made in the USA
Monee, IL
27 May 2022

97101550R00207